# Politics and the Labour Movement in Chile

*The Royal Institute of International Affairs is an unofficial body which promotes the scientific study of international questions and does not express opinions of its own. The opinions expressed in this publication are the responsibility of the author.*

*The Institute gratefully acknowledges the comments and suggestions of the following who read the manuscript on behalf of the Research Committee: Raymond Carr, Laurence Whitehead, and Philip Williams.*

# POLITICS
# AND THE LABOUR MOVEMENT
# IN CHILE

# ALAN ANGELL

*HD
6617
.A63*

*Published for*
THE ROYAL INSTITUTE OF INTERNATIONAL AFFAIRS
*by* OXFORD UNIVERSITY PRESS
London
1972

159066

*Oxford University Press, Ely House, London W.1*

GLASGOW NEW YORK TORONTO MELBOURNE WELLINGTON
CAPE TOWN IBADAN NAIROBI DAR ES SALAAM LUSAKA ADDIS ABABA
DELHI BOMBAY CALCUTTA MADRAS KARACHI LAHORE DACCA
KUALA LUMPUR SINGAPORE HONG KONG TOKYO

ISBN 0 19 214991 1

Printed in Great Britain by
Richard Clay (The Chaucer Press), Ltd.
Bungay, Suffolk

# Contents

## Abbreviations not given in the text*

AIFLD    American Institute for Free Labor Development
ANEF    Agrupación Nacional de Empleados Fiscales (National Association of State Employees)
ASIch    Acción Sindical Chilena (Chilean Trade Union Action)
CC    Central Committee
CEPch    Confederación de Empleados Particulares de Chile (Chilean Employees' Confederation)
CGT    Confederación General de Trabajadores (General Workers' Confederation)
COMACh    Confederación Marítima de Chile (Confederation of Maritime Workers)
CORFO    Chilean Development Corporation
CP, PCch    Communist Party, Communist Party of Chile
CTC    Confederación de Trabajadores de Cobre (Confederation of Copper Workers)
CTch    Confederación de Trabajadores de Chile (Chilean Workers' Confederation)
CUT    Central Unica de Trabajadores (United Workers' Federation)
FIFch    Federación Industrial Ferroviaria de Chile (Chilean Railway Unions' Federation)
FOCh    Federación Obrera de Chile (Chilean Workers' Federation)
FOF    Federación Obrera Ferroviaria (Railway Workers' Federation)
FONACC    Federación Obrera Nacional de Cuero y Calzado (Federation of Shoemakers & Leatherworkers)
FORch    Federación Obrera Regional de Chile (Regional Workers' Federation)
FRAP    Frente de Acción Popular (Popular Action Front)
HAHR    *Hispanic American Historical Review*
ILPES    Latin American Institute of Economic and Social Planning
ICIRA    Institute for Training and Research in Agrarian Reform
INSORA    Institute for Administration and Organization
IWW    International Workers of the World

* Excluding those in common usage.

JUNECh   Junta Nacional de Empleados de Chile (National Council of Chilean Employees)

MAPU     Movimiento de Acción Popular Unitaria (Movement of United Popular Action)

MIR      Movimiento de Izquierda Revolucionaria (Left Revolutionary Movement)

MUTCh    Movimiento Unitario de Trabajadores de Chile (United Movement of Chilean Workers)

ODEPLAN  National Planning Office

OLAS     Organization for Latin American Solidarity

ORIT     Inter-American Regional Labour Organization

PAL      Partido Agrario Laborista (Agrarian Labour Party)

PDC      Partido Demócrata Cristiano (Christian Democratic Party)

POS      Partido Obrero Socialista (Socialist Workers' Party)

PS       Partido Socialista (Socialist Party)

PSP      Partido Socialista Popular (Popular Socialist Party)

RILU     Red International of Labour Unions

UECh     Unión de Empleados de Chile (Union of Chilean Employees)

UTRACh   Unión de Trabajadores de Chile (Union of Chilean Workers)

*Note:* Unless otherwise indicated, Chilean books and journals referred to are published in Santiago.

# Acknowledgements

CHAPTERS of this book were read by Andrés Bande, Harold Blakemore, Emanuel de Kadt, and David Lehmann and I am grateful for their advice and comments. Raymond Carr and Philip Williams read the entire manuscript and their criticisms and suggestions were of great benefit to me. I owe much to Raymond Carr's general support and encouragement over the past five years. Laurence Whitehead read early versions of this book and his detailed and meticulous comments led me to rewrite most of it.

Generous financial assistance for two visits to Chile was provided by St Antony's College and Chatham House from a grant made by the Ford Foundation.

Dr Claudio Véliz and the Instituto de Estudios Internacionales were kind and considerate hosts in Chile. The provision of working facilities and of an extremely congenial academic environment helped to make fieldwork productive and enjoyable. Sandra Barbosa, of the Institute's library, Alicia Claro of the Library of Congress, and Patricio Rogers of the National Library provided invaluable assistance in tracing and locating essential material. Jorge Barría and Emilio Morgado of INSORA, and Adolfo Gurrieri of ILPES were always ready to discuss their own work with me and to provide invaluable guidance at the outset of my research. In Chile I enjoyed several conversations with Pat Peppe on trade union affairs.

Several versions of this book were typed with speed and patience by Diana Greenfield. Her ability to cope with long and very untidy manuscripts was of great assistance. Moira MacQuaide kindly helped with the final version. Faced with an overlong and overdetailed manuscript, Hermia Oliver brought to the task of editing a degree of firmness, concentration, skill—and tact—for which I am indebted (and the reader has been spared many repetitions and much unnecessary detail). I am also grateful to Mrs Helen Baz for preparing the index.

A great deal of my research was based on interviews with trade unionists and political leaders. My requests for information were invariably received with great courtesy and, usually, with readiness to converse at length. Without their assistance this book could not have been written.

The author of a first book may be permitted the opportunity to acknowledge less specific help. I would like to thank Professor S. E. Finer and my former colleagues in the Politics Department at the University of Keele for their encouragement when I started developing an interest in Latin America; my friends at St Antony's and Chatham House for making it a pleasure to sustain that interest; and finally my wife for many things.

*September 1971*                                                    A.A.

# 1. Introduction

THE Chilean labour movement is distinguished by the multiplicity and consequent weakness of most of the trade unions, which are as a result compelled to rely on the support of political parties to a greater degree than is usual in other countries. Thus Chilean unions have conflicting loyalties, for if they exist to protect the economic interests of their members, they have to try to reconcile this with the loyalties of most of their leaders to a particular party. Even if the leaders are able to do this because of a happy coincidence between the aims of the party and of the labour movement, another source of conflict arises between the expressed union aim of unity of the working class and party conflict and competition, since the relations between all the four main Chilean parties most actively concerned with the labour movement (the Socialists, the Communists, the Radicals, and the Christian Democrats) are rarely cordial and are sometimes very bitter. The extent to which a union emphasizes one or other value—internal unity or the demands of the party—reveals the extent and type of politicization of the Chilean labour movement.

Because most union leaders profess allegiance to one of the chief political parties, and because these parties are active amongst unionists and in unions, any study of Chilean labour must also be largely concerned with the political parties. Union-party relations throw much light on the structure, aims, and ideas of the parties, two at least of which, the Socialists and the Communists, consciously base themselves on the working class. The Christian Democrats, and even the Radicals, though they concentrate on the white-collar workers, also actively try to secure as wide as possible a base in the labour movement. Parties use the unions in their quest for political power; but unions are not simply their docile instruments. Unions have their own specific functions, their independent strength, their separate organizations. It is the interaction between party and union, when neither completely dominates the other, which illuminates the study of Chilean politics and labour, especially since in Chile political parties are more important than in most Latin American countries.

There is no simple formula by which one can judge whether the labour movement of a particular country is *non-political*, i.e. performs only the function of collective bargaining; if it is *political*, i.e. it acts also in the arena of national politics but as a kind of independent pressure group; or if it is *politicized*, i.e. acts in national politics but at the behest of a party or ideological group. Elements of all three modes of action are present in the behaviour of many labour movements and the Chilean one is no exception. But the Chilean movement is unusual in Latin America for a number of reasons, which are also the ones that make it highly interesting for those who wish to explore the political activities of unions. First, the union movement is large enough, and, more important, sufficiently representative of the active labour force to escape the charge of simply being an aristocracy of labour with no ties with the broader working class. In Chile there is a fair degree of coincidence between the aims of union movement and the interests of working class as a whole; even in rural areas unionization has recently spread rapidly and dramatically. Secondly, unions are not controlled by the state or by employers. Company unions, though they exist, are not common except in the smallest enterprises. Unlike the union movement in say Brazil or Mexico, in Chile trade unions have never been dominated by the Ministry of Labour or the official party. This does not mean that labour relations are not closely regulated by the state; the fact that they are has often been detrimental to the unions. But it does mean that union leaders are not appointed and controlled by the state, and it does mean that, broadly speaking, union policies are made by union leaders democratically elected by the rank and file.

Another factor which adds interest to a study of Chilean labour is that several parties of diverse and sometimes conflicting ideologies actively compete to win the loyalty of unionists. No one party dominates the unions to the exclusion of all others, and even though the Socialist and the Communist parties consider themselves marxist, this by no means implies uniformity of aim and method in their relations with labour. Although both these parties co-operated to secure the election of President Salvador Allende, a Socialist party leader who headed the Popular Unity Alliance in

1970, they maintain their separate identity in the unions, and neither is anxious to cede positions of influence to the other.

The contrast between the Chilean labour movement and similar movements in other Latin American countries parallels that between the Chilean political system and theirs. In no other country in the continent has representative government such firm constitutional and popular roots. In no other country is there such open and relatively equal competition between a number of important political parties, ranging from the far right to the far left. Chile was the only Latin American country to elect a Popular Front government in the late 1930s and the first to elect a Christian Democratic President. Most significant of all, Chile was the first country in the world to elect by fully democratic means, a marxist President (and may well become in 1976 the first in which a marxist President presides over fully democratic presidential elections).

Since the election of President Arturo Alessandri in 1920 as the supposed champion of the rising middle class, experiment and change have characterized the Chilean political scene. Although she did not escape the wave of military dictatorships in Latin America in the interwar period, Chile did witness the unusual spectacle of the group of politically romantic military officers, and rather more calculating politicians, establish—for a brief 100 days in 1932—the so-called Socialist Republic—an episode which was more important for the origins of the Socialist party than for any legislative or political achievements. A more durable and important experiment was the formation of a Popular Front movement in 1936, made up largely of the Radical, Socialist, and Communist parties, with the participation also of the major labour confederation. Two years later the Popular Front elected a Radical as President. Although Radicals were to hold executive power for the next fourteen years, during which time Socialists and Communists were to hold cabinet positions, friendly relations between the three parties lasted little more than two years, to be succeeded by bitter rivalry between them, culminating in the persecution and outlawing of the CP in 1948 by the Radical President González Videla, supported by a faction of the by now divided Socialists.

In 1952 the former military dictator of the interwar period, General Carlos Ibáñez, now posing as a populist, was elected to the presidency on a wave of popular enthusiasm and with the support of the majority Socialist party. If the populism of Ibáñez produced no solutions to Chile's economic and social problems, the return of conservatism with President Jorge Alessandri (1958–64) was to end in similar disappointment. Perhaps the Chilean electorate is so prone to experiment with new political formulas precisely because nearly all of the experiments have failed to deal with the problems of endemic inflation, low agricultural productivity, inadequate industrial investment, erratic economic growth, enormous external indebtedness, and increasing social tension.

The most sustained effort to deal with those problems was undoubtedly made by the Christian Democratic government of President Eduardo Frei (1964–70). In the 1960s the whole Chilean political spectrum moved perceptibly to the left, as a rapidly expanding electorate—votes cast increased from 1,250,350 in 1958 to 2,954,799 in 1970—showed increasing desire for fundamental reform of the political, economic, and social system. Both the main competitors in the presidential election of 1964 promised revolution, but the majority of the electorate preferred the Christian Democrat offer of revolution in liberty to that of the marxist revolution offered by the Socialists and Communists organized in the FRAP. But if the Christian Democratic government was faithful to its promise to maintain liberty, it found that revolution was much more difficult to promote than it had expected. In some ways the major impact of Christian Democratic policies was to increase demands for urgent change. Thus the government enabled and encouraged the rural farm workers to organize militant trade unions; but agrarian reform was too slow to satisfy the demand for land, and agricultural productivity did not increase sufficiently to satisfy union demands for higher wages. In the urban sector the government encouraged the growth of trade unions, but alienated the union movement when it unsuccessfully tried to curb the rate of inflation by a severe and strictly applied wages policy.

The 1970 election saw the rise of a strong right-wing challenge in the person of former President Jorge Alessandri, who offered a return to stability and order after the hectic years of social change under the Christian Democrats—an appeal that aroused a strong response amongst the Chilean upper and middle class, and indeed in sectors of the lower class as well. But both the Christian Democratic candidate and that of the Popular Unity

Alliance (composed of Socialists, Communists, Radicals, a break-away group from the Christian Democrats—the MAPU, and two minor parties) offered electoral programmes more radical than those of 1964, and the votes for the Alliance outnumbered those of the right-wing candidate. Unlike 1964, the victorious candidate was elected on a minority vote, gaining only 36·3% of the poll, compared with 34·9% for the right-wing candidate and 27·8% for the Christian Democratic candidate.

At the time of writing it is too early to forecast the changes likely to be made by the Allende government. There will no doubt be very considerable economic, political, and social reform, but it must be emphasized that the government is a coalition, with all the weaknesses and instabilities of multi-party coalitions in which the members have distinctive beliefs and represent different social sectors. Moreover, the largest single party in Chile is still the Christian Democratic party, determined to hold Allende to his pledge to respect the democratic and constitutional system.

It is thus difficult to foresee how the labour movement will develop under the new administration, though unions are likely to become stronger and politically more powerful. Nevertheless reform of the labour code will not be easy, for if all parties—apart from the right-wing National party—agree on the need for reforms, there is little agreement on their precise nature. Partisan loyalties are unlikely to diminish in the labour movement, even between Socialists and Communists in the governing coalition, and the Christian Democrats will certainly oppose, both in Congress and elsewhere, any measures that would weaken their position in the unions relative to the members of the coalition. Nor can union reform be separated from industrial reform generally, and from the pressing problems of inflation and unemployment which are likely to preoccupy the new administration for much if not all the period of Allende's presidency. The trade union movement will obviously occupy an important role in the economic strategy of the government. To understand that role, and the general political involvement of the union movement, it is necessary to understand the structure, traditions, aims, and political develop-ment of the labour movement, which is precisely the objective of this book.

Sociologists of union movements stress the importance of the origins of unions in creating a tradition which exerts and main-tains a strong influence over later developments, especially at the

B

level of leadership. As chapter 2 shows, compared with many other Latin American countries the union movement in Chile did soon develop its own structures, aims, and political organization, mostly under the leadership of committed Communists, though the activities of anarchists and of members of the Democratic and Radical parties were far from insignificant. Further, unlike developments in, say, Argentina with the rise of Perón, or Brazil with Vargas, there was no massive upheaval in the union world dividing its development into two defined stages—a kind of prehistory when marxist and anarchist influences were strong though confined to a small number of unionized workers, and then a sudden transition to mass unionism under the leadership of a populist ruler, in which the earlier ideas and affiliations became insignificant. (This oversimplifies the Argentinian case.) Continuities in the attitudes, aims, and political activities of Chilean labour are very marked; it is thus important to become acquainted with the origins of the Chilean union movement.

To estimate the power and influence of unions in any country it is necessary to know how many of them there are, their proportions in relation to the total labour force, and their occupational distribution. In Chile such basic statistics (which are set out in chapter 3) are especially important because of the large number of small unions and the small number of powerful national federations, even though by comparison with labour movements elsewhere in Latin America, the number of unionists as a proportion of the total labour force is relatively high—c. 30%. The reasons for this unusual structure must be sought in the labour code, for this lays down two basic types of unions (outside the rural sector, where there has been since 1967 a distinct system). Most blue-collar workers (*obreros*) are organized in plant unions (*sindicatos industriales*), where membership is obligatory if in any establishment of at least twenty-five workers there is an affirmative vote of at least 55% of them to establish a union. There can be only one union per establishment, and the unions are forbidden to form federations with other unions for the purposes of collective bargaining. The other type of union is the craft or professional union (*sindicato profesional*) for skilled blue-collar and white-collar workers (*empleados*), which is not confined to a single establishment. However, membership is not obligatory, and the craft unions, unlike the plant unions, have no right to share in profits. Any federations that may be formed by craft or professional unions are so circumscribed by legal regulation that the possibility of such a federation becoming a strong agent in a national collective-bargaining process is remote indeed. There are strong national federations in Chile, but these exist in spite of, not because of, the legal code.

The effect of the code on the internal structure of unions and the part that unions play in the industrial-relations system form the subject of chapter 4. First promulgated in 1924, the labour code embraces nearly all aspects of union affairs and has profoundly influenced the development of unions. But an industrial-relations system is not the product of legal regulation alone; it depends also on the country's economic structure and on the relations between unions and employers and between unions and the state. In the Chilean case I have come to the conclusion that the labour movement has developed radical and strong political affiliations because the effects of the labour code, the attitude of employers, and the activities of the state have combined to weaken unions as economic bargainers, thereby driving them to seek political allies and political solutions.

Part II deals with the relations between the major political parties and the unions. Socialism and communism are treated jointly because of the close relationship between the two in the unions as well as in the political system at large. The major confederations in Chilean labour history since the decline of the first, Communist-dominated, FOCH have in their turn been dominated by Socialists and Communists, and the state of party relations has been mirrored inside these confederations. The Popular Front produced a close alliance between unionists of both parties in the CTCH; the hostility between the parties with the onset of the Cold War and specific internal disagreements resulted in the division of the CTCH into two warring factions. Finally, party co-operation in the 1950s resulted in the formation of the CUT (which is difficult to translate—it approximates to the Unique or United Workers' Federation or Central). It would, however, be misleading to give the impression that the direction of influence is one way only, from party to union. Unions influence the parties as well, and one of the major achievements of the unionists in the CUT was to strengthen and preserve the original intention of unity and co-operation between the two marxist parties, sometimes in the face of open disagreement between the parliamentary leaders of those parties. Nevertheless, the relative weakness of Chilean unions makes them dependent to some extent on the parties, and the degree and effect of this dependence is also examined.

Socialists and Communists do not monopolize the political loyalties of Chilean unionists. The Radical party has also long enjoyed support, though very largely confined to the white-collar workers, especially in the public sector. Of greater importance, though more recent development, are the activities of the Christian Democrats in the labour movement. The relationship between Christian Democrats and other groups in the unions has always been uneasy, partly because of the internal divisions of opinion inside the party itself. Some, usually politicians, were of the opinion that the Christian Democratic unionists ought to collaborate with Catholic groups to set up a rival to the marxist-dominated CUT; others, usually unionists, emphasized the importance of unity of all the working class rather than Catholic sectarianism. The impact of six years of Christian Democratic rule was to strengthen the second tendency, as unionist dislike of the anti-inflationary policy of the government, based on a strict wage policy, resulted in radicalizing Christian Democratic labour.

The last chapter attempts to assess the extent and meaning of politicization at a variety of levels in the union movement. Obviously the major confederation, the CUT, is by any definition a political body, but the individual federations and unions, the leaders and the rank and file, are to a lesser or greater degree, creators of or participants in a union movement that as a whole is very politicized. Politicization is not the same as, nor does it imply, control by parties; as I try to show, the relationship is more complicated than that.

Two appendices deal with rural unions and external influences. Effective rural unionization dates only from the 1967 law, though there was considerable activity in rural areas immediately preceding and in anticipation of the law. The situation in the countryside is still rather confused, but it is at least clear that urban unions have played little or no part in the formation of their rural counterparts. It is the parties that have played and are playing a vital role, although there are points of comparison and contrast with the urban unions. Because external groups have been active, though not particularly successful, in trying to orient the political attitudes of Chilean labour, it seemed relevant to try to outline the activities of two of the most influential of them, those of the United States and of the Catholic international labour organization—for part of the reason for the failure of external influences has been a misconception and underestimation of the political loyalties of Chilean labour.

Inevitably in a book covering a wide range of relations between unions and parties there will be omissions, or perhaps misplaced emphases. In extenuation, one can plead that there are few studies of Chilean labour or political parties covering the same ground. Though in this book I am sometimes critical of the interpretations made by the authors of the INSORA survey of union leaders, I am nevertheless very thankful to have been able to use some empirical evidence in a field where there is very little. Secondary sources I have relied upon in particular sections I have acknowledged in the footnotes. Union and party publications are few and scattered, but have been used where available and appropriate. A great deal of this book, however, is based on interviews and conversations with trade unionists and politicians. Except where I wished to give specific authority for a particular point, I have not normally acknowledged all the information gained from such interviews, because some of it was given in confidence—to be used but not attributed—and because it is not always helpful or necessary to indicate the source for every point of interpretation. Interpretation is often a composite of a number of different points emerging from a number of different interviews. Moreover, statements about unions by unionists, especially interpretations rather than statements of fact, may not necessarily be true or accurate, although even false statements, sometimes made to mislead, may be useful evidence.

# PART 1

## 2. History of the Labour Movement and its Legacy

In the 1920s Chilean politicians debated the need for a labour code to restrict and contain the increasing, and increasingly radical, activities of organized labour. When a labour code was passed by Congress in 1924 legislators were more concerned about military interventions in politics than working-class radicalism, but fear of the spread of radicalism undoubtedly lay behind the legislation. The fear was not without grounds. By 1924 important sectors of the Chilean labour movement were led by committed Communists or anarcho-syndicalists. Sociologists stress the crucial role of the character and structure of union leadership in forming a tenacious political and industrial tradition,[1] and it is necessary to examine this tradition to understand the present political composition and attitudes of the Chilean labour movement.

The concept of radicalism is ambiguous. On the one hand there was a radicalism in the Chilean movement that essentially represented a rejection of the 'system', a spurning of involvement in the intrigues of a despised parliament, a refusal to compromise

[1] W. McCarthy, 'Why workers join unions', *New Society*, 26 Oct. 1967. This is also a starting point for one of the finest studies of British trade unions, H. A. Turner's *Trade Union Growth, Structure and Policy* (London, 1962). McCarthy refers to leadership, not membership. There must be some relationship between leadership and rank and file for the tradition created by the leadership to develop and survive. For the majority, Henry Pelling's comment on the working class of late Victorian England is not inappropriate—'The picture is on the whole one of political apathy and social conservatism, associated however with a profound class-consciousness and quite commonly a marked sense of grievance' (*Popular Politics and Society in Late Victorian Britain* (London, 1968)).

principles for short-term gains; and on the other hand there was a radicalism which aimed, at least in theory, at a complete and final transformation of society, but which was prepared to work inside the parliamentary system and the political game. This is the division between anarchists and orthodox Communists. But, though this was the earliest, it was not the only division in the labour movement. The CP itself was considerably divided, reflecting the later Stalinist–Trotskyist split. With the formation of the Socialist party in the 1930s yet another division appeared. However, until the turbulent political period of the late 1920s and early 1930s, the major development in the labour movement was the creation and consolidation of the authority of the CP.

## Origins

The political and union activities of the Chilean working class crystallized with the formation of the POS in 1912; and the development of the FOCH from a mutualist society to a revolutionary federation of unions. But there is considerable evidence of earlier political and union activity.[2]

The War of the Pacific (1879–83) and its aftermath had effected considerable changes in the society and economy. Whereas in 1880 in the northern provinces of Antofagasta and Tarapacá, there were only 2,848 workers in the nitrate industry, by 1890 this number had increased to 13,060, with a corresponding increase in employment in related port and transport work. By then in the country as a whole the numbers employed in the non-rural manual labour force had risen by almost 50% in a decade, to 150,000 workers.[3] Though money wages were rising in the period 1890–1914, given the rate of inflation it has been estimated that real wages overall were falling.[4] A rapidly depreciating currency was a spur to working-class protest at this time and one of the first minor working-class parties formed was a party advocating a convertible currency.[5]

[2] The most useful publications dealing with this period are: H. Ramírez, *Historia del movimiento obrero* (1956); J. C. Jobet, *Recabarren* (1955); M. Poblete, *Organización sindical en Chile* (1926); and two university theses or *memorias* by J. Barría, *Movimientos sociales en Chile 1900–10* and *1910–26* (1952 and 1960).

[3] Ramírez, *Hist.*, pp. 190–1.

[4] Solberg, 'Immigration and Social Problems in Argentina and Chile', *HAHR*, May 1969.

[5] J. H. González refers to a contemporary Radical senator who affirmed

The end of the nineteenth century and the beginning of the twentieth witnessed the great massacres of Chilean working-class history: the first general strike of the nitrate workers in Iquique in July 1890, which spread to Valparaíso and was severely repressed by the army; the merchant marine strike in Valparaíso in mid-1903 that started the fight for an eight-hour day and resulted in some forty workers losing their lives; the 'red week' in Santiago in October 1905 when many workers were killed in protests against the rising cost of living; the railway workers' strike in 1906 in Antofagasta; and, the most infamous of all, when between 1,000 and 3,000 nitrate workers were mown down by the army in a school yard in Iquique in 1907 while protesting against conditions in the mines and the policies of mass dismissals at the onset of recessions in the industry.[6] Estimates of dead and wounded are of course very uncertain, but the pattern of action seems clear. Worsening conditions brought about mass protest which provoked quick, brutal army and state repression. The causes of the protests were very similar: intolerance on the part of employers; the 'truck system' of payment which meant further abuses by company shops; bias of the authorities favouring employers; appalling working conditions that endangered life.[7] The demands made were often very similar and seem quite modest by present standards: payment in legal tender; freedom to buy from non-company shops; the right to meet and to form associations; no illegal deductions from salaries; safer working conditions.[8]

that the only cause of strikes was the rise in the cost of living produced by depreciation of the currency. And the workers of Valparaíso in 1914 petitioned the President against the state saving banks, claiming that inflation reduced their savings to nothing (*Constitución de 1925* (1950), pp. 91–2; M. Segall, *Desarrollo del capitalismo en Chile* (1953), p. 39).

[6] G. Kaempffer, *Así sucedió* (1962); also 'Masacres en la historia chilena', *Punto final*, 2 Jan. 1968.

[7] These were the grievances in the first recorded workers' strike in Chile, of a group of miners in September 1864 (C. M. Ortíz & P. I. Ljubetic, *Estudio sobre el origen y desarrollo del proletariado en Chile durante el siglo XIX* (*Memoria*, Inst. Pedagógico, Univ. Chile, 1954), pp. 274–6).

[8] These were the demands made by the nitrate strikers in Iquique in 1890. Their other demands throw light on working-class conditions (and aspirations): they included free and compulsory primary education; security for money in savings accounts; prohibition of alcoholic drinks in mining camps; no tampering with the mail; drinking water; prohibition of prostitutes and gambling on company property (Jobet, *Recabarren*, p. 89).

The workers' short-term response to oppression and exploitation was unorganized and spontaneous. They seemed to think that
a mass assembly would by sheer numbers draw attention to their
demands; this and the occasional act of violence exhausted their
tactics. Thus after a massacre in 1908 a labour newspaper berated
the working class for its stupidity, lack of purpose, and reliance on
violence as its only method.[9]

There were two long-term responses to these working conditions; one was to establish and support a number of reformist and
revolutionary political parties;[10] the other was to form unions.
There were three sorts of unions—the mutualist societies, important in the artisanal sectors, the 'resistance societies' or
'unions for the protection of labour', important for anarchist-
influenced workers, and the *mancomunales* or brotherhoods, predominant amongst the Northern miners and port workers.

### 1. The mutualist societies

Mutualist societies started very early in the history of Chilean
working-class organization. By 1870 13 had been recognized by
the government; by 1880, 39; and by 1924 there were 600, with
90,000 members, apart from those societies that had not sought
legal recognition.[11]

Their aims were mutual co-operation amongst members and
the provision of a rudimentary social-security system that neither
state nor employer was likely to provide. Though at first they
included only artisans they seem later to have been organized
amongst other workers. Their relationship with trade unionism
was ambivalent. By the educational services they provided and
the experience of organization, they trained leaders of more

[9] *La voz del obrero* (Taltal), 13 Jan. 1908, quoted by O. Millas in *Principios*
(the official CP monthly), July–Aug. 1962, p. 9.

[10] Of the effect of government and employer repression on the early Russian
labour movement, S. Perlman writes: 'Had Russian labor unions been let
alone during the dozen years that lapsed between the two revolutions it is not
at all unlikely that they might have permanently re-made the ideology handed
down by the intellectuals, in the pragmatic mold of a trade unionism that
seeks primarily to enlarge labor's opportunity. . . . Consequently, when the
government drove the trade unions back underground, it only succeeded in
foisting upon labor for good the leadership of the revolutionary parties' (*Theory
of the Labor Movement* (New York, 1928), p. 47).

[11] Poblete, *Organización sindical*, p. 24. The first one he cites is the Society
of Artisans of Valparaíso, formed in 1858, though Ramírez (*Hist.*, p. 166) refers
to one of the same name in Santiago in 1847.

'typical' unions. They themselves under pressure of events could act like unions, but their stated aim was co-operation, not conflict, with employer and state. In their first national congress in 1901 they excluded the resistance societies from membership, and it seems that the congress was held with government support and protection.[12] By this action they made clear their desire to break from the radical working-class groups that had been associated with them, and confirmed the artisanal and co-operative character of the movement. They were linked with the Democratic party rather than with any of the socialist groups, preferring to work inside the law, and susceptible to clerical influences which held that the mutualist societies were the Christian solution to working-class problems.[13] Though the later growth of the societies took place rather separately from the unions,[14] early on at least the two were interconnected. Mutualist societies demonstrated the possibility of organization, they spread ideas, they showed that co-operation could bring benefits, but their organization was intended to serve purposes outside the workplace, for their aim was to establish the social position of their members.[15] Unlike the Northern working class, they had enjoyed the support and inspiration of middle-class liberals like Santiago Arcos and Francisco Bilboa, who were influenced by mid-nineteenth century European ideas.

Mutualism was not a prehistory of the labour movement. As

[12] Jobet, *Recabarren*, pp. 112–13; A. Escobar, *Compendio de la legislación social* . . . (1940), p. 198. Escobar was an ex-Labour Inspector.

[13] Ramírez, *Hist.*, p. 170. Ramírez, ever anxious to look for ideological antecedents also suggests (p. 148) that one of the reasons for the growth of mutualism was the widespread reading of Proudhon amongst the Chilean petty bourgeoisie (using as evidence booksellers' catalogues of the times).

[14] The report of the president of the Congreso Social Obrero de Chile, the major mutualist federation, in 1927 affirms that the essential aims guiding the movement from its inception are first, the organization of workers based on concord, solidarity, and mutual co-operation, secondly, popular education as the only way of spreading culture, dignity, consideration, and happiness amongst workers, thirdly, national colonization schemes, industrial development, and protection, fourthly, fighting the vices of gambling and drinking, (causes of ruin amongst workers), and lecturing on hygiene. He reported an active campaign to abolish taxation on Argentinian meat; to solve unemployment in the nitrate and coal industries; to build cheap houses; to form co-operatives, etc. The workers also congratulated Ibáñez personally as the 'saviour of the country'—at a time when he was busy deporting union leaders (Bernardo Quiroga, 'Memoria anual', *Congreso Social Obrero* (1928)).

[15] A. Gurrieri & F. Zapata, *Sectores obreros y desarrollo en Chile* (1967), p. 27.

long as there was a numerous artisanal sector in Chile, the mutualist societies continued, especially until the state began to fulfil some of the basic social-security functions originally performed by them. That they influenced the union movement seems to be indicated by the fact that the FOCH started as a mutualist society. At the political level it has been suggested that the society members, lacking a firm Socialist ideology, could easily be incorporated into populist movements, such as that of Alessandri in 1920, whose programme contained many promises central to the mutualist movement.[16]

## 2. The resistance societies

Resistance societies and unions for the protection of labour were more common among the industrial and port workers than among the miners. They were not so important or numerous as the *mancomunales* in the North. Rather than the influence of Proudhon brought by Bilboa and Arcos, their intellectual antecedents lay more in the diffusion of anarchist and socialist ideas from Argentina.[17] They concentrated their activities at the level of the workplace, not outside it, and fought for the eight-hour day, salary increases, and better conditions. Though anarchists were represented amongst them, there were also more moderate sectors linked to the Democratic party. The resistance societies were concentrated geographically in the central zone of the country, especially in Santiago and Valparaíso, though there were some in the North until they were generally replaced there by the *mancomunales*. They were based in such industrial activities—often of an artisanal or near artisanal character—as printing, shoemaking, transport, and carpentry. Among this group also fall the unions for the protection of labour, as they were then called. These were distinct from the anarchist groups, which generally used the name of resistance societies, but the distinctions were far from clear and there was much overlapping. By the end of the nineteenth century, one estimate is that there were thirty unions of this type, of which ten called themselves resistance societies. They were active amongst port workers, who in 1893, with a nucleus of Valparaíso anarchists, made the first attempt in Chile

[16] Ibid., p. 29; see also B. G. Burnett, *Political Groups in Chile* (1970), pp. 102–3.

[17] Gurrieri, 'Consideraciones sobre los sindicatos chilenos', *Aportes*, July 1968, p. 88.

to organize a national (later intended to be continental) federation, the South American General Federation of Unions for the Protection of Labour; but it collapsed in the year of its creation.

The resistance societies declined with the decline of anarchism and they tended to be replaced either by a more professional non-political type of unionism on mutual lines, or by politicized marxist unions. Very often their existence was fleeting, called into being by a protest and disappearing shortly after, and they tended to decline in importance as industry developed larger and more modern units.

### 3. The mancomunales

The core of Chilean unionism lay in the *mancomunales* or brotherhoods, though their development must not be isolated from the mutualist and resistance societies which influenced their growth. If the brotherhoods bore traces of both these forms of worker unions, their role in the economy, social composition, geographical isolation, and conditions of work made them distinctive.

The labour force grew rapidly in the North following the War of the Pacific. Whereas in 1884 5,505 workers were employed in the nitrate industry, 19,345 were employed in 1896 and 48,476 in 1912.[18] Most of them came from the Southern and Central zones, though a considerable number of foreign labourers, especially Peruvians, Bolivians, and Chinese was employed.[19] Peruvians and Bolivians constituted close on a third of the total population of Tarapacá in 1907. The foreign capitalists who controlled nitrate production preferred foreign labourers, alleging that they gave far less trouble than the Chileans.[20] But there does not seem to have been much racial tension between the different groups of workers; in the protests and uprisings in that area the great stress was on wages, living and working conditions, and the solutions proposed by the workers did not refer to the problem of foreign labour.[21]

[18] F. Recabarren Rojas, *Historia del proletariado de Tarapacá y Antofagasta, 1884–1913* (*Memoria*, Inst. Pedagógico, Univ. Chile, 1954), p. 13. Other sectors of the economy serving the nitrate industry grew too.

[19] The numbers of Chinese labourers is not known exactly; but rather doubtful census returns for 1907 produce a figure of 2,000 (ibid., p. 36).

[20] According to evidence given to a Commission sent by Congress to examine labour conditions in the area (quoted ibid., p. 29).

[21] At least this is categorically asserted by Elías Lafertte, for many years secretary-general of the FOCH and leader of the Chilean CP, in his *Vida de un*

The labour force seems constantly to have been shifting from one nitrate mine to another, which made working-class organization difficult. Partly this was a search for better conditions,[22] but mostly it was a consequence of the fluctuating employment between times of restricted production and of maximum production caused not only by world demand but also by the ability of the producers to form combines to limit production and force up prices. Thus in 1884 employment fell by half, and the employers were often readier to dismiss their Chilean workers first; in 1896 in the course of two months alone some 6,000 workers were dismissed.[23]

The Congressional Commission of Inquiry in 1904, reflecting the values of Catholic paternalism, reported that low wages were not the main cause of misery, for they found wages on average high enough to purchase the necessities of life. They also felt that the dangers of work and the issue of abuses by company shops had been overrated (though worker protests at the time place these high on their list of complaints). They did, however, point to genuine enough grievances. Apart from work, there was little to do in the nitrate pampa; labourers lived completely abandoned by employers, state, and church, often without their families. The fact that owners and manager were largely foreigners caused grave social tensions. The Commission also found that nearly all the judges in the area were either employees of the companies or received payment from them.[24]

The situation of the nitrate workers is typical of the one-industry town noted for its bad labour-relations system.[25] On the one hand there was a relatively homogeneous labour force, or at

*comunista* (1961), pp. 63–4. For some time Lafertte worked in the nitrate areas and claims that blame was laid on foreign capitalists, not workers. On the other hand, Kaempffer (p. 105) claims that owners put Peruvians or Bolivians in charge of groups of Chilean workers to discharge tensions at a lower level than the management. While this undoubtedly did occur, it does not seem to have displaced economic grievances directed at the capitalists from the first attention of the workers.

[22] Lafertte, pp. 38–9, who worked in a 'large chain of nitrate centres' by the time he was twenty.

[23] Recabarren, pp. 81–91. They could either drift to the towns, or, as many did, return to rural areas in the South and await the next demand for labour from the North. See also Ramírez, *Hist.*, p. 279.

[24] F. Recabarren, p. 156.

[25] Clark Kerr & A. Siegel, 'The Interindustry Propensity to Strike', in Kerr, *Labor and Management in Industrial Society* (New York, 1964), pp. 105–47.

least one with similar labour conditions; on the other, an intransigent employers' group, foreign in nationality, out of sympathy
with the workers they employed, and backed up by state and
army. Unlike neighbouring Argentina, there was no large immi-
grant workforce with its own traditions and culture. Immigration to Chile was much smaller and more middle-class; the 1907
census showed only 4% of the population foreign-born compared
with nearly 30% in the case of Argentina on the eve of World
War I.[26] This did not stop the Chilean bourgeoisie for blaming
'foreign agitators' for the labour problems, but, as Recabarren,
the foremost labour leader and founder of the CP insisted in
Congress, the agitators in the country were Chileans, and, moreover, manual workers and not intellectuals.[27] The Chilean labour
movement was less advanced, less radical, less aggressive, less
urban, and less persecuted (at least in a systematic way) than in
Argentina. The European working-class radicals who came to
Chile were more likely to be urban anarchists than socialists in the
mining areas.[28] The Chilean mining labour force mostly came
from rural areas; its value systems derived from the traditional
rural social structure, and required time and upheaval to convert
into union militancy; it was not, as in Argentina, already
anarchist or socialist willing to challenge the state on arrival
from Europe. The Chilean working class was hardly accepted
or represented in the social and political system, but until the
growth of FOCH it was too weak to try to undermine or even
reform that system.

The homogeneity of the mining labour force made it a fairly
solid social group, with its own culture and class consciousness,
even if still affected by its rural background. Despite the fewer

---

[26] Solberg, *HAHR*, May 1969, p. 216. Only about 100,000 Europeans
settled in Chile from the latter half of the 19th century to World War I.

[27] L. E. Recabarren, 'Los albores de la revolución social en Chile', *Obras
escogidas*, (1965), p. 23. Recabarren insisted that the protests of the first years
of the century were the genuine work of the proletariat.

[28] Ramírez refers to 300 French Communists who arrived in the South
following the Paris Commune; but though these and other similar groups
brought ideas, they were not large enough to provide the rank and file of union
and socialist movements ('Tuvo influencia la Primera Internacional en
Chile?' *Principios*, Sept.–Oct. 1969, p. 39). The activities and writings of
Argentinian socialists, esp. J. B. Justo & J. Ingenieros, were also important
theoretical influences (Jobet, 'Alejandro Escobar Carvalho', *Arauco*, Jan. 1967,
p. 54).

European immigrants, the influence of European ideas helped to lead the early unions towards radicalism.[29] There were divisions among the workers; the more advanced and more politicized tried to improve conditions by organizing and by conflict with employer and state; the less advanced, who were a powerful restraining force, tended to demand benefits from employer and state, to alternate between passivity and protest, and thus to suffer exploitation and repression. Both groups were nevertheless bound together and relatively isolated from the other sectors of society. In this working-class attitude, opposition to the foreign capitalist played an important part, for most of the nitrate areas were controlled by British and American companies and this tended to drive capital and labour into two clearly defined groups. As the nitrate concerns also needed to control transport, port facilities, and in fact the greater part of the economic structure of the North, the labour movement had a clear image of the extent of the power of capital. The workforce was also relatively homogeneous, mostly consisting of unskilled rural migrants, possibly earning better salaries than the national average, but suffering similar deprivations and always subject to regular periods of unemployment.[30] Given the crucial importance of nitrate in the state economy, it was natural that the government should seek to maintain regular production. It therefore chose to repress labour rather than cause difficulties with the employers. Thus, while there was a continuing and strong tendency in certain sectors of the labour force to seek support and benefit from the state, the constant use of the army to put down protest, the regular use of the legal system against the workers, the abandonment of the workers by the state in all matters pertaining to living conditions, were bound to impress on the workers' leaders the notion of the state as an enemy of the people and an ally of capital.

The union organization created to combat these conditions, the *mancomunales*, reflected the situation of the Northern worker. They were territorially based, not organized by craft, for there were few distinctions of this sort in the labour force; they made general

---

[29] The Bolivian labour movement—sectors of which were to become, and to remain, very radical—received some of its first socialist ideas and organizers from Bolivians returning from work in the Chilean nitrate mines.

[30] Gurrieri & Zapata, p. 20. And as the workforce had few internal professional distinctions, worker demands tended to be general and applicable to all, rather than seeking differentiation and privilege for a specialized sector.

demands about wages and work and living conditions; they were weak and constantly subject to harassment by state and employer, which made their existence temporary and dangerous; but because they represented the demands of a majority of the labour force they were constantly reappearing.

The *mancomunales* did not preclude other forms of organization in the area. The mutualist unions were quite strong, with an estimated membership of 10,000 in 1910 in the two Northern provinces.[31] There were more of them in the towns than in the mining camps. Many of them developed into *mancomunales*,[32] whilst many of the *mancomunales* continued to perform mutualist functions.

In essence, the aims of the *mancomunales* were more akin to the resistance societies than to the mutualist associations, even if in many cases they had been consciously set up in opposition to the anarchist models. They started in the ports of the nitrate areas, and also in the coal-mining districts near Concepción in the South, but soon spread to the nitrate mining camps proper. They were basically organizations of manual workers, and it was often stipulated that members had to belong to the working class, and that the leaders should be active workers. They usually began by starting a shortlived newspaper or periodical. The first *mancomunal* to be founded seems to have been the Combinación Mancomunal de Obreros in Iquique in 1901. By 1904 it had about 4,000–6,000 members, and had created in 1903 a shortlived political party.[33] Though at least some of them seem to have had radical ideas (the *mancomunal* of Tocopilla expressed solidarity with the Russian workers in the 1905 revolution)[34] the first *mancomunal* convention passed a relatively moderate set of resolutions, most of which demanded that the state should provide services like education and request employers to improve safety standards.[35] There was a strong streak of puritanism in the *mancomunales*; they insistently demanded education for their children and themselves, and the prohibition of alcoholic drinks, gambling,

[31] F. Recabarren, *Hist. del proletariado*, p. 174.

[32] Such as the Sociedad Gran Unión Marítima, formed in Iquique in 1892, which organized port workers.

[33] Ramírez, *Hist.*, p. 269; Jobet, *Recabarren*, p. 106.

[34] Ramírez, *Hist.*, p. 270; and it also condemned the 'authoritarian and bourgeois despotism that in all parts of the world weighs like a granite mountain on the shoulders of the workers'.

[35] This was held in Santiago in 1904, with 15 organizations represented by

C

and prostitution. One ex-labour inspector affirms that unlike many other movements their funds were never fraudulently misused, but that almost all were spent on schools, libraries, newspapers, and mutual help during sickness.[36]

The *mancomunales* were the expression of the social cohesion and solidarity of their members, and in this sense followed the example of the mutualist societies; but in their demands and actions they looked forward to more modern trade unionism. All the important strikes of the period in the North were their work.[37] Yet they were weak organizations, based on a relatively small part of the total working population for their regular functioning, and as such they were vulnerable. After the great period of strikes from 1905 to 1907, with subsequent prolonged unemployment, they practically disappeared. Their leaders enjoyed no immunity from dismissal and were easily singled out by the employers. Early political rivalries in the *mancomunal* movement, often between the Democratic party groups and others such as the early socialist parties, or even sections of the Radical party, were an additional source of weakness. They revived again in the later part of the second decade of this century to take part in the activities of the foch and the cp. Their role had been crucial in training leaders, in spreading ideas and organization, often through a lively press, and in preparing the way for later union developments.

Parallel to the organization of the workers in unions, there were organizations of a more political nature, both by and for the working class.

------

25 delegates on behalf of 20,000 members. They asked for the abolition of whipping in the army and navy; state acquisition of public services like water and transport; free and compulsory primary education; night school for adults; hygienic housing; employers to indemnify injuries at work; and the appointment of factory inspectors (Jobet, *Recabarren*, pp. 108–9). Some resistance societies withdrew from this convention on the grounds that workers should ask nothing from the government (Barría, *Breve historia* (1967), p. 19).

[36] Escobar, p. 198.

[37] Gurrieri & Zapata, p. 31. And more strikes took place in the Northernmost provinces than in any other areas of Chile.

## Early political movements

There were three early working-class political organizations: the Democratic party, the anarchists, and the socialist movements which gave rise to the POS, which later became the CP.

### 1. The Democratic party

This party originated in the efforts of a group of young middle-class Radicals to organize centres for workers, artisans, and middle-class members of the liberal professions to unite in order to deal with the 'social problem'. Their activities were not welcomed by the Radical party and they broke away to form the Democratic party, holding a founding convention in 1887.[38] Its first programme proclaimed as its object the political, social, and economic emancipation of the people;[39] and it emphasized the need for education, social services, and elimination of corruption from public life in a manner that was to be echoed in many of the manifestos of the mutualist societies and early unions.

As if to back up its words with actions it organized demonstrations protesting against the railway companies for raising fares. As these ended in the burning of coaches, the party executive was arrested and jailed.[40]

The main emphasis of the party, however, was liberal rather than socialist. Its most consistent platforms were free elections, popular representation, administrative decentralization, promotion of manufacturing, and the provision of welfare services.[41] It was also essentially a parliamentary party; and in its early years had a notable record of legislative projects for reform, most of which were not passed, though in 1920, after many years of effort, the law on compulsory free primary education was enacted. But the party became closely involved in the corruptions, intrigues, and alliances of the so-called 'parliamentary period' in Chile; by

[38] P. F. Iñiguez Irarrazaval, *Notas sobre el desarrollo del pensamiento social en Chile 1901–6* (*Memoria*, Univ. Católica, Santiago, 1968), p. 21.

[39] Ramírez, *Hist.*, p. 214. It also wanted to reduce the size of the army, grant municipal autonomy, assert state supremacy over all other associations, protect national industry, and replace taxes on food by a tax on wealth.

[40] Jobet, 'Estudio preliminar', in Recabarren, *Obras escogidas*, pp. 6–7.

[41] G. Feliú Cruz, *Chile visto a través de Agustín Ross* (Santiago, 1950), pp. 126–8. It also opposed immigration of 'low social classes of old Europe with all the evils and vices of spent nations'.

1920 it was well entrenched in the political system and no longer a notable reformist force.

Its social basis was artisanal and petty bourgeois rather than working class; it was associated with the mutualist societies rather than the more radical forms of worker organization. But it did attract many leaders who were later to become socialists and communists, such as Recabarren himself, for many years a Democratic party militant. Its newspapers helped to spread reformist ideas among sectors of the population which received no periodicals except the irregular anarchist publications. Democrats were prominent in the Valparaíso strike of 1903; and Democratic unionists spread ideas on unions and helped to found unions in areas in the North.[42] They early took up the battle against the anarchists and their mutual polemics antedate those that were later to take place between Communists and anarchists. If at first an educative and training force, they were later to become a restraining influence; the labour movement outgrew the party's limited reformism.[43]

The Democratic party had indeed established quite radical branches in Santiago and especially among the coal miners in the Concepción area, who were later reluctant to abandon those who had first helped them to organize. At the 1921 convention the more advanced elements suffered defeat and many of them left to join the CP and the FOCH (which established local organizations in the coal areas only in 1920, blocked in earlier attempts by the hold of the Democratic party), leaving a Democratic party more conservative, more middle class, and enmeshed in the parliamentary and political system.[44] Recabarren himself had finally broken with the party in 1912 over the choice of party candidate for deputy in a district that he wished to contest but where the sitting Democratic member refused to withdraw.[45]

[42] Kaempffer, pp. 75–6; F. Recabarren, *Hist. del proletariado*, p. 177.

[43] Escobar (p. 197) refers to the Democrats' assumption that they were the real leaders of the working class. But he notes their conservatism in always opposing new ideas and independent action.

[44] Ramírez, 'El movimiento obrero chileno desde 1917 a 1922', *Principios*, Jan. 1960, p. 32.

[45] Lafertte, p. 81. The historian of the Democratic party claims that Recabarren was expelled from the party for indiscipline (H. de Petris Giesen, *Hist. del partido democrático* (1942), p. 41).

## 2. The anarchists

The anarchists stood for a diametrically opposed form of action. Their ideas influenced Recabarren (whose early writings rely heavily on the works of Reclus, Kropotkin, and Malatesta), though he had rejected these ideas before he left the Democratic party. As early as 1904 he was to affirm against the anarchists that it was necessary to enter the world of politics to realize the aims of the working class.[46]

The lines between socialists and anarchists in many cases were not clearly drawn before the impact of the 1917 Russian revolution in Chile; and there were many libertarian socialist groups that could be fitted into both camps. It seems, however, that at least in the first decade of this century the anarchists were the best organized, most advanced, and most publicized of the radical groups, especially in their resistance societies. They were also the first to receive the brunt of attacks by employer and government. They were principally organized in the Santiago and Valparaíso area, in occupations such as printing, baking, and shoemaking, and in the port area, with some strength also in the coal mines near Concepción and in some Northern districts. Many of these early anarchists were immigrants from Spain, Italy, and Germany who had mostly settled in Santiago.[47] The anarchists attempted the first real organization of workers there with the Federation of Carpenters and Similar Trades, which played an important part in the strikes in Santiago in 1906–7. Though they rejected alliances with politicians, they co-operated with students, and many prominent student leaders of the time were anarchists.

The anarchists' ideas were typical of such movements elsewhere. They emphasized direct action and rejection of external aid, especially from politicians, for they regarded politicians, whatever their expressed affiliation, as exploiters of the working class. They were especially opposed to the organization of working-class parties. They attacked Recabarren and attempted to prove that he had sold out to the bourgeoisie.[48] Relations inside the worker movement deteriorated even more after the Russian

---

[46] Ibid., p. 12, quoting from Recabarren's article in the newspaper *El Marítimo* (Antofagasta), 20 Aug. 1904.

[47] Barría, *Movimientos sociales 1900–10*, p. 128; Jobet, *Recabarren*, p. 41.

[48] G. Ortúzar & I. Puente, *Hacia un mundo nuevo* (1938), p. 12; Osvaldo Arias, *La prensa obrera en Chile* (*Memoria*, Univ. Chile, 1953), p. 45.

revolution, the formation of the Chilean CP, and the conversion of the FOCH to a section of the RILU. The anarchists argued that the FOCH had become totally dependent on Moscow, and acted as a divisive force inside the working class; they constantly attacked the CP with the slogan 'down with all governments, proletarian or bourgeois'.[49]

Anarchists were active in many of the protest movements of the time. They claimed involvement in the Valparaíso strike of 1903; and in the Red Week (*Semana roja*) of 1905 when they had helped to organize the Committee for the Abolition of Tax on Argentinian meat, the failure of which one anarchist writer attributed to a lack of theoretical knowledge of the general strike. They were strong in the Shoemakers' Federation, which organized a series of successful strikes and direct action in 1917–18. They were also prominent in the early FOCH, which was by no means initially an exclusively communist group. In 1913 the anarchists established their most successful newspaper, *La Batalla* (The Struggle), which ran until 1925.[50]

The real heyday of organized anarchism was reached with the creation of the Chilean branch of the IWW, which held its first congress in 1919. This was anarcho-syndicalist rather than purely anarchist. Its newspaper saw syndicalism and anarchism as two parts of a common ideal. The IWW, it argued, was not anarchist; industrial unionism was the most modern syndical form, avoiding the anti-organizational impotence of anarchism and the state bureaucracy of socialism.[51] At this congress the Chilean branch adopted the tactics of the IWW—the strike, boycott, and sabotage; and announced its enemies—capital, government, and the church.[52]

The Chilean IWW remained united until 1925 and was strong amongst the port workers of Iquique, Valparaíso, and Antofagasta. It was organized in seven associations, on an industrial

---

[49] Arias, p. 49. Apart from the work of Arias there is not a great deal written, especially by anarchists themselves, apart from newspapers of the time. One work which does reflect on the anarchist tradition and which tries to offer some (pessimistic) guides to the future is by Luis Heredia (who introduces himself as a worker of little formal education) in *Como se construirá el socialismo* (1936). This comes down very firmly on the side of Bakunin against Marx.

[50] Fanny Simon, 'Anarchism and anarcho-syndicalism in South America', *HAHR*, Feb. 1946, p. 52.

[51] From *Acción directa* (Santiago, 1920–6), cited in Arias, p. 49.

[52] Simon, p. 53.

basis, with an estimated 9,000 members.[53] It declared all paid posts abolished, leaving only a secretary-general whose function was to summon meetings of the executive. The IWW found considerable support amongst the students and one or two teachers' organizations, especially the Chilean Primary Schoolteachers' Association. Though the IWW had unions in a number of industries—bakers, construction, shoemakers, printers—it was never as strong as the FOCH, and indeed was outnumbered by some of the Catholic and clerical unions. It was not to remain united for long; port workers, printing workers, and bakers soon broke away from its ranks. A major dispute took place over the type of organization, some preferring a federal or regional structure by profession rather than industrial unions; and the former group broke away to form the FORCH in 1925–6.[54]

The anarchist unions suffered heavily from repression by both government and employer. In 1920, for example, many of the IWW leaders were arrested for having dynamite in their offices in Valparaíso, though they firmly held that it was planted there by the police.[55] They suffered particularly under the dictatorial military regime of Carlos Ibáñez (1927–31), partly because they were the group most opposed to him, partly because Ibáñez pressed for the application of the labour code and crushed opposition to it, strongest amongst the anarchists.[56] Their organizations were virtually destroyed and their leaders were exiled.

Though the formation of the CGT in 1931 falls outside the period covered in this chapter, it is convenient to deal with it here, for it was the last time that the anarchists achieved any organizational importance. The CGT was organized on a regional rather than an industrial basis, and united the remnants of the IWW and FORCH. It drew its members from the same groups, and estimates of its numbers at its peak vary from 15,000 to 25,000;[57] it included among its members some of the best-paid workers in Chile at the

[53] Poblete, *Organización sindical*, p. 36. This was its peak in 1928; in 1924 it had an estimated 2,000 (Simon, p. 53).

[54] Barría, *Breve hist.*, pp. 27–8.

[55] Heredia, p. 47.

[56] In 1924 the civilian regime was overthrown by the military. Ibáñez—then a major—emerged as the dominant leader and held formal (as well as informal) power from 1927 to 1931. In 1932 he was overthrown and the regime returned to civilian rule with the election in 1933 for the second time of Arturo Alessandri as President.

[57] Barría, *Breve hist.*, p. 36; Escobar, p. 217.

time, for many of them were skilled artisans and their unions very combative—for example, the Leatherworkers' Industrial Union. Their tradition was carried on to the present day in FONACC.

Yet by 1946 the CGT was reduced to little more than a skeletal organization. As industrial structures became less artisanal and more modern, the social basis of much anarchist support declined. By its total opposition to legal unions, it lost the support of many who saw advantages in legal protection and profit-sharing. By rejecting conciliation and arbitration it suffered more repression than other unions. The violence of its activities lost it supporters when those tactics not only proved unsuccessful but brought about mass dismissals of workers.[58] In the waves of popular enthusiasm that swept the electorate and the Chilean people— Alessandri in 1920, the Popular Front in 1936–8—it lost a great deal of the mass support among the marginal elements that it had been able to mobilize in mass protests, most notably against taxes on food, high rents, and the cost of living.[59] In comparison with the communist and socialist giants in the labour movement, it looked and became irrelevant. Heredia, a convinced anarchist, writing in 1938, was very pessimistic about the prospects for his movement; he no longer believed that it could overthrow the state by a general strike, and he admitted that he did not know what force would make the revolution, though he added that in any case a European, or at least major Latin American, upheaval was necessary first. Chilean anarchism, he concluded, had no future by itself;[60] and events proved him right.

Yet the influence of anarchism on the labour movement was far from negligible. Many future CP leaders, both intellectual—like Carlos Contreras Labarca,[61] a CP secretary-general—and pro-letarian—like Juan Chacón, a former port worker in Valparaíso and later a member of the Central Committee and spokesman on agrarian affairs—had passed through the ranks of anarchism.[62]

[58] Even the Trotskyists of the time, then concentrating their attacks on the 'conservative' and 'bureaucratic' Communist party, condemned the CGT for adventurism and irresponsibility (CPCh, *En defensa de la revolución* (1933), p. 113).

[59] Gurrieri, p. 89.          [60] Heredia, pp. 78–9.

[61] A student leader in the 1920s. The anarchist journal *Acción directa* circulated widely among students and their own journal, *Claridad*, carried many articles on anarchism (A. Chelén, *Trayectoria del socialismo* (?1968), p. 33).

[62] Only briefly, but his account pays tribute to the energy and enthusiasm of the anarchists of the period 1910–20 (J. M. Varas, *Chacón* (1968), pp. 21–7). He refers also to active contacts with Argentinian anarchists at that time.

Similarly, in the Socialist party Oscar Schnake, a leading Socialist and cabinet minister in the Popular Front, had been a member of anarchist movements; and the old disputes between Marx and Bakunin were echoed in the debates of the Socialist party congresses until the mid-1940s. The radical stance of anarchism, its hostility to state, church, and capital, was an important element in the tradition of the Chilean labour movement.

### 3. Socialist movements and the POS

The period from 1890 to 1910 was marked by the frequent formation and usually rapid decline of socialist and anarchist clubs, movements, and parties. Nearly all were founded in Santiago and Valparaíso, and a few in Punta Arenas, Iquique, and Antofagasta. Many of their members were middle-class intellectuals, together with some artisans.[63]

The first antecedents of such movements can be traced to the Sociedad de la Igualdad (the Equality Society) set up by Santiago Arcos and Francisco Bilboa in 1850. From the Europe of 1848 the founders of this society had conceived the overriding need to destroy the aristocracy by a truly democratic and popular movement. The original society lasted only seven months; but it aroused interest by its meetings, and it organized protests and educational activities. It set off many imitators, such as the Club de la Opinión in Valparaíso, where the 'working classes would for the first time breathe the air of philosophy and glimpse for the first time their own dignity and importance'.[64] If the founders of such groups were middle class, many of the members were artisans and workers. The societies were not socialist and utopian; rather they urged upon the working class the need for education and political action. In this sense they were the forerunners of the Radical and Democratic parties rather than the POS, but they were also the school through which many leaders of that party had passed.

The first real attempt at founding a Socialist party came in 1897 with the Partido Socialista. It was a confused but active group, many of whose leaders, like Alejandro Escobar Carballo, were later to opt for 'libertarian socialism' and anarchism. Its programme was advanced for the times: demands for an eight-hour day; councils of workers and employers to solve industrial disputes and to regulate factory conditions (with payment of

[63] Jobet, *Recabarren*, p. 101.
[64] Ramírez, *Hist.*, pp. 80 & 82 (quoting its statutes).

council members by the state); direct and progressive taxation; abolition of monopolies and privileges; salaries related to production and profits.[65] Yet, it added cautiously, it would work through legal means to achieve its ends. It was never a mass party, and it had little following in the North. Most of its leaders were very young and soon opted for anarchism. The party lasted little more than a year.

The socialist groups in Punta Arenas had little to do with the movements elsewhere in Chile. European immigration was much more important in the South and there was considerable mobility of labour between Punta Arenas and Argentina, so that in some ways the movement in Magallanes province can be seen as an extension of the Argentinian rather than the Chilean one.[66]

The POS was formed in 1912 as a breakaway from the Democratic party rather than as the creation of an autonomous socialist movement. Socialist groups had moved into and out of the Democratic party for some time; as early as 1891 a Protectionist party had broken away, on the grounds that the Democratic party was not sufficiently concerned with the economic conditions of the working classes. Movements of this sort, usually shortlived, with some members returning to the Democratic party and others to anarchism, were fairly common occurrences.[67] But the crucial break was to take place with Recabarren's formation of the POS, the forerunner of the Chilean CP.

The POS was founded in Iquique in June 1912 by a group of militant workers from the Democratic party; independently in August a similar organization was founded in Punta Arenas that was to unite with the POS, though at first the Punta Arenas group was much more reformist.[68] By 1915 it had organized sixteen sections in various parts of the country, when the first congress, over which Recabarren presided, was held. It was decided to call the party the POS in order to distinguish it clearly from the social democratic parties of Europe that had, in Recabarren's eyes, betrayed the working class by their attitude towards World War I.[69] Apart from resolving to fight for the eight-hour day, the English Saturday', and Sunday rest-day, the party resolved to

[65] Full text, ibid., p. 235.
[66] Ibid., p. 245; Chelén, p. 23.
[67] Ramírez, *Hist.*, pp. 225–6, 243.
[68] S. M. Martínez, 'El primer congreso del POS', *El Siglo*, 7 May 1967.
[69] Ibid. The 1915 POS congress condemned World War I.

take part in political and electoral struggles without seeking alliance with other groups or parties. Some members wished to see the POS and FOCH unite in a single body, but Recabarren insisted on the need to keep union and party separate, though co-ordinated. From this time, therefore, dates the dual development (not always followed in practice) of the more narrowly-based political party organizing the militants, and the wider union confederation accepting all members of the working class, though hoping to convert them into party supporters.

In its early days the POS was a far from rigid group. As Lafertte writes:

People came from all camps. There were Democratic party militants, anarchists, people with no party, workers, small businessmen, intellectuals, professional people. But the working class was predominant, from the nitrate pampa, from Iquique, from the bakers' unions. Many anarchist ideas and customs flourished in our ranks: for instance, resistance to the law, free love, anti-clericalism. We were not really marxists. Marxism came in good time to the POS after study, after reading the books from Europe, from international contacts, from the travels of our comrades, from the contact with the Communist International. But we had in our midst . . . the capacity to fight, to resist injustice, to organize, the sentiment of unity, the pride of the proletariat and above all class consciousness (p. 101).

The influence of Recabarren's ideas and philosophy on the formation and development of the party cannot be overstressed. His strongly puritanical sentiments were present in the constant stress on hygiene, in pressure for the prohibition of alcoholic drinks and the spread of education.[70] His vision was reflected in the emphasis on the classless society and the equality of the sexes. His tactics were embodied in the formal division between party and union, yet with the obligation for party members to be active in the unions. He also insisted on the need to reject anarchist prohibitions on party and parliamentary activity. (He himself was twice elected as a deputy. After not being permitted to take his seat, he was then successfully elected for Antofagasta, together with another POS, member in 1921).

[70] He once wrote: 'Two fatal circumstances determine to a large extent the permanent, progressive, and inherited misery of the masses: improvidence and vice' ('Ricos y pobres', *Obras escogidas*, pp. 90–1). One of the offences justifying expulsion from the present-day CP, according to its statutes, is 'habitual drunkenness' (PCCH, *Estatutos* (1965), p. 20).

The POS, however, was transformed by the simultaneous impact of the Russian revolution and postwar unemployment. The social situation grew tense, and Chile's first popular leader, Arturo Alessandri, started his successful campaign for the presidency in 1920. The POS set out on the path that was to take it into the Comintern. Recabarren refused to allow the party to support Alessandri's campaign, and himself stood (though in gaol) against the 'lion of Tarapacá', gaining, however, only a handful of votes. But it seemed at least to be a challenge to the old, established parties, and an assertion of independence.

At the fourth congress in Valparaíso in December 1920 it was resolved to seek admission to the Third International after the local branches had had time to discuss and approve the move. And, as a foretaste of what was to come, it was resolved to purge the party of reformist elements who served only to deflect the proletariat from its task of liberation,[71] to adopt the name of Communist party and, as its immediate programme, that of the FOCH. The proposals were subsequently ratified at the congress in Rancagua in January 1922, practically without dissent, though not before strenuous efforts had been made by some sectors to try the alternative model of a Labour party on the British model, to be formed of the FOCH, the Democratic party (much abused, but like the present-day Radical party, available to be used), and the POS. Yet it was to be some time before the CP transformed itself into a 'correct' marxist-leninist body as approved by Moscow. By 1926 the South American Bureau of the Comintern still felt that the process of 'bolshevization' had not proceeded far and fast enough.[72] Indeed, the party was accepted only as a candidate member until 1928; full status was not granted until it had been declared illegal in 1927 by Ibáñez.

## The FOCh

In 1908 the State Railway Companies, arguing financial crisis and the need for economies, reduced their workers wages by 10%. A conservative lawyer helped the workers to organize, in September 1909, the Workers' Federation and to mount a successful

[71] Ramírez, *Origen y formación del* PCCH (1965), p. 124.
[72] Barría, *Movimientos 1910–26*, p. 400. There were an estimated 2,000 members in 1923 organized in 50 sections (Ramírez, *Origen*, p. 182; see also S. Clissold, *Soviet Relations with Latin America 1918–68* (1970), p. 119).

campaign for the reinstatement of the cut. In 1911 railway workers held their first congress, where they called their union the Grand Workers' Federation of Chile. They were organized as a mutualist society for railwaymen, with a very moderate programme stressing co-operation with employers and the government.[73] Their union was incorporated as a mutualist society under the civil code.

The Federation was severely criticized by Recabarren for being an instrument of the bourgeoisie to control the workers. But it did provide relatively strong organization in the days of generally weak unions. Some of its more militant sections in Valparaíso used it to launch a general strike in 1913 in protest against the decree compelling railwaymen to carry photographs as a means of identification.[74] The Federation itself started to develop militant tendencies. Union organization elsewhere was in disarray. The *mancomunales* and the resistance societies were suffering from the repressions of the period. In 1917, at its second congress in Valparaíso, representatives of the *mancomunales* were allowed to participate and it was decided to open the Federation—now renamed the FOCH—to all workers. Workers from many industries and of all political persuasions were attracted; like the POS, the Federation brought together initially socialists, Democratic party supporters, anarchists, and non-political unionists.[75] It was far stronger in the North and South of the country than in Santiago itself, where it had little support, compared with the anarcho-syndicalists.[76]

The postwar period was one of considerable social tension and the years 1917–20 were marked by an increasing number of strikes and of mass movements like the Asamblea Obrera de Alimentación Nacional (the Workers' Assembly for National Food Supply), formed in late 1918 to combat the high cost of food (with representatives of the FOCH, the students federation, the POS, and the Democratic and Radical parties).

The FOCH itself began to reflect this sharpening of tensions. At its 1919 congress in Concepción it changed its structure and character. The basic organizational unit became the union, which grouped all workers of an area without distinction of

---

[73] Barría, *Breve hist.*, p. 23. This programme and extracts from later ones is reproduced in Troncoso, *Organización*, pp. 83–88.

[74] Barría, *Movimientos*, p. 114.

[75] Lafertte, pp. 149–50.

[76] L. Vitale, *Discursos de Clotario Blest* (1961), p. 49.

function or profession. The FOCH demanded the abolition of the capitalist system and proposed that industry should be run by the unions. Recabarren estimated that just after the war it had close on 60,000 members but that by 1922 they had dropped to 30,000 because of unemployment and repression by state and employer.[77]

The period 1920–2 was vital in the development of the FOCH, for this was the time of the great debate over the formation of one single political party on the style of the British Labour party, and over entry into the RILU. A congress in 1920 with Recabarren as chairman considered the idea, which had the approval of FOCH's executive, of forming a mass popular political party. The congress agreed that discussions should be opened with the POS and the Democratic party; and hoped that the 1921 FOCH congress would be able to celebrate the fusion of the three bodies. However, the Democratic party could not accept the idea of forming only one party which would not enter into alliances with any other group; but it did accept in principle the idea of co-operating with the FOCH in its fight against capitalism and of making electoral pacts with it to the exclusion of other groups (which it soon repudiated in favour of an alliance with the Radicals). At the 1921 congress, however, the FOCH resolved that, because of the reformism of the Democratic party and its collaboration with the government, it would have no further contacts with that party. This resolution was carried by only 77 votes to 33, and the minority (mostly of the Democratic party) retired from the congress.[78] The POS had also, in its 1920 congress, agreed to the formation of a united party and had participated in the fruitless negotiations with the Democratic party.[79]

The 1920 FOCH congress had also resolved that its branches should consider entry into the RILU, and at the 1921 congress this

[77] These he divided into 10,000 miners (nitrate, copper and coal) 10,000 in transport, 1,000 peasants, and 9,000 in other occupations. By 1924, when the economy had picked up, according to Ramírez the numbers had risen to 140,000 (*Origen*, p. 93).

[78] Barría, *Movimientos*, p. 145.

[79] There is contradictory evidence on the role of Recabarren in this episode. According to Chacón, Recabarren advised against making the FOCH the basis of a political party (at the FOCH Rancagua Congress in 1920) (Varas, p. 38). Vitale (a Trotskyist) alleges that, on the other hand, it was Recabarren who promoted the venture, p. 56. An article in *El Siglo*, 22 Dec. 1968 (the official CP daily) gives the impression that he changed his mind between 1920 and 1921.

was approved by an overwhelming majority.[80] That congress passed a radical statement of policy about the need to control the means of production, as well as the usual resolution on the need to combat especially gambling and drink. The organization was again changed; the Federal Councils which existed in most cities on a professional basis were reorganized on an industry basis, classified in six major groups. The FOCH resolved to work with the POS for their common ends, which were to be propagated by jointly owned newspapers.[81]

Part of the reason for the move of both party and union into the camp of international communism was the quick disappointment after Alessandri's election in 1920. The candidature of Recabarren was little more than a gesture (and could hardly be more considering that he was imprisoned at the time). Little attention was paid to the election in the contemporary working class press,[82] for workers in general did not have the right to vote. Even so, the 1920 election was the first one to engage the sympathies and interest of many members of the working class. However, a massacre of nitrate workers in San Gregorio led to disillusionment when Alessandri refused to repudiate, and, indeed, even supported, the sections of the army responsible for it. As he was blocked in Congress by a conservative majority, he could do little to fulfil his electoral pledges.

If the ideological clarity and political unity produced by the entry into the RILU and the increasing identification with the CP (which name the POS now adopted) brought some benefits to the

[80] At the 1921 congress there were 128 delegates representing 102 organizations comprising 80,000 workers. A motion to postpone affiliation for a year was defeated by 74 votes against, 34 for, and 6 abstentions. The motion to seek affiliation was carried by 106 for, 12 against (mostly railway union delegates) and 7 abstentions (Barría, *Movimientos*, p. 143).

[81] Poblete, *Organización*, pp. 34–5.

[82] Apart from that sector controlled by the Democratic party which was strongly pro-Alessandri (Arias, p. 178). Chacón vividly describes the appeal of Alessandri to the working class (Varas, pp. 35–6). But not many workers could have voted for Alessandri. In 1920, of a total population of 3,785,000, and a potential male, adult electorate of 898,000, the actual number of electors registered was 370,314, of whom only 166,917 cast votes (a decline from the 295,000 votes cast in the 1912 congressional elections), a narrow majority going to Alessandri. Tampering with the electoral register, widespread fraud and corruption are factors in explaining both the low poll and the low number of registered electors (Atilio Boron, 'Movilización política y crisis política en Chile', *Aportes* (Apr. 1971, pp. 47–51)).

union movement, it had disadvantages too. The movement became more concerned with political, and less with economic, ends; and it lost supporters, like the members of the Democratic party, who did not accept its ideas. It lost unions as well, like the railwaymen in 1923, who felt that their interests did not receive enough attention in the new FOCH.[83] The FOCH tended to concentrate its activities where the CP was also active, i.e. in the coal and nitrate sectors, to the neglect of the urban centres, so that in Santiago it had scarcely 1,000 members.[84] Communist historians now regard this period as one in which the wrong tactics were drawn from the right conclusions. The right conclusion was that the emancipation of the workers could only be the product of their own efforts; but the movement was far too inward-looking and far too pessimistic and mistrustful of other social groups. These tactics were not changed until the formation of the Popular Front.[85] Moreover, according to official party historians, the FOCH underestimated the staying power of capitalism and overestimated its own strength to change the system; and the virtual identification of the FOCH and the CP caused the FOCH to decline and groups like IWW to grow. Yet party historians are too critical. The IWW, with its open membership policy and radical tactics, was attacked and destroyed. The CP and the Communist unions suffered, but survived and later continued to grow.

The FOCH probably reached its peak in 1924 before the combined effects of military intervention in politics, Ibañez's dictatorship, and the world depression threw the whole labour movement

[83] Though they later affiliated to the RILU separately (Jobet, *Recabarren*, p. 140).

[84] Barría, *Movimientos*, p. 146. The then secretary-general of the FOCH, C. A. Martínez, attributed this to ideological competition and factionalism in the working class.

[85] Ramírez, *Movimiento*, pp. 45–6. In his *Origen* he writes: 'The outstanding participation of communist militants in the FOCH, and the recognized leadership of Recabarren both in the party and in the union, the fact that the FOCH had expressed its sympathies for the Russian revolution and had joined RILU, the circumstance that—from the very beginning—the party had intimate and harmonious links with the FOCH, were factors that created the impression that, for Communists and enemies of the working class alike, the party and FOCH were one and the same thing.' This tended to divide the working class on the one hand, and on the other seemed to make FOCH, which was a mass organization, the guiding force of the Communist movement, which lessened its political weight (pp. 209–20). In 1933 the Comintern S. American Bureau made the same criticism.

into confusion and decline as it felt the joint impact of persecution and unemployment. The approximate size of the labour movement is shown in the table below.

*Federations and* obrero *unions, 1925*

| | Unions | Members |
|---|---|---|
| Railway Workers' Federation (affiliated directly to RILU) | 30 | 15,000 |
| Coal-miners' unions (in FOCH) | 12 | 10,000 |
| Metallurgical unions (some only in FOCH) | 15 | 16,000 |
| Nitrate workers' unions (in FOCH) | 40 | 40,000 |
| Seamens union (divided between FOCH & IWW) | 30 | 11,000 |
| Rural unions (in FOCH) | 10 | 5,000 |
| Tram workers' unions (in FOCH) | 7 | 5,000 |
| Other unions in FOCH | 50 | 60,000 |
| Other unions not in FOCH | 20 | 40,000 |
| | 214 | 204,000 |

*Source:* Poblete, *Organizacion,* annex 5. Poblete was an official at the Ministry of Labour and played an important role in drafting the labour code.

From 1924 onwards the FOCH became embroiled in the turbulent politics of the time and suffered accordingly, as did most political parties and unions.[86] Recabarren's suicide in 1924 was a great blow;[87] the establishment of legal unions drew support away from the movement, for the FOCH was ambivalent towards seeking legal status; the movement and party suffered divisions over the attitude to adopt towards Ibáñez, when a Communist senator and four Communist deputies (the party had elected two senators and seven deputies in 1924) advised support for him at a time when he was persecuting many FOCH and Communist leaders.[88]

[86] Between 1925 and 1933 it was unable to hold congresses and by the latter date had been reduced to a quarter of its size, though there was a convention in 1931, basically to engage in the Stalinist–Trotskyist disputes of the time. This convention expelled the allegedly Trotskyist group of Manuel Hidalgo (which had captured the party CC for a time under the Ibáñez dictatorship when almost all members of the Lafertte–Contreras Labarca group were in exile or imprisoned) which favoured working with the legal unions. Hidalgo's group also attacked the current Communist line on 'social-fascism' (R. J. Alexander, *Communism in Latin America* (1957), p. 185).

[87] The reasons are not known, but he was ill and disillusioned and there was a bitter internal CP struggle at the time.

[88] Varas, p. 60.

D

The FOCH was active in the creation of the Social Republican Union of Chilean Wage and Salary Earners in 1925, which claimed 100,000 members from workers, teachers, and white-collar employees. It supported the candidature of far from Communist José Santos Salas[89] for the presidency, who gained 80,000 votes against 180,000 for the right-wing candidate. But this precursor of the Popular Front was taken over by groups seeking to build up a reformist party (though it ended by supporting Ibáñez—who later banned it), and the Communists split from the organization, taking along the FOCH.

### Conclusions

By 1924 it is possible to define some general and persistent features of the labour movement. In the first place it is a highly politicized movement. Union divisions are party or ideological divisions; there is little room for the leader who advocates the complete separation of union from party or non-political unionism, even though this is a theory to which many pay lip-service. The issues debated are political ones—whether there should be a revolutionary syndical movement or whether the task of the political revolution should be left to a separate political party; whether the inspiration of the unions should be Marxist, Bakuninist, or Christian (and later Trotskyist, Christian Democrat, or North American). The fact that this political debate takes place in the unions sets up a tension between inclusivity (all members of the working class including white-collar workers) and exclusivity (party faithful only), and this debate has been a continuous one. Each party believes it alone follows the correct union policy; but on the other hand members of other groups speak for large sections of the working class. The question of the relationship between party and union had already arisen by 1924—which view was to predominate, that of the union or that of the party? As early as this the union movement, and especially the FOCH, had started the process of seeking allies, theoretically to the right of the movement, in the interest of securing political power and influence. By 1924 the problem of retaining ultimate political control over a movement intended to incorporate disparate groups of varying ideologies was a familiar one for Communist leaders.

[89] He modestly proclaimed that his programme was 'not of the left, not extremist, but of national salvation' (cited in Ramírez, *Origen*, p. 149).

It must not be assumed that all unions and all workers were engaged in debating political issues. Even at its peak there were more workers outside the FOCH than inside; and even amongst unionized workers, party militants or union militants were a minority. Because many objected to or were unmoved by a debate couched in party terms, many workers, even those formally attached to a party, were open to the appeal on national grounds made by a genuinely popular leader such as Alessandri in 1920, who stood outside the internal union debate. But if populist figures sweep along many voters with them they do not sweep along the union leadership. The CP was well served by those union leaders who in spite of persecutions and dismissals remained faithful to the party and its ideology, and kept in operation a much reduced party apparatus in the unions even at times when the party itself was outlawed.

The CP was not operating in a working class unfamiliar with or hostile to its ideas. Even if union groups disputed bitterly in the early years, there were at least certain shared assumptions: of opposition to the capitalist system; of the desirability of united action; of the need for workers to seek their own salvation (even if this is modified by the formation of political parties, they are still parties of the working class); of arbitrary treatment by the state; of a common class situation. At least this was so in the Northern mining areas, and this radical tradition was spread by the nitrate workers who lost their jobs with the development of artificial substitutes after the World War I, and with the depression of the interwar period. Of 100,000 workers employed in nitrates in 1928, 60,000 had left by 1932. Migration patterns are not easy to establish, but there is evidence of the role of these workers in spreading the Northern style of unionism to other parts of the country.[90] The autobiography of Lafertte, a former FOCH secretary-general, supports this.[91] Even before he became a Communist of any note he had migrated to several parts of Chile, driven from the North by unemployment and political persecution. He claims that his wandering existence was typical of the unemployed nitrate worker in this period.

[90] Poblete ('Movimiento sindical en Chile', *Combate* (Costa Rica), July–Aug. 1962, p. 26), estimates that 20,000 workers (with families, a total of 100,000 people) were moved from the North to the Santiago region by the government because of the unemployment following World War I.

[91] Lafertte, pp. 17–68.

Not only did these union leaders move around geographically; they also held positions of leadership for long periods of time—Lafertte himself was prominent as a labour leader for many years. There was not in Chile, as there was in Argentina, a sharp break between an 'old class' of labour leaders and a 'new class' formed by different circumstance in response to different pressures (such as massive industrialization or the emergence of leaders like Perón or Vargas). The continuity of ideas, attitudes, structures, and leaders makes it important to understand the tradition of the Chilean labour movement.

The ten years after 1924 were very eventful ones in the history of the Chilean labour movement. Legal unions started, and the whole system of industrial relations became regularized under procedures laid down by the state; a military dictatorship broke Chile's long spell of civilian rule, banned the CP, and persecuted the FOCH; unemployment reduced the size of unions in the early 1930s, and industrialization altered their form in the late 1930s; a new marxist party emerged to challenge the Communists now that the anarchists were a spent force; and the Comintern swung from a policy of 'class against class' to one of Popular Front.

The labour movement faced many dilemmas. Should the unions accept the legal code or not? If so, how far? What should their reaction be to the military coups of 1924 and 1925? Indifference, support, or hostility? (In fact the reaction was a mixture of all three in varying proportions at different times.) [92] There was also difference of opinion over the form of political action: should it be autonomous or organized in alliances with other groups? For the Communists in the unions there arose the tension between their own internal assessments and policies and those of the Comintern. And after 1933 the question of the relationship with the Socialist party became important—and difficult. Nevertheless, the Communists had secured a firm base in the union movement; if their support was to decline at times under attack, it was never to disappear. And they had helped to create a labour movement with strong traditions of politicization and radicalism.

---

[92] The FOCH and the CP certainly supported the 'second' coup of January 1925 which promised to bring in a more reformist military group (Chelén, p. 65). C. Vicuña alleges that they were ready to mount a general strike in September 1924 if certain conditions (support of Congress, arrangements for feeding strikers) were met; but they were not (*La tiranía en Chile* (1938), i. 156).

In 1924 the pattern of civilian rule in Chilean politics was severely disrupted. A military coup heralded a period of subordination to the armed forces, until the leading military figure, Colonel Carlos Ibáñez, assumed the presidency himself from 1927 to 1931. In July 1931 Ibáñez, like many other Presidents in Latin America, fell victim to the effects of the economic depression. There followed eighteen months of political turbulence before civilian rule was firmly re-established under Arturo Alessandri, elected to the presidency for the second time.

Organized labour was a spectator rather than an active participant in these events. A new constitution, a labour code, social legislation—all were passed without consultation, with the unions. The military rulers at first made several half-hearted attempts to woo the workers to their cause, but soon switched to rather more effective attempts to persecute and disrupt the labour movement.

The intention of this chapter was to outline the major traditions of the labour movement before the code of 1924 imposed a new structure on the unions and regulated their activities. It is convenient at this point therefore to change from historical description to contemporary analysis. Before examining the politics of labour following the formation of the Socialist party in 1933, the next two chapters will deal with the size, structure, and growth of unions, and with the impact of the labour code.

# 3. The Size and Structure of the Chilean Labour Movement

APART from rural unions, the growth of the Chilean labour movement since the 1930s has been gradual and slow rather than, as in many Latin American countries, rapid and abrupt. There has been no explosion in numbers comparable to that in Argentina with the rise of Perón (even if, admittedly, much of that explosion was on paper only). Nor has the Chilean movement been tamed and incorporated into the state apparatus, as in Brazil or to a lesser extent in Mexico. It is true that the rural sector is being transformed as a result of the law of 1967 allowing for the formation of rural unions, and that numbers of unions and unionists have grown in other sectors of the economy. Nevertheless, the proportion of the labour force organized into unions has changed gradually rather than dramatically in the last thirty years, and, more important, the style, structure, and political role of the movement have not assumed radically new forms.[1]

If this is convenient for the investigator in some ways, it also imposes on him the need for some historical explanation because—as the last chapter has shown—the origins of the movement in many ways determined its style and political role. And since, apart from the rural sector, the legal framework is substantially the same as it was when first promulgated in 1924, its effects must be described. The political and industrial role of any labour movement depends to a considerable extent on its size, distribution, structure, and growth, and this is the starting point for the present chapter.

[1] The election of a marxist President in late 1970 brings about the possibility of an increasingly important role for the unions, but as I will try to show, the structure of Chilean politics and unions are such that changes are likely to be gradual, and often difficult to achieve.

## 1. Size

The latest available official figures claim that 18·2% of workers belong to unions, representing an increase compared with 10·3% in 1964, when President Frei's Christian Democratic administration first took office.[2] Numbers of unions and members are as follows:

*Unions & members, 1969*

|  | Unions | Members |
|---|---|---|
| Plant unions | 1,342 | 196,101 |
| Professional or craft unions | 2,413 | 232,946 |
| Rural unions | 421 | 104,666 |
|  | 4,176 | 533,713 |

*Source:* As n.2, pp. 362–4. The figures refer to late 1969. The ODEPLAN calculated the labour force in October 1967 as 2,822,500, of which 136,900 or 4·9% was unemployed (*Informe sobre la actividad económica en 1967* (1968), p. 29).

There are, however, three major sources of error in these figures, two of which, when corrected, increase the real proportion of the labour force in unions. In the first place, official figures include only legal unions, but public-sector organizations, which are not 'legally' unions, in fact function as such. Civil servants and municipal employees are not supposed to form unions, but may form 'associations' or other collective bodies. In reality these associations perform all the functions of unions without suffering the restrictions imposed by the labour code. For reasons that will be explained later, a very high percentage of the public sector, including state, municipal, and autonomous enterprises, is unionized. One estimate is that of the approximately 250,000 public-sector employees, over 90% are in union-like organizations, and most estimates put the figure at over 80%.[3]

The proportion of unionized labour in Chile also rises if we exclude from the total active population those who cannot or who are most unlikely to form unions. There are, for example, some 330,000 workers between the ages of 12 and 17, but the legal age for joining a union is 18; there are some 70,000 persons in the

[2] *Sexto mensaje del Presidente Frei . . . 21 de Mayo 1970*, p. 345.

[3] Clotario Blest, 'La organización de la clase trabajadora chilena', *Prensa firme*, 22 Apr., 1969, pp. 22–3. Blest is a radical Catholic, heavily influenced by Castroism, once president of the CUT and a former president of the largest organization of state employees (ANEF). But more detached observers agree with his figures (see E. Morgado, *Libertad sindical* (1967, p. 120).

police and army who may not form unions; and there are some 50,000 employers in the active labour force.[4] The self-employed normally do not form unions, but they cannot be totally excluded, for some groups, like newspaper street vendors, in fact have a quite well organized and political union. Domestic servants, who in 1960 made up 34% of the total female labour force, are difficult to organize, but even here the CP has made efforts to start a union.

Labour force: distribution by employment status, 1960

| Status | No. | % |
| --- | --- | --- |
| Employer | 32,842 | 1·4 |
| Self-employed | 449,116 | 18·8 |
| Salaried employee | 488,056 | 20·4 |
| Wage-earner | 1,081,188 | 45·3 |
| Domestic service employee | 196,478 | 8·2 |
| Unpaid family worker | 38,826 | 1·6 |
| Unspecified | 102,161 | 4·3 |
| | 2,388,667 | 100·0 |

Source: Dirección de Estadística y Censos, Población del país: Características básicas de la población (censo 1960) (1964), pp. 62–3. The most accurate figures on the distribution of the labour force by employment come from the decennial censuses; the figures for 1970 will not be available for some time, so the table summarizes the position from the 1960 census.

At the other end of the scale the CUT, the major labour confederation in Chile, by reducing the labour force as much as possible (to 2,169,000 potential unionists), and by increasing the number of unionists as much as possible (to 734,000), estimates the proportion of unionized labour at 34% of the total. But this includes the third major source of error: classification as unions of associations that are not really trade unions, double counting of members, and the inclusion of inactive unions. For example, the CUT figures, and also the official figures, include 26,000 members of legally registered employers' associations as unions;[5] and the

[4] Blest, p. 21. His figures go up to Dec. 1968 and are taken from the Ministry of Labour and CORFO.

[5] F. Zapata, Estructura y representatividad del sindicalismo (1968), p. 35. This most useful work is based on the Ministry of Labour figures for legal unions only (which means most, though not all unions in the private sector, but not unions in the public sector) as of 3 May 1967.

figures for the rural unions also include a couple of thousand rural employers.[6] Estimates for the number of workers who are members of more than one union vary considerably; given the nature of the data they can be no more than guesses.[7] Data on unions which have to all intents and purposes ceased functioning are a little more reliable. Though as high as 20% of all unions (which organized 15% of all unionists) in the late 1950s, by 1967 the figure for inactive unions had fallen to only 2·3% of unions (1% of all unionists).[8]

Because of these ambiguities it is clearly not possible to give precise figures for actual union membership as a proportion of total potential union membership. It does seem that the CUT figure is the more accurate one, both in its estimate of the base for potential union membership and in its inclusion of public-sector organizations as part of union membership. If the overall percentage of the labour force in unions is not as high as 34%, it is nevertheless probably not far short of 30%.

## 2. Distribution by occupation

Global figures are not very satisfactory indices of the representativeness of union organization, which is better conveyed by looking at the distribution of unionization in the various sectors of the labour force.

First, it is necessary to look at the distribution of the active labour force in the various economic sectors. Historically the greatest changes took place as a result of the import-substitution based industrialization policies pursued by the Popular Front and

---

[6] Blest, in *Prensa firme*, 22 Apr. 1969, p. 21.

[7] J. O. Morris & R. Oyaneder, *Afiliación y finanzas sindicales* (1961), estimate double affiliation at one-sixth of union membership (p. 27). Morgado (p. 120) thinks this is exaggerated and reduces the figure to 6%. Zapata (p. 71) also argues for a similar figure.

[8] Morris & Oyaneder (pp. 26–7) give the earlier figures. These estimates are made on the basis of (legally required) union returns on election of executives and of their financial statements to the Ministry of Labour. Official figures do not disclose whether unions ceased functioning because of apathy or the closure of plants by employers. The register of unions was greatly improved in 1958 by the removal of many inactive unions (generally those in small plants). The decline in the number of inactive unions is also due to a change in the political and administrative climate in favour of unions since 1965. The later figures are taken from M. Barrera, *Participación social y los sindicatos industriales* (1970), pp. 12–16.

later governments. Since the 1950s there have not been any dramatic changes in the employment structure of the labour force. Secondly, the extent of unionization in each economic sector must be examined—and here the greatest changes have taken place in the rural sector following the 1967 law passed by the Christian Democratic government permitting the formation of effective rural unions. These figures must also take into account the average size of unions in the different economic sectors, for a sector in which there is a very large number of small unions may well have an industrial relations system distinct from one in which there is a small number of large unions. The figures are shown in the following table.

| Sector | Distribution of active population by economic sectors (%) | | | Level of unionization of different economic sectors (%) | | No. of members | Ave. size of unions |
|---|---|---|---|---|---|---|---|
| | 1930 | 1952 | 1965 | 1965 | mid-1968 | mid-1967 | mid-1967 |
| 1. Agriculture | 37·5 | 30·1 | 27·7 | 3·3 | 14 | 22,700 | 72 |
| 2. Mining | 5·7 | 4·7 | 3·8 | 65·3 | 62 | 57,800 | 321 |
| 3. Manufacturing | 15·9 | 19·0 | 18·0 | 38·9 | 40 | 163,200 | 127 |
| 4. Construction | 4·3 | 4·8 | 5·7 | 17·8 | 27 | 16,100 | 125 |
| 5. Electricity, gas, water | 0·8 | 0·9 | 0·8 | 45·0 | 36 | 9,400 | 151 |
| 6. Commerce | 11·4 | 10·3 | 10·1 | 16·6 | 22 | 42,600 | 96 |
| 7. Transport & communications | 5·4 | 4·4 | 4·9 | 20·7 | 48* | 37,700 | 110 |
| 8. Services | 16·1 | 22·2 | 22·8 | 4·6 | 35* | 22,400 | 93 |
| 9. Non-specified | 2·9 | 3·6 | 6·2 | | | 900 | 58 |
| | 100 | 100 | 100 | | | 372,650† | 124 |

\* These figures, unlike those for 1965, include the public as well as private sector.
† Except for the original total, figures have been rounded to nearest hundred.

*Sources:* Distribution of population by economic sector up to 1952: C. H. Ruíz Tagle, *Concentración de población y desarrollo económico: el caso chileno* (Santiago, 1966), p. 186; 1965: CORFO, *Geografía económica de Chile: primer apéndice* (1966), p. 153. For extent of unionization for 1965: Gurrieri, *Aportes*, July 1968, p. 95; 1968: *Memoria del consejo directivo al 5° congreso de la CUT, 19–24 Nov. 1968*, p. 51. For ave. size and members of unions, Zapata, p. 36.

Figures for the average size of unions can be further refined. In most countries the larger the size of the establishment, the more likely there is to be a union, and Chile is no exception to this rule. In manufacturing industry, if we use the *total* industrial labour force as the base for our calculation of the level of unionization, we arrive at a figure of just over 30%; if, however, we use as our base only establishments with 10 or more workers, we arrive at a level of 60%; but if we consider only factories with 25 or more workers—the legal minimum for forming a union in Chile the level is 70%. It is important to bear these points in mind when talking about the representativeness of trade unions, for many accusations that the organized workers in Chile constitute a small 'aristocracy of labour' are based on unreal calculations of the gap between the actual and the potential level of union organization. In Chile it is legally impossible to form unions in factories of 10 or fewer workers, and in factories of between 10 and 24 workers, they can form only union 'committees' which are allowed to perform few functions. Workers in such small concerns are naturally less inclined to form unions. If a more realistic base is used, it can be seen that the Chilean union movement, at least in manufacturing industry, is far from unrepresentative of the labour force that can effectively be organized.

The same is true for other sectors. Copper mining, for example, has a high rate of unionization at well over half the labour force. But if we exclude from our calculations the labour force in the small and medium-sized mines, largely privately owned, and consider only the 'Gran Minería', until recently largely North American owned but now owned by the Chilean state, then the percentage of the mining labour force in unions rises to almost 90%.

As with economic sectors, so there is considerable geographical variation. The highest level of unionization—32%—is in the Northern mining province of Antofagasta. In several rural provinces it drops to 3%. In Santiago and its surroundings, where almost half of all unionists live and work, the figures rises to about 12%, though this would be much higher if the public sector were included. Nearly 90% of all unionists live in or near four large cities: Santiago, Antofagasta, Valparaíso, and Concepción.

## 3. Structure

The structure of Chilean unions is laid down in the law of 1924 for urban unions and the law of 1967 for rural ones. Not all unions are inside the legal framework; some operate outside in a condition of non-legality rather than illegality. This is especially true of the 'political' confederations like the CUT, and also of some federations, like the FONACC, which find that greater freedom compensates for the advantages of legal recognition. Since these advantages are largely confined to plant unions, it is not surprising that they should constitute the most important sector of legally recognized unionism.

Before the 1967 law altered the situation in the rural areas, the law established three major classes of unions, though there are also a number of sub-classes.

There are first the *sindicatos industriales*, or plant unions. There must be at least 25 workers for a union to be formed (though if there are more than 10 they can form a union-like association, as is quite common in the construction industry), and in a free vote at least 55% must be in favour of starting a union. The decision once taken is binding on all members and there can be only one union. Only *obreros* may join the union. Once formed, it may share in the profits of the enterprise; half the profits distributed to the workforce go to the individual members and half to the union. Plant unions may form federations with other plant unions, but not for the major ends of union activity such as collective bargaining. The functions of the federations are meant to be largely educational and social, although the labour code normally prevents them from getting sufficient membership dues to finance these uncontroversial activities.

Secondly, there are the *sindicatos profesionales*, or professional (or craft) unions. In theory these are formed of similar trades or crafts across plant lines as well as inside plants. They can include *empleados* or *obreros*, and even employers. It is possible for members of a plant union to belong also to a craft union. Though there are numerous craft unions, they are on average smaller, weaker, and less important than the plant unions. *Empleados* who can only form craft unions enjoy higher legally established minimum wages than *obreros*, a better social-security system, and a higher social status independent of union organization; thus their incentive to form unions is weaker than that of the *obreros*. Membership in craft unions is not compulsory; they do not share in profits; their collective-bargaining activities are largely extra-legal for they are not supposed to strike. While the craft unions can legally form federations, mostly they are confined to single establishments.

*Sindicatos agrícolas*, or rural unions, used to be constituted under the very strict provisions of the 1947 law. Besides the usual difficulties of organization in the countryside, the law demanded that each union must have a minimum of 20 workers (which only a sixth of all farms had), all of whom must have worked on the same farm for a year (which ruled out most of the rural labour force), and at least 10 of these had to be able to read and write (when rural illiteracy at the time was over 50%). Moreover limitations on the right to strike made it hardly worthwhile to form unions, even if the low level of rural wages had made this possible. The intention of the 1947 law was more to prevent unionization than to encourage it, and was part of the deal made by the then Radical President, González Videla, to gain the support of the right-wing parties.[9] The 1967 reform allowed rural unions to be formed and function in a way not unlike plant unions.[10] Though a rural union was supposed to have a minimum of 100 members based on the geographical *comune* (thus combining the union branches of several farms), it could be organized with 25 members, with the permission of the local labour inspectorate. Rural unions have full freedom to form federations and confederations, as do the craft unions (though not the plant unions), but they may belong to only one federation. The law also allows for the formation of employers' unions in order to facilitate collective bargaining. Union leaders enjoy protection from dismissal in the performance of their duties and in the creation of the unions. Union dues are deducted by the employers at source (2% of taxable income, the employer to pay the same) and are used to finance not only the base organizations but also the provincial and national organizations. Unlike the urban law, the rural law does not establish only one union per *comune* or farm, but it recognizes the right of the most representative union to defend the interests and to engage in collective bargaining for all local union members. Strike provisions are much less restrictive than under the old laws. Unions may belong to only one federation, and federations to only one confederation.

With the passing of the 1967 law union growth was very rapid; though often this meant only legal recognition of those unions that had been formed in anticipation of the law and with the stimulus and funds of various governmental and private agencies. Thus virtually all rural unions have been created since 1965.

The plant union is the most important and the most numerous as compared with any one of the other types of craft union.

---

[9] See F. Walker Linares, 'Trade unionism among agricultural workers in Chile', *Internat. Labor R.*, 68/6 (1953).

[10] For text of the law see *La Nación*, 1 May 1967. See also J. Petras, *Chilean Christian Democracy* (1967), ch. 4, *passim*. A useful discussion of the text is contained in G. Arroyo, 'Sindicalismo y promoción campesina', *Mensaje*, June 1966, pp. 244–9.

Though inside the plant-union system there are undoubtedly company unions under employer control, especially in the smaller enterprises,[11] this class also includes the large modern union engaged in a collective-bargaining situation not unlike that in modern industry elsewhere. The average plant union is larger than the craft union, and plant unions are concentrated in the largest towns and in the mining areas. Well over 80% of all plant unions are organized in the secondary sector and mining; a special statute governs the organization of the copper mines.[12] Plant unions in the agricultural sector are virtually all in fishing and in forestry. In the tertiary sector, on the other hand, plant unions are less important than professional ones. If there is not a higher proportion of unionized labour in the manufacturing sector it is more because the labour code prohibits the organization of plant unions in establishments of fewer than 25 workers than because there are vast sectors of unorganized workers ignored by some hypothetical aristocracy of labour. To look at it another way, 51% of all *obreros* in the manufacturing sector are in unions (compared with 30% for *empleados*). There is also a high correlation between industrial concentration and extent of unionization.[13] The effects of this pattern on the industrial-relations system will be examined in the next chapter, but it is clear that in the manufacturing sector most union activity is at the plant level.

The craft unions are much more varied than the plant unions. They can consist of very specialized craft groups seeking legal

[11] This is a fairly general phenomenon. S. M. Lipset and others write that 'over a hundred years ago Marx noted that workers in small craft shops who work side by side with their employers associate with them informally, and develop personal ties with them, are markedly less class conscious and less involved in workers organizations than are workers in large industry. The personal ties of small shop men with their employers tend to weaken their identification with organizations predicated on a conflict of interests. . . . To the small shop man the problems of the boss are more persuasive and the chances for individual recognition and rewards through personal relations with the shop owner are felt to be greater than in larger shops of even fifty or a hundred workers' (*Union Democracy* (1956), p. 172).

[12] Zapata, p. 42. In 1967 75% of all plant unions (and 65% of all unionists) were in manufacturing industry; and 8·2% of unions (with 23% of unionists) in mining (Barrera, *Participación*, p. 19).

[13] Zapata, pp. 113 & 127. Over 95% of workers in industries organized as monopolies are unionized, compared with 55% of workers in competitive industries.

upgrading from *obrero* to *empleado* status because of the material advantages that it brings. On the other hand they can be a less developed form of unionism than the plant unions, characteristic of small industrial units in backward areas, with objectives sometimes more akin to the classic mutualist society than the modern trade union. Some craft unions can include employers as well.

In contrast to the plant unions, there are also several types of craft union. Their relative distribution is shown in the table below.

*Types of union, mid-1967*

| Type | Unions | Members | Ave. size |
|------|-------|---------|-----------|
| Plant | 1,054 | 179,500 | 170 |
| Craft | | | |
| *Obrero* by establishment | 80 | 9,000 | 112 |
| *Obrero:* independent | 504 | 50,600 | 100 |
| *Empleado* by establishment | 471 | 57,700 | 122 |
| *Empleado:* independent | 262 | 27,400 | 104 |
| Employers or self-employed | 299 | 25,800 | 86 |
| Mixed by establishment | 96 | 7,700 | 79 |
| Mixed: independent | 28 | 3,700 | 131 |
| Rural | 199 | 11,300 | 56 |
| Total | 2,995 | 372,650 | 124 |

*Source:* Zapata, p. 35. Figures for members have been rounded to nearest hundred, except for the total.

The professional union of independent *obreros* organizes those who practise the same craft but who work in different enterprises, yet reside close enough to form unions, for these are not massive federations but very small local unions. In this category falls part of the double membership, those affiliated both to a plant union and to a professional union. This type of union exists in the developed areas, and is the most common form in several of the underdeveloped Southern provinces, partly because the small size of establishments there does not permit the formation of plant unions; it often exists for the pursuit of mutualist ends rather than collective bargaining. It is a type more common than the plant union in the primary and tertiary sectors of the economy and is also found in the construction industry, where labour mobility impedes the formation of the more settled plant union.

The professional unions of *obreros* by establishment are a very small group. These basically organize the mechanics and electricians of specific establishments who are also members of the plant union, since collective bargaining by the plant union usually includes them as a separate section. They predominate in the Concepción area where there are a larger number of modern industries; and most of these unions have been created in the last ten years.

The professional union of *empleados* by establishment is the *empleado* equivalent of the plant union for the *obreros*. Its smaller average size is indicative of the lower propensity of *empleados* to join unions (and of the smaller number of *empleados*). It has grown as a group quite considerably—by almost two-thirds since 1965[14]—because of legislative changes of status from *obrero* to *empleado* of skilled groups such as mechanics, electricians, etc. Nearly half its members are found in the tertiary sector, in commerce, transport, and personal services.

The professional union of independent *empleados* also organizes those sectors employed in commerce and transport but who do not work in the same enterprise. They are practically all in the tertiary sector, with a large proportion of drivers of public transport (*choferes*).

The professional union of employers (*empresarios*) are basically self-employed workers, such as small retail salesmen, bakers, butchers, etc. Practically all are in the tertiary sector, especially in commerce and transport. Very often they are the employers of those who are grouped in the professional unions of independent *empleados*.

The mixed union of *empleados* and *obreros* by establishment is again characteristic of small enterprises such as printing, commerce, and personal services like hairdressing establishments. Very often in such unions it is difficult to distinguish between functions of *empleados* or *obreros*, or the small size of the establishment means that the legally necessary number of 25 can be reached only by both categories combining. Most of these unions were created after the victory of the Christian Democrats in 1964 and 1965.

There are very few mixed unions of independent *obreros* and *empleados*. They are mostly in very small manufacturing or service occupations, though there is oddly enough one very large union of almost 2,000 members in this group, accounting for almost half

[14] Ibid., p. 72.

its total membership. This is the Professional Union of Textile Workers and Employees in the province of Santiago, which groups workers in a large number of small textile establishments.

Separate from the legal forms of Chilean trade unionism, however, are the public-sector organizations, and it has been estimated that there are some 2000 associations of varying size and name.[15] Unlike the private sector, most of them have constituted real federations. Their distribution is shown below.

*Federations of public-sector organizations, 1967*

|  | *Members* |
| --- | --- |
| National Government Employees' Group (ANEF) | 43,130 |
| Chilean Teachers' Federation (FEDECh) | 51,603 |
| National Semi-Government Employees' Group (ANES) | 9,812 |
| Union of Professors and Employees of the Univ. of Chile (UPECh) | 6,731 |
| Industrial Railway Workers' Federation (FIFCh) | 27,252 |
| National Health Workers' Federation (FENATS) | 33,560 |
| National Association of Municipality Workers & Employees | 26,000 |
| Other independent state enterprises (petroleum, transport (ETCE), port, airlines, housing (CORVI) | 10,031 |
|  | 208,118 |

*Source:* Blest, *Punto final,* 26 Mar., 1968, p. 17.

## 4. Growth

The number of workers in unions, defined as paid-up members of a permanent organization, is not necessarily a guide to the numbers which may be mobilized for specific industrial or political action. In the late nineteenth century, though there existed only a rudimentary organized labour movement, far more than the theoretically sparse membership could be mobilized for protest in times of crisis or hardship, if often more in the nature of spontaneous mass protest than planned union agitation. Today the relationship between formal union affiliation and the number of workers who may be mobilized for industrial action such as factory seizures or strikes is much closer, though there are still variations between occupational groups.

Estimates of the numbers in unions are very speculative for the early years of the Chilean labour movement. Some put the mem-

[15] Barría, *Breve hist.,* p. 45.

E

bership as high as 63,000 in 1903; and by 1928 the first of the major confederations, the FOCH, claimed to have 136,000 affiliated unionists.[16]

Rather more reliable figures, for legal unions only, start in 1932 when the Labour Ministry began to collect figures.[17]

*Growth of union membership*

| Year | Plant | Craft | Rural | Total |
|------|-------|-------|-------|-------|
| 1932 | 29,400 | 25,400 | — | 54,800 |
| 1942 | 122,400 | 71,600 | — | 193,000 |
| 1952 | 155,000 | 128,300 | 1,000 | 284,300 |
| 1964 | 143,000 | 125,900 | 1,700 | 270,600 |
| 1969 | 196,100 | 233,000 | 104,700 | 533,800 |

*Sources:* Up to 1964: Morgado, p. 153. From 1964: *Sexto mensaje del Presidente Frei*, p. 362. Figures refer to legal unions only, and have been rounded to nearest hundred.

Growth and decline of legally-recognized unions seems to depend very largely upon economic and administrative factors. The acceleration in the pace of industrial development with the coming of the Popular Front government produced a rise in the numbers in unions. Official encouragement to form unions and the easing of the administrative obstacles to the granting of legal recognition help to explain their growth in the Christian Democratic era. Obviously the change of law in the rural sector and technical assistance to unions explain the rapid growth in rural union membership. Even in the non-rural sector, with no dramatic change in the law, there was an increase of 12% in 1967 alone. The variation in numbers affiliated to the federations and the major confederations, though obviously affected by economic and especially administrative factors too, are also affected by party political factors. Bitter party infighting between Socialists and Communists in the late 1940s led to the break-up and decline of the then major union confederation, the CTCH. The size of the CUT depends upon whether at the moment of calculation the Christian Democrats and Radicals, with the unionists they control, form part of it or not.

[16] Ramírez, *Origen*, p. 93.
[17] These have been usefully summarized in Morris & Oyaneder.

## Conclusion

It is not easy to see sectors in the economy where unionization could expand easily and rapidly; the sectors where there are few unions are those where it is difficult to organize unions in any circumstances. With a manufacturing structure where almost half the labour force works in establishments of ten or less, the only appropriate union structure would be the professional union of *obreros*; but while the legal code provides few advantages to this form of organization, there is unlikely to be much union growth in these small concerns. Nor are the advantages of unionization for the *empleado* grades so great that there is likely to be much change from the present situation.

Most unions in Chile are small. In mid-1968 the average size of the plant union was 155; 63% of all these unions have less than 100 members and these account for 21% of all workers in them.[18] An earlier survey found that only 26 unions had over 1,000 members.[19] The average size of professional unions is even smaller, with only 98 members. Moreover, 77% of these unions have fewer than 100 members, and there were only 5 with over 1,000 members.[20] The growth of unions now taking place in the urban sector is reducing the average size still more. Of the 449 formed between 1967 and mid-1968, the average membership was 61 (for plant unions alone it was 69).[21]

There are few strong federations of plant or professional unions to offset this picture of fragmentation. Collective bargaining, as the law envisages, is very largely the concern of the individual plant union negotiating with an individual employer. The local plant union in manufacturing industry is the 'typical' Chilean trade union.

The relative absence of federations at regional or national level apart from the public sector is not surprising. Federations of plant unions are not supposed to engage in collective bargaining; and in the professional sector they are in practice largely limited to mutualist ends. At the beginning of 1967 there were 7 legally recognized federations of plant unions, 21 of professional unions, and the copper workers enjoyed a special legal statute which

---

[18] *Memoria al 5° congreso de la* CUT, p. 20.
[19] Morris & Oyaneder, pp. 28–9.
[20] *Memoria*, p. 20; Morris & Oyaneder, p. 29.
[21] *Memoria*, p. 20.

helps to make their union by far the most powerful federation in Chile.[22] There are, however, powerful federations outside the legal structure such as the COMACH and the FONACC. Apart from these, the millers (Confederación de Molineros), the printing workers (Central de Obreros Gráficos de Obras), and the bakers (Federación de Panificadores) are the only ones that engage in collective bargaining for all their members with a comparable employers' association.[23] However, there are another ten or so federations that play a real co-ordinating and information role in the process of collective bargaining of their constituent members even if they do not initiate it. Figures for membership in federations are not particularly reliable, but in the private sector it is probable that fewer than ten can claim more than 10,000 workers, and of these the largest is the Miners' Federation, with 30,000 members.[24] The three major rural confederations all claim large membership and, given the growing numbers in the rural unions, are likely to expand far more rapidly than any in the urban sector, unless the Allende government succeeds, as it has promised, in transforming the labour code.

The striking feature of the Chilean union scene is not so much the lack of unionization as its limitations. One reason for this is obviously the economic structure and the occupational groupings to which it gives rise. Another factor of great importance is the all-embracing labour code. These two factors, and the way they interact to produce the Chilean system of industrial relations, are the subject of the next chapter.

[22] Morgado, p. 146–8.

[23] Barría, *Relaciones colectivas del trabajo* (1967), p. 52.

[24] Barría, *Trayectoria y estructura del movimiento sindical chileno* (1963), pp. 387–9.

# 4. The System of Industrial Relations

The unions established in conformity with the provisions of this [code] will be institutions of mutual collaboration between the factors of production, and therefore those organizations which impede discipline and order in work will be considered contrary to the spirit and norms of the law.

Art. 367, Labour Code.

## The legal code and its effects on the unions

THE legal code was devised in the 1920s and in fundamentals it applies today, except for the modifications in the rural sector and the special statute for the copper miners.[1] Its origins lie in the legislative proposals devised by the two major political forces of the time, the Conservative party and the Liberal Alliance. The projects were in essence authoritarian and restrictive, the main difference between them being that the Conservatives wished to see labour organizations controlled by employers (with the more advanced wing of the Conservative party advocating a form of Catholic paternalism), whereas the Liberals were prepared to see the government as the final authority. However, neither inside the parties nor between them was there agreement on the need for legislation; most deputies were quite happy to see the unions unrecognized and preferably non-existent.[2] Even those intel-

---

[1] J. Morris, *Elites, Intellectuals and Consensus* (1966), deals fully with the historical background. Alexander, *Labor Relations in Argentina, Brazil and Chile* (1962), describes the impact of the legal code on the industrial-relations system. A Christian Democratic projected reform presented to Congress in February 1965 was blocked because of left-wing and internal party opposition to several provisions. Allende's first initiatives in labour-code reform—the legalization of the CUT—were also defeated in Congress.

[2] Not that the code did apply immediately. Morris (p. 292) writes: 'In fact, not until the unification of the labor movement in 1936 and the election

lectuals whose concern with the 'social problem' had led them to devise measures for legal regulation of labour conditions had done so because they feared the radicalism of the existing labour movement. They wanted to eliminate radical influences by setting up unions easily controlled by state and employers.

Organized labour itself was consulted neither by the politicians nor by the military, whose eruption into the political scene in 1924 allowed President Alessandri to push through a number of reforms that Congress had blocked for several years. Given the political turbulence of 1924 and 1925, the labour movement was as much preoccupied by the general political situation, and in particular the proposed constituent assembly to reform the constitution, as it was by the proposed labour code. The unions' attitude to the code was ambivalent. United in agreement that it was a capitalist conspiracy, they were divided over whether they should reject it outright or accept it and try to manipulate it for their own ends.[3] The majority, however, was attracted by the idea that government protection might allow it to extend its influence into areas where unions had previously made no impact, and by the financial attractiveness of the profit-sharing schemes. But union acceptance of the code was not widespread until the change in Communist policy at the start of the Popular Front period.[4]

---

victory of the Popular Front government two years later did development of the legal industrial relations system take on a real and lasting momentum'. Indeed, until the codification of laws in 1931, many attempts at organizing legal unions (especially in the nitrate regions by the FOCH) and running them according to the law were broken up by the employers with the help of the police force (ibid., pp. 250–1). Thus although the law was passed in 1924, only 61 unions had been formed by 1929. The Ibáñez administration in 1930–1 backed up the laws, firstly by codification and then by developing the necessary administrative apparatus. Ibáñez wanted to develop his own union movement under the aegis of the code but was overthrown before he could do so.

[3] Morris, pp. 243–7. In its December 1925 congress the FOCH decided that it must reject reformism *and* a completely anti-political stand; that it would use bourgeois legislation to fight the capitalists; and that it would therefore work for the implementation or the repeal of laws in accordance with the dictates of the working class and its long-term objectives. The Communist leader and deputy, Recabarren, had, on his own initiative, introduced proposals on labour legislation which were ignored by congress.

[4] Indeed, hostility to the laws grew in 1927 when the Ibáñez administration tried to drive the left out of the unions and used the government apparatus of labour laws for this purpose (ibid., p. 247).

As well as the overall structure for unions, the code also closely regulates their internal workings. However, its application is far from uniform; to mention only two anomalies, there are the tacit recognition by the state of public-sector unions that are not supposed to exist, and the development by a few unions of strong federations outside the law.

The hand of the state lies heavily on the labour movement. In many ways the code is successfully aimed at limiting the economic power of the unions, so contributing, amongst other factors, to making them relatively weak agents in the system of industrial bargaining. This does, however, produce one effect entirely unintended by its framers. Economic weakness tends to increase political influence and commitment, for weak unions are forced to seek political allies to take the fight to areas where they are likely to have more success than if they acted alone on the industrial or economic front.

The way that the state changes labour law to suit its own purposes is another factor that explains why unions must seek political protection. The prime example of the arbitrary use of state power against unions was the Law for the Defence of Democracy passed in 1948 and not repealed for ten years. This law was intended to eliminate the CP from the political scene. All union leaders of Communist affiliation were removed from their posts and all Communists were banned from standing for office. Surveillance over union leaders was entrusted to the Political Police, who had the right to prevent candidates standing for union office if they were suspected of sympathy with the CP.[5] This naturally gave employers ample opportunity to denounce union leaders and activists to the Political Police.[6] The law, and the subsequent regulations issued by the Ministry of the Interior, considerably increased the government's powe 10ver unions. All political groups were banned in public-sector organizations; strikes were

---

[5] W. Thayer, *Trabajo, empresa, y revolución* (1968), pp. 25–6.

[6] The two circulars of the Ministry of the Interior enlarging police interference in union affairs were known as the Koch–Yañez decree and the Holger–Letelier circular. Under these regulations, for example, the executive of the plant union of the Huachipato steel works was removed from authority for having supported a general strike called by the CUT in January 1956 to protest against the government's economic policy. The enterprise used the opportunity to get rid of known trouble-makers. The new executive chosen to succeed the dismissed one ran into strong opposition from the rank and file (T. Di Tella & others, *Sindicato y comunidad* (1967), pp. 89–90).

virtually prohibited in that sector and made more difficult in the private sector; even more control was established over unions' funds and property; acting 'against the economic interest of the country' could result in a union losing its legal standing. The pursuit of legitimate union ends might be turned into crimes against the state.[7] Though the law was repealed in 1957, it was not until the election of a Christian Democratic President in 1964 that the Ministry of Labour could be seen as at least in some ways an ally rather than an enemy of the labour movement. Nevertheless the Frei administration, while helping new unions to form, did not succeed in passing new labour legislation, so that the rules regulating the internal structure of unions are still (at the time of writing) those of the original code.

The labour code closely prescribes the form of internal organization for the different types of union. The supreme union authority is a general assembly of all its members. Leadership consists of a five-man directorate and all five, both in office and in campaigning for office, enjoy immunity from arbitrary dismissal from their jobs.[8] Three of them serve as president, treasurer, and secretary, though they do not stand for these offices as such, since the executive itself allocates these positions. Elections are held annually (except for the copper unions, where they are held triennially). The voting system in plant unions is rather unusual. Workers who have been employed for three or more years in the same concern are entitled to double votes; and as votes can all be given for one candidate, such workers can cast all their ten votes, assuming that there are at least five candidates, for one person. This system allows small minorities to be represented on union executives if only a small number of senior workers cast all their votes for a given candidate. It can also lead to well-organized large minorities obtaining three of the executive posts, thereby monopolizing the offices of president, treasurer, and secretary, even if these three posts are held by candidates who came third,

---

[7] A. Bowen Herrera, *Nuestro derecho del trabajo y la ley de defensa de la democracia* (1950), pp. 12–37; Comité de Solidaridad y Defensa de la libertades públicas, *El estado policial—o la ley de las defensa de la democracia*, I (1951), pp. 29–30. The organization publishing this pamphlet, a Communist 'front' group, estimates that 15,000 workers were dismissed and moved to other, and usually remote, areas of the country.

[8] Though this was not granted until 1931; hence one reason for the slow growth of unions.

fourth, and fifth in the poll.[9] Until 1965 union leaders were not supposed to receive compensation for lost earnings in performing their union functions, and indeed were expected to work full-time at their employment tasks. The only exceptions were unions that reached *de facto* agreement with employers and, by special legal statutes, the officials of the merchant marine unions and the copper unions.[10] Even with the reforms of 1965, the barest justice is accorded to union leaders; and if the union lacks funds and the employer is unwilling to pay the leader while engaged in union duties, then his situation is no better.[11] In no case does he receive extra payment over and above his salary for carrying out union duties.[12] This has obviously hindered the development of a bureaucratic structure, though it has the advantage of reducing the gap between leader and rank and file.[13] The effect of the

[9] Morgado, pp. 70–1. All voting has to take place in the presence of a member of the Labour Inspectorate.

[10] Amendments in 1965 (and in 1967 for the rural sector) extended the right to compensation to all union leaders. When authorized by the union general assembly, leaders receive pay and expenses from the union when they must attend to union business during normal working hours. Only in the rural area are full-time leaders envisaged. Directors of the CTC are still supposed to work at their regular jobs a minimum of 30 consecutive days each three months. It does not seem that this is inflexibly applied in practice (US Dept of Labor, *Labor Law & Practice* (1969), p. 31).

[11] In one survey of presidents of plant unions in the Santiago, Valparaíso, Concepción area 32% said that the enterprise paid them unconditionally; 16% said that the enterprise paid but with some conditions, such as always asking permission and always performing duties inside and not outside the factory; 13% said the union paid for hours lost; 2% said that the enterprise paid for work inside the factory and the union outside; 19% said neither union nor enterprise paid—so presumably they lost pay. In some large factories all or some of the executive were paid; more often than not it was only the president (Barrera, *Sindicato industrial* (1965), p. 28).

[12] There are obviously some material compensations, like occasionally travelling to Santiago, or even to Moscow or Washington. But these are relatively few and far between and hardly an incentive for seeking union office.

[13] Nevertheless, there is a surprising amount of stability in office. A survey of the incumbents of the presidency (the most important post) of nearly all the industrial unions in the Santiago, Valparaíso, Concepción area found that 23% had been president for 10 years or more, and 44% for 5 years or more (Landsberger & others, *Pensamiento del dirigente sindical* (1963), p. 22). However, another survey, for Gran Santiago only, covering *all* union posts found, that 77% of unions had 50% or more turnover in the period 1959–63 and that 10% changed leadership every year. Of the leaders elected in 1963, nearly 40% had never held office before. Professional unions showed greater instability

present system, in the absence of substantial status, financial or power inducements for seeking union office, is to increase political commitment as a motive. Unionists are certainly encouraged by their parties to do so, for all the main Chilean parties involved in the union movement invoke the need for their union militants to seek office or to help organize the efforts of those from their party who do.

Unions are forbidden to set funds aside for strike purposes; though there is considerable evasion of this law, in financial matters the state closely regulates the the unions. Union budgets must be submitted to local labour inspectors; union treasurers may keep only a derisory amount of cash in hand, and the rest in a supervised bank account. When unions need to act they must, because of the inadequacy of their own resources, either seek political help or mount only a 'guerrilla' strike—short, sometimes violent, often accompanied by seizure of the plant. Except for the few large federations they do not have the means to sustain prolonged action.

Linked to the problems created by state control is the general one of inadequacy of union funds, especially when constant inflation means that union dues must be constantly increased to maintain their real value. Much of the revenue of plant unions comes from profit-sharing schemes rather than from the members.[14] In 1948 it was estimated that two-thirds of total revenue came from profits paid over by employers directly to the unions, in 1959 this proportion was estimated at 52 per cent.[15] Yet there is still widespread evasion by employers; of the 608 plant unions entitled to receive profits in 1960, for example, only 265 received them.[16] Much union time is spent in squabbling with employers

---

than plant ones. There was especially great rotation amongst young leaders. No real difference was found according to the size of enterprise. The office of president was much more stable than any other, which helps to explain the discrepancies with the Landsberger survey (E. Latorre Díaz, *Rotación de dirigentes sindicales*, *Memoria*, Escuela de Economía, Univ. Chile, 1964).

[14] The 'check-off' system is legally possible, but it is difficult. The legal formalities are complicated; there are possibilities of employer interference, for the employer collects the dues; and union assemblies prefer their executives to exhaust the possibilities of profit-sharing first.

[15] Alexander, *Labor relations*, p. 296; Morris & Oyaneder, p. 40. Employers also paid over a share of profits directly to their employees. Half goes to the union; half to the employee.

[16] US Dept of Labor, *Labor in Chile* (1962), p. 37.

over profits. As the original Conservative scheme foresaw, the system of profit-sharing increased employer domination and weakened worker solidarity. Craft unions and federations do not normally receive profits, and given the usually low revenue from dues, their financial weakness prohibits much activity. The CUT is in a state of continuous financial crisis.[17]

In general, income from dues and profits is low, and limitations on power to invest prevent unions from using their scarce resources to advantage. Plant unions may not pay dues to a federation to which they belong. One study estimates that the average income per union member per month in industrial unions in 1959 was E° 0·62; for the professional unions it was E° 0·29. Average real income per member has been declining since 1940,[18] partly as union membership has spread to less skilled, and less well-paid, sectors.

Unions have little power or influence over the terms of employment of members. Contracting of labour is on an individual basis, and usually unions have little power to prevent dismissal of employees, though under the Frei government dismissal became more difficult and expensive for employers.

The importance of the plant union in the overall union structure, and the impotence of most craft unions and federations, is heightened by legal restraints on the system of collective bargaining, which is essentially an affair of the local plant union. The table (p. 64) shows the distribution by type of union of *pliegos de petición* (in effect union demands for wages and working conditions).

The agreement signed between an employer and his workers only applies to the signatories; it does not extend to other similar establishments unless they sign similar agreements.[19] Very often, of course, they do, but the need to go through the legal procedures and to ensure that employers do grant similar provisions to those established elsewhere occupies a great deal of union time in Chile. It also tends to work against the creation of larger units, for if agreements have to be negotiated locally, then the basic union

---

[17] Barría, *Trayectoria*. Though it wishes to keep clear of international commitments (or so it claims) it was at one point forced to seek a loan from the WFTU (ibid., p. 373).

[18] Morris & Oyaneder, p. 42. In 1960 the Chilean escudo (E°) was worth roughly $US 1.

[19] Barría, *Relaciones colectivas*, p. 37.

unit will be the local one. Every year sees a similar large number of *pliegos* presented, and this very high number signifies the virtual need of every establishment to go through the legal formalities of collective bargaining. Though the great majority of plant unions present *pliegos*, only a small number of professional unions and an even smaller number of *empleado* unions do so. For the year illustrated (1964), this was partly because salary readjustments for *empleado* groups were specifically exempted from the scope of the *pliegos* as these were fixed by law, but even though there was some relaxation of that provision in 1966, the number of *pliegos* from *empleado* unions is still low, reflecting the weakness and small numbers of these unions.

*Union* pliegos *by type of union, 1964*

|  | No. of demands | Workers covered |
|---|---|---|
| Plant unions | 525 | 137,486 |
| Professional unions of *obreros* | 194 | 29,373 |
| Professional unions of *empleados* | 74 | 14,737 |
|  | 793 | 181,596 |

*Source:* Barría, *Relaciones colectivas*, p. 46. He also indicates that *pliegos* came from union *comités* (the legal form for establishments of 10–24 workers) in the following numbers: 297 from *comités* of *obreros* covering 20,398 workers, and 20 from *comités* of *empleados* covering 1,412 workers. These figures refer to legal unions only.

Even for plant unions, the items that may be included in the *pliegos* are severely restricted. On the one hand labour legislation regulates many potential items of collective bargaining, such as minimum wages, conditions of work, social-security provisions, and so on. On the other hand over the past decade official attempts to control inflation have, with varying severity, tried to fix limits to amounts of annual wage adjustments to take account of the rate of inflation.[20] The effect of this type of regulation is constantly to involve the state as an agent in the collective-bargaining process, though there is obviously a certain amount of ritual, with employers arguing that they cannot grant greater increases than the state permits, and then the inevitable recourse to the state as mediator.[21] Faced with what often seems a dual alliance of em-

[20] Barría, *Breve hist.*, p. 6.

[21] 'In recent years it has been rare to conclude an agreement in the copper industry without government intervention. . . . Union leaders with whom we

ployer and state, unable to form alliances of much immediate purpose with other unions, the plant union is weak and in need of political allies; its problems transcend the local situation and become national issues, but often not so much national economic as national political issues.

There are a number of federations that have achieved some sort of national collective bargaining, and indeed this has been a long and constantly expressed aim of the labour movement. Moreover, with the increasingly stringent attempts to control wage increases under the Frei government, the CUT became more important as the only national counterpart to the state.

One national federation that has achieved an unusually favourable collective-bargaining position is the FONACC, working outside the legal framework. It is a relatively well-financed federation, has a national industry-wide coverage (except for the very largest factory, which by its size would tend to dwarf the rest), paid leaders, and is co-administrator of a fund for pensions and social-security benefits worth several million escudos.[22] This process started in the late 1950s and owed a great deal to the willingness of the employers (about 100 in all) who accepted the union offer to rationalize production procedures in the industry, with the proviso that it should share in the resulting increased profits.[23] The copper workers are also well organized, but in a different way; they enjoy high wages because of the vital role of the industry in the economy and its high profits.[24] A handful of

---

conversed appeared convinced that the intervention of government during the Alessandri regime yielded higher wage increases than would otherwise have been attainable. And to be sure, the copper companies never do make their final offer in private negotiations, but this is merely a matter of tactics, born out of a conviction that the union will always hold out for government inter-vention. If such intervention could be irreversibly ruled out, there is no reason to believe that the ultimate settlement through private negotiations would differ significantly from the actual mediated results' (P. Gregory, *Industrial Wages in Chile* (1967), p. 71).

[22] Barría, *Convenio colectivo en la industria de cuero y calzado* (1967).

[23] Gregory, p. 68. Both unions and employers benefited from the agreement. FONACC groups 67 unions and 8,000 workers. It arrived at a position of organi-zation via a long and combative union tradition before it was recognized by the employers.

[24] Unions are formed at the work centres, with a minimum of 50 *empleados* or 200 *obreros*. *Empleados* and *obreros* may each form a single union. When a single union of *obreros* includes 55% of those employed in the work centre, it automatically includes all workers and shares in the profits. Where these single

other federations plays some role in the process of collective bargaining, but in many sectors of industry, there are only one or two large firms and many small ones. Often the large firms have powerful unions that stand apart from the smaller ones, and this makes the process of forming federations difficult, aside from the legal obstacles that have to be circumvented. Few employers' associations have shown such willingness to deal with unionists as those in the shoe and leather industry.

One very important distinction established in the original labour code of 1924, and strengthened by statute and convention since, is that made between 'manual' and 'intellectual' labour, between *obreros* and *empleados*. White-collar workers are very favourably treated compared with blue-collar workers. In manufacturing industry, *empleados* receive on average salaries three times as high as those of *obreros*, with automatic adjustments for cost-of-living increases. Moreover, social services and benefits (an important part of salaries and pensions) also favour the *empleado*.[25] Indeed, the *empleado* grades received their legally-protected minimum wage in 1942, well before the *obreros*. A general minimum for industrial workers was not established until 1960.[26] The minimum wage for the *obrero* category is less than half—sometimes as low as 40% that of the *empleados*. The family allowance is about three and a half times greater for *empleados*. There tends also to be less 'spread' in the *empleado*-level wage structure, partly because their minimum wage is more realistically related to earnings, and partly because the wage costs of their grades total less than those of *obreros*, because there are far fewer of them,

---

unions exist, other (craft) unions are not allowed. The 1956 statute also makes legal provision for the CTC, to which only unions from the large copper mines may affiliate: it is governed by a 13-member executive, elected every 3 years by a national council of delegates from affiliated unions and is entitled to a direct checkoff of dues from the members of its affiliates (US Dept of Labor, *Labor Law*, p. 30).

[25] Though wage-earners, in 1961, made up three-quarters of all insured persons, they received only one-third of benefits paid out; whereas *empleados*, one-quarter of the employed population, received two-thirds of all benefits. And within the *empleado* sector, those in public employment received disproportionately more than those in the private sector—reflecting the Radical government's favourable treatment of one of its bases of support (US Dept of Labor, *Labor in Chile*, p. 34; see also T. Davis, 'Dualism, stagnation and inequality: the impact of pension legislation in the Chilean labor market', *Industr. & Labor Relations R.*, Apr. 1964, pp. 380–98).

[26] Though there were partial ones before (Gregory, p. 91).

and so employers tend to conform more to the national standards. Their skills in industry tend to be in short supply. Socially they are more akin to the managerial and employer groups, and enjoy far greater identification with them as a class.

Certainly trade union organization would not seem to be an important factor in their relatively privileged position. In manufacturing industry only 30% of *empleados* were members of unions (compared with 51% for *obreros*) and in commerce only 23% (24% for *obreros*).[27]

The division between *obrero* and *empleado* has important repercussions in the union system. It tends to emphasize social distinctions inside the labour movement and so weakens its potential as a unified bargaining force. It weakens the *obrero* group as well by tempting skilled workers to seek upgrading to *empleado* status. This reflects the weakness of the skilled workers in establishing what they consider to be an adequate differential by the usual means of collective bargaining. Hence the appeal to Congress for their reclassification as *empleados* in order to benefit from the higher minimum wages and social-security advantages.[28] Since Congress fixes these often unclear dividing lines, this gives politicians, and especially the executive if it has a majority in Congress, considerable influence over the labour movement. Even though the craft unions to which *empleados* belong are less able than plant unions to carry out normal trade union functions, the individual benefits of white-collar status outweigh the advantages of plant union membership.

Outside the legal framework are also those unions that have developed in the public sector. It is stated flatly in the labour code that workers in this sector are not allowed to form unions;[29] nor

[27] Zapata, pp. 113 & 115.

[28] As a typical example, Gregory (p. 99) cites the case in 1958 of the operators of excavating machines who appealed to Congress, which reclassified them not only in the railway shops but throughout private industry as well. Huachipato, Chile's large steel mill, started operations in 1952 with a labour force made up of about one-third *empleados* to two-thirds *obreros*. Reclassification has reversed these proportions and soon, it seems, all workers will be *empleados*. All political groups seek this reclassification; in Huachipato Socialists and Communists are in the majority.

[29] Though practice abounds in contradictions, e.g. the 2,500 state petroleum employees are organized in unions and associations of workers and employees. Though in law such public-sector unions are not supposed to present *pliegos*, in fact, thanks to a ruling by the Contraloría General, their *pliegos* are presented

are they supposed to join groups of a political character.[30] In theory the prohibition is complete; in practice it is ignored. Unions exist, if not in name, and political groupings exist inside them. Moreover, membership in these associations is very high. There are a number of reasons for this. Because these government *gremios* or associations are not deemed by the state to be unions, they are not subject to the manifold restrictions of the labour code. The *empleado/obrero* distinction is not so important as in the private sector, for most state employees are *empleados*, and they share common wage levels and social-security systems. There are many material advantages in belonging to these associations, such as subsidized government shops, preferential treatment for mortgages, special holiday facilities, and so on that must tempt the most reluctant civil servant into his union. Official associations have often been encouraged to expand by political parties and government. Direct encouragement was especially forthcoming in the period 1938–47 when Radicals, Socialists, and Communists, all at some time in government and the Radicals all the time, sought to build up strength in the public sector as they had (at least Socialists and Communists) in the private sector. Given the middle-class self-identification of many of the public sector employees, the Radical party built up considerable support amongst them and still has strong support today. The major government associations, especially those with clerical and administrative staff, normally have Radical majorities. Government employees also share an advantage denied to most workers in Chile—one employer with whom to negotiate and one who is used to spending more than he receives, meeting the difference by borrowing. Instead of perhaps 100 employers or more, as in many sectors of manufacturing industry, the public-sector association faces the executive or municipal power. Though this may involve dealings with several ministers or councillors, it is a far less cumbersome procedure than in the private sector.

---

annually and go through the usual procedures (Barría, *Relaciones colectivas*, p. 99).

[30] Art. 166 of DLF (Decreto con Fuerza de Ley) 338 of 6 Apr. 1960 states that '*empleados* and *obreros* who work for the state cannot form or join any union (*sindicatos*) nor form brigades, teams or functional groups of an essentially political character'.

## The role of the unions in the economy

The industrial-relations system is also shaped by a number of economic factors, such as the structure of the economy, the power of the unions as economic agents, the relations with employers and with the state.

### 1. The structure of the economy

An obvious explanation of the fragmented union structure is the fragmented economic structure. The large number of small unions mirrors the large number of enterprises too small for effective unions to be formed. The table below shows the extent of the artisanal sector.

*Industrial employment, 1925–60*

| Year | Labour force artisanal* | (000) industrial† | % artisanal | % industrial |
|------|-------------------------|-------------------|-------------|--------------|
| 1925 | 198 | 82 | 70·7 | 29·3 |
| 1930 | 161 | 96 | 62·6 | 37·4 |
| 1940 | 140 | 138 | 50·4 | 49·6 |
| 1950 | 194 | 189 | 50·7 | 49·3 |
| 1960 | 207 | 240 | 46·3 | 53·7 |

\* Establishments of 4 workers or less.
† of 5 workers or more.

*Source:* R. Lagos, *Industria en Chile* (Inst. de Economía, 1966), p. 146.

Of the 6,100 enterprises in the manufacturing sector in 1960 only 190 employed 200 or more workers; there were 70,000 enterprises employing 5 or fewer workers, comprising about half the industrial labour force.[31]

Salaries and union strength vary in proportion to the size of the undertaking, partly because in the larger enterprises unions and management face each other in a collective-bargaining situation like that of modern industry elsewhere.[32] In smaller factories employers tend to dominate their employees and many unions in small enterprises are company unions. The traditional environ-

[31] US Dept of Labor, *Labor Law*, p. 15.
[32] Davis writes 'higher wage costs for larger firms result as a consequence of the fact that minimum wages and related protective labor legislation, as well as social security contributions (that may constitute as much as 50% of take-home pay) can only be enforced, together with tax and regulatory laws, upon the large scale, highly capitalized establishments' (as n. 25, p. 384).

F

ment of these factories and the docility of the workforce are often explained in terms of the workers' social background. It is argued, and the observation has been made for most Latin American countries, that workers are recent rural migrants, whose value systems are conceived in the dependency terms of the rural *patrón*–peasant relationship.[33] This is unlikely to be the true explanation, at least in Chile. One study showed that most migrants move not from the rural areas to the major towns, but through a variety of intermediate stages starting in small towns, before moving to the capital. It also found that recent migrants to Santiago had no special problems of adjustment to life in the city; their problems were those of the urban poor generally.[34] Another study, comparing the modern steel mill of Huachipato with the traditional coal mines of Lota, found that in both cases recent rural migrants were very active in unions.[35]

In addition, the proportion of the labour force made up by rural migrants is so small that one would expect the migrants to adopt the social values of the majority. Economic development in Chile has not, in the last decade, favoured the growth of an industrial proletariat, which might constitute the basis of a more extensive and powerful union movement. Manufacturing productivity between 1953 and 1965 grew faster than the extra number of workers employed, who increased by only 6·5% (though the number of *empleados* rose by nearly 40%). In

[33] See E. Faletto, *Incorporación de los sectores obreros al proceso de desarrollo* (ILPES 1965, mimeo), *passim*. A different sort of argument can also be advanced to explain the lack of class consciousness, which is that they 'see membership of the industrial labour force as being only a transitional phase in a movement of social ascent which will eventually bring them to at least petit-bourgeois status. Thus, while greatly concerned with the economic returns from their work they tend not to adopt the solidaristic, class-conscious ambitions of the established working class. Thus they retain the more individualistic and basically conservative values of their original culture' (J. H. Goldthorpe & others, *The Affluent Worker* (London, 1968–9) iii. 13).

[34] B. Herrick, *Urban Migration and Economic Development in Chile* (1965), pp. 51 & 100.

[35] In Huachipato the rural migrants came from the higher strata of their original society, were more ambitious than many of their fellow industrial workers and often more active than them in the unions. In Lota, though the recent rural migrants were not markedly more educated, more ambitious, or more prosperous than others from their peasant communities, their strong rejection of the dominant social structure led to a high level of participation in the union (Di Tella & others, p. 274).

mining the workforce fell by 12% between 1957 and 1965.[36]
The trend is similar in the modern steel plant of Huachipato.[37]

## 2. Unions in the economy

The most pressing problem facing Chilean union leaders is that of
keeping money wages rising at the same rate as, or a little ahead
of, the rise in the cost of living.[38] In considering the economic
role of unions there are two questions at issue; the first is that of
real wages and how well the workers have been doing relative to
other groups; the second is whether the role of unions is important
or irrelevant in accounting for the real wage performance. These
are not questions that can be answered easily. It has been argued
that the unions' economic importance has been generally overestimated and that the relative share of wages in the national
income has only been altered by them significantly in the short
run, when 'hard' unions and 'hard' markets have co-existed.
Governmental redistribution of income has been more important
—but one force pushing for such redistribution has been the
unions. Clark Kerr writes that 'the general level of wages has
been drawn up more by full employment (of which unions are
co-authors) and economic growth and the monetary policies
accompanying them than pushed up by union action'.[39] This
amounts to saying that the (unmeasurable) political significance

[36] CUT, *Política de remuneraciones* (1966), p. 14. But 1957–65 were poor years
for economic growth in Chile. The CORFO projection for 1978 is for a labour
force in copper mining of about double the 1967 total of 31,500 (CORFO,
*Geografía económica*, p. 205). But even if this happens, it is not likely to be
typical of the increase in employment opportunities.

[37] In 1953, a year after it was opened, it was producing 313,073 tons of steel
ingots with a total labour force of 6,203 workers. But by 1964–5 it was producing 541,095 tons with a smaller workforce of 5,510 (Ca. de Acero del Pacífico,
*Memoria anual, 1965–6* (Concepción), pp. 10 & 20).

[38] A. O. Hirschman gives the following figures for the average annual price
increases in the decades 1910–20, 6%; 1920–30, 3%; 1930–40, 7%; 1940–50,
18%; 1950–60, 36% (*Journeys Toward Progress* (New York, 1965), p. 216).
These conceal some fairly dramatic fluctuations from year to year. Recently,
the lowest annual increase for the Christian Democrats was 17% in 1966. In
1964 it was over 40%.

[39] *Labor & Management*, p. 263. He adds that 'a case might almost be made
that there are nearly as many illustrations of the union movement (in the USA,
Great Britain, Holland and Sweden) restraining wage increases over the past
decade as there are of spurring them on'. A similar analysis doubting the
significant impact of unionization on wage levels is J. Ramos, *Labor and Development in Latin America* (New York, 1970), pp. 174–8.

of unions is greater than the (assumedly measurable) direct economic impact.

Until 1965 the answer to the first question would appear to be that workers were not doing very well. Average per capita income rose by 30% between 1940 and 1954, but this was made up of a rise of only 9% for *obreros* as compared with 38% for *empleados* and 43% for employers.[40] However, calculations for the period from the middle-1960s look much better for those earning wages and salaries. Compared with 1964, when wages and salaries accounted for something like 42% of the GNP, they had risen by 1969 to something slightly in excess of 50%.[41] The index of real wages (*obrero* and *empleado* combined) shows a rise from 93·8 in mid-1964 to 162·2 in April 1969.[42] In a sector that had previously been much neglected, the minimum agricultural wage, rose by 40% in real terms from 1964 to 1969.[43] Nevertheless the unequal distribution of income in Chile still leaves plenty of opportunity for the Allende government to implement its promises of socialism.

[40] N. Kaldor, 'Problemas económicos de Chile', *Trimestre económico* (Mexico), Apr.–June 1959, p. 179. See also O. Sunkel, 'La inflación chilena: un enfoque heterodoxo', ibid., Oct.–Dec. 1958; and Hirschman, pp. 215–16.

[41] AID evidence to the House of Representatives' Sub-Committee on Inter-American Relations, *New Directions for the 1970s: towards a strategy of inter-American development* (1969), p. 774. For 1940 the share was only 40% (J. Gavan, 'Sobre la distribución funcional del ingreso en Chile', *Cuadernos de economía*, Aug. 1968, p. 34).

[42] Barrera, *Participación*, p. 95. The base year was 1959 = 100.

[43] Minister of Agriculture, Hugo Trivelli, quoted in *El Mercurio*, 12 Oct. 1969. However, the statistical base of these calculations has been much queried, (though this does not necessarily affect the trend of real wages). The calculation of the share of factors of production in the national income appears to be based on several errors; e.g. the actual wage paid to rural labour is greater than the legal minimum, yet it is this latter figure which has been used to calculate the distribution between factors. One analysis even arrives at a figure of 65–70% of the share of labour in the national income (Gavan, p. 46). But his calculations too are subject to a good deal of statistical uncertainty; those for income of labour were based on surveys, and for capital partly on adjusted tax returns. And he includes in his total for wages and salaries most of the earnings of the self-employed (not normally included in this type of calculation). See the objections to Gavan's calculations by a director of ODEPLAN in *Cuadernos de economía*, Apr. 1969, pp. 78–81. However, this shows that arguments about wages cannot be based simply on the legal minimum wage. From 1953 to 1967 the *sueldo vital* (legal minimum wage) fell in real terms from 150 to 109. If real wages had followed this, they would have fallen by 30%. In fact they went up by 50% (J. R. Ramos, *Política de remuneraciones en Chile* (Inst. de Economía, MS., 1968), p. 14).

In 1967, for example, the employers, who made up 1·56% of the active population, received 5·95% of the total of personal income; the self-employed, 23·32% of the active population, received 23·60%; *empleados*—26·30%—received 44·82%; and the *obreros*—48·2%—received 25·5%.[44]

The increasing share of labour in the national income since 1965 obviously owes more to governmental policy (in a number of fields, not only wages) than some sudden sharp increase in union strength. However, official legislation is a poor guide to the actual level of wage increases; the government was unable to control the process it had unleashed. Even in the public sector, the level of wages and the amount of increases do not bear much relation to official policy. Many public agencies are autonomous and can defeat government wage policies by such tactics as increasing the number and type of promotions granted, the amount of overtime allowed, and so on.[45] In the private sector the government authorized wage readjustments of 38% in 1965, 26% in 1966, and 17% in 1967. In fact money wages went up 53, 37, and 37% (in real terms 19, 11, and 13%).[46] Central government wages in the same three years went up in money terms by 50, 33, and 32%. Wage policies are poor indicators of actual wage movements.

One reason why government policy on wage increases rarely corresponds to actual increases is the difficulty of enforcing such a policy, given the peculiar nature of Chilean inflation with its erratic rate of increase. Ramos points out that in a persistently inflationary situation wage demands and offers are made with an implicit anticipated rate of inflation, and that if not the exclusive source of wage increases, forward adjustment based on expectation of a certain rise of the rate of inflation, plays a very important role. His findings are that in the 36-year period 1929–30 to 1965–6 real wages fell 14 times, and that 13 of these occurred in years of accelerating inflation. Real wages rose 19 times; in 14 of these cases inflation was decelerating, and in five cases was accelerating

[44] I. Heskia, *Análisis estadístico de la distribución del ingreso personal en Chile en 1967* (1967), cited in Barrera, *Participación*, p. 57.

[45] Ramos, *Política de remuneraciones*, p. 23.

[46] Ibid., p. 10. However, though real wages in manufacturing doubled from 1937 to 1966, the wage share in value-added in manufacturing was actually lower at the end of the period than at the beginning, because in the long run output increased strongly. Wages and productivity have grown more or less together, especially in the 1957–66 period when a 75% rise in real wages was accompanied by a similar increase in output per worker.

(though never more than 5 per cent); and in periods when changes in the rate of inflation from one period to the next were 10% or less, fluctuations in real wages were essentially random. On his analysis, labour organization is not an important factor, for even without it wage bids and offers will incorporate an implicit expected rate of inflation.[47] But this argument looks at industrial relations in an almost purely economic way, ignoring the political element. It is difficult to imagine a situation where unions were abolished and the political climate was hostile (as in Brazil after 1964) and where labour would not suffer.

The general structure of unions in Chile would not lead one to expect that they are in a strong bargaining position, for there are many small, weak, and poor unions. Moreover, the single plant union is generally handicapped as an instrument for collective bargaining when compared with unions covering a number of enterprises. Since a plant union covers the whole enterprise, wage demands fall heavily on the employer—whereas the demands of a craft union, though they may be greater, fall on a number of employers, so that the cost to any one is a relatively small part of his total wage-bill. Unions with branches in several factories can aid a branch on strike, but the single plant union on strike, if not a member of a powerful federation, is more isolated and exposed.[48] There is also a large labour pool and a low level of average skill in the industrial labour force, and the legal restrictions hampering the unions apply to nothing like the same extent to the employer who wishes to get rid of troublesome labour. One of the few unions which controls labour supply for the whole industry is FONACC, and its members have benefited from productivity increases which might otherwise have gone to the other factors of production or in lowering prices.[49] There are only a few other cases in Chile where unions have comparable power where an industry is dominated by a single firm and where there are inelasticities in the supply of labour, for example where a high level of skill is required of the labour force.

[47] 'I think that persistent inflation awakens individuals to anticipate it and react accordingly even without any labour organization' (ibid., p. 58).

[48] M. Urrutia writes of the Colombian single-plant union that it 'can only depend on its own limited strike fund when it goes on strike, and given the monopoly structure of the Colombian product market, the defeat of an enterprise union usually does not affect the union standard in other firms' (*Development of the Colombian Labor Movement* (Yale, 1969), pp. 155–6).

[49] Gregory, p. 69.

It is clearly difficult to determine the impact unions have had on wages, and micro-economic case-studies of a particular industry do not solve macro-economic queries about their effect on the rate of increase of the general level of wages. Even for the United States, with more reliable statistical data, there is little agreement on the magnitude of the effects of unions on wages.[50] Whatever the theoretical problems, however,[51] it is clearly the case that as long as the original labour code remains substantially unreformed, unions in Chile will be unable to organize and operate to their maximum advantage.

### The unions and the employers

There are two rather somewhat contradictory sources for the state of labour relations. Survey material tends to show a more or less grudging acceptance of one or the other. The record of strikes in Chile shown in the table on p. 76 seems to indicate a different and rather more hostile state of affairs.

Strikes are short, frequent, localized, and mostly undertaken by plant unions on issues of wage demands and work conditions, rarely for wider issues such as union rights or a share in decision-taking. There are far more illegal than legal strikes, usually caused by spontaneous workers' protest against unilateral action by the management.[52] Less organized than legal strikes, they are shorter

[50] Thus there is a positive correlation between size of firm and wages paid, and a positive correlation between unionism and size of firm—but there is little agreement on which element, size of firm *or* the existence of union, causes higher wages (Uruttia, p. 240).

[51] Gregory (p. 72) tried to show that for the period 1959–63 his calculations indicated that larger productivity increases and greater inelasticities of demand for labour were associated with higher rates of wage change, but that neither labour market forces nor trade union organization was instrumental in translating these into higher rates of wage change. In spite of this, however, he stressed that industries which reported lower real wages at the end of his period of investigation were known to be amongst the most poorly organized, concluding that 'trade unionism thus is probably a contributing factor by explaining (by its mere absence or presence) part of the diversity in the rates of wage change'.

[52] A. Armstrong Verdugo, *Huelgas en Chile en 1962: su magnitud y causas* (thesis, Univ. Chile, 1964), *passim*. Petras (p. 19) offers a similar conclusion for the rural areas. He writes that 'the leading factor contributing to the growth of militancy, union consciousness and social solidarity in the countryside has been the violation of agreements by the landowners'.

—an average of five days as compared with twenty-two days for legal strikes. Hence the record of man-days lost often is far greater for legal strikes, which usually include prolonged national strikes of large unions, such as the copper or mining unions.[53] Strikes become legal only after a long process of arbitration.

*Strikes, 1960–9*

| | No. of strikes | | | No. of strikers (000) | | | Man-days lost (000) | | |
|---|---|---|---|---|---|---|---|---|---|
| | Total | Legal | Illegal | Total | Legal | Illegal | Total | Legal | Illegal |
| 1947–50* | 121 | 39 | 82 | 45 | 13 | 32 | 1,195 | 951 | 244 |
| 1960 | 257 | 85 | 172 | 88 | 47 | 41 | .. | | |
| 1961 | 262 | 82 | 180 | 111 | 20 | 91 | .. | | |
| 1962 | 401 | 85 | 316 | 83 | 19 | 64 | 1,020 | 465 | 555 |
| 1963 | 413 | 50 | 363 | 117 | 22 | 95 | 786 | .. | .. |
| 1964 | 564 | 88 | 476 | 138 | 17 | 121 | 835 | .. | .. |
| 1965 | 723 | 148 | 575 | 182 | 41 | 141 | 1,902 | .. | .. |
| 1966 | 1,073 | 137 | 936 | 195 | 32 | 163 | 2,015 | 1,261 | 754 |
| 1967 | 1,142 | 264 | 878 | 225 | 60 | 165 | 1,990 | 1,290 | 700 |
| 1968 | 1,124 | 223 | 901 | 293 | 60 | 233 | 3,652 | 1,311 | 2,341 |
| 1969† | 997 | 206 | 771 | 275 | 54 | 221 | 972 | 592 | 380 |

* annual average.    .. not available.    † approx. 9 months

Sources: J. Petras, *Politics & Social Forces*, table 38; Barría, *Relaciones colectivas*, p. 42; US Dept of Labor, *Labor Law*, p. 41; *Sexto mensaje del Presidente*, ii.366; *Memoria al 5° congreso de la* CUT, p. 53. Separate figures for *obreros* and *empleados* have not been given as *obreros* always well exceed *empleados* in all categories (in 1966–8 by proportions of roughly 5 to 1).

Many unions try to avoid these lengthy procedures, but they run the risk of having their strikes declared illegal and so of being ordered back to work. Strictly speaking, it is illegal to strike to enforce agreements made with employers. That this should be the most common cause of strike action, however, illustrates the weakness of the unions in face of hostile employers, and the lack of union confidence in the legal system of conciliation. The sharp increase in strikes since 1965 need not be interpreted as a marxist attempt to heighten the class war. It was more likely due to the fact that the government was more sympathetic to unions; that the numbers of unions and unionists increased considerably; that a larger labour inspectorate meant more attempts at conciliation and less use of police repression; and, of course, to national strikes, especially in 1967–8, against national-incomes policies.[54]

The conclusion must be that the great majority of strikes result from failures on the management side. But the process occurs so regularly that it seems possible that there is a strong element of

[53] Armstrong (p. 45) refers to one mining strike in 1962 that lasted over a year because of non-payment of salaries by an insolvent enterprise.

[54] Landsberger, 'Ideology and Practical Labor Politics', in M. Zañartu & J. J. Kennedy, eds., *The Overall Development of Chile* (1969), p. 134; *Sexto mensaje del Presidente*, ii.388.

routine about the whole affair. Employers try to avoid their obligations if they can, but strike action serves to show them how much (or little) they can get away with. In this sense collective bargaining functions largely to obtain from individual employers what has been granted legally, or what the conciliation boards have recommended as a standard for the industry.[55]

Collective bargaining does not only deal with wage negotiations. Managements often provide housing, medical attention, company shops, social-security provisions for the whole family, and even leisure-time entertainment; and many unions demand these in their *pliegos*. These demands are made partly because state social-security provisions are deficient and partly because the unions are too poor to provide these services themselves. Management is often glad to grant these facilities as a price for industrial peace, for making unions unnecessary, or at least converting them into docile bodies under management supervision.

Employers do not seem to be too unhappy with the present state of industrial relations. One survey showed that over 82% were in favour of maintaining the present situation of fragmented unionism or even of increasing state control over union activities; and fewer than 15% were for giving more freedom to trade unions.[56] They should have little reason to dislike the labour code, for in general it has no sanctions against employers who do not follow its provisions, unlike the many sanctions that threaten the unions. The code, moreover, permits a great deal of employer interference in the unions' affairs.[57] Employers do not seem to regard unions as one of their major problems; another survey showed that management was much more concerned about the instability of economic policy than about the power of the unions.[58] When asked who took decisions on the social policy of the enterprise, 64% indicated management alone compared with

[55] Barría asserts that it is very likely that all the *pliegos* presented in the period he studies (1956–63) resulted in agreements to apply the legal readjustments to salaries. In other words, collective bargaining served to make employers face their legal obligations (*Relaciones colectivas*, p. 57).

[56] G. Briones, *Empresario industrial en América Latina: Chile* (1963); quoted in Petras, 'The harmony of interests', *Internat. Socialist J.*, Nov. 1966, p. 496.

[57] Morgado, p. 87. Early employer reaction to the labour laws was adverse; encouraged by government slowness to act they successfully sabotaged many attempts at forming unions (Morris, p. 249).

[58] C. Fuchs & L. Santibáñez, *Pensamiento, política, y acción del ejecutivo industrial* (1967), p. 46.

26% for managements and unions.[59] Towards the union they were moderately co-operative.[60]

A survey of the presidents of nearly all plant unions in the Santiago, Valparaíso, and Concepción region roughly confirmed this attitude towards unions; 49% thought that the employers helped the unions. But 18% thought employers tried to eliminate the union in their establishment and 27% that they tried to block its growth.[61] A majority agreed that relations between the enterprise and the union were good. About a quarter thought that the attitude of the employers towards the workers leaders was discourteous and arbitrary. In another survey, when asked to identify who they thought were working against them, of a sample of workers (not leaders) in industry only 13% chose the employers.[62]

The picture that emerges from these surveys is hardly one of an industrial-relations system in which embittered marxists are locked in combat with hardened capitalists. Chilean trade union leaders seem to be able to make a distinction between their long-term political beliefs and their actual conduct of day-to-day union affairs; or between the way they act in the political arena and the way they act in the economic arena. One survey concludes that

the union struggle at the local level does not have either a revolutionary orientation or even a reformist view of the social order. It attempts to bring about a slight improvement in the economic and social conditions of its workers. In this sense the union movement expresses the workers' efforts which are aimed at diminishing the distance between their standard of life and their standard of expectation.[63]

However, the problem in surveying the whole group of union leaders is that one may lose sight of the active minority, who are

[59] When asked why the unions played such a small part, reasons given were: no unions (in half the enterprises), low level of education and competence, too much politicization (which meant that unions had no interest in co-operating) (ibid., p. 57).

[60] Where unions existed, 44% thought relations were good and 41% 'more good than bad'. Only 7% gave politicization as a reason for bad relations (ibid., pp. 77 & 79).

[61] Barrera, *Sindicato*, p. 21.

[62] The other candidates for chief enemy were: great landowners 38%; foreigners 30%; financiers and commercial interests 17% (V. Nazar, *Imagen sociológica del obrero industrial chileno*, Memoria, Univ. Chile 1967). This was based on a survey directed by a section of ECLA for Alain Touraine.

[63] Barrera, *Sindicato*, p. 106.

more concerned to bridge the gap between industrial and political action, especially at the federation rather than plant-union level. Moreover, it hardly seems likely that the leader of a small plant union is going to offer grandiose propositions about revolution in a context where the social system seems relatively secure—or at least immune from the attacks of a leader of 100 or so unionists mainly preoccupied by the impact of inflation on their wages. But this does not imply by definition that they become reformist and purely concerned with economic gains—if so, why do so many of them support marxist parties? If union leaders see the ends of their own local union largely in economic terms it does not follow that they expect only the same of their federation, their confederation, and their political party.

## The unions and the state

For a political system in which corporate interests have considerable representation in government institutions at all levels, the unions stood out, at least till the election of Allende in 1970, by their absence and isolation from the main areas of decision-making. One study found that the four major business associations in Chile were all voting members of several semi-autonomous key financial policy institutions such as the Central Bank (monetary policy), the State Bank (credit, subsidies), and CORFO (which controls a great deal of government investment); and each major business association usually voted on the boards of the many specialized government committees concerned with its particular economic sector.[64] Trade unions had 1 representative on the Central Bank's board (compared with 6 for other private interest groups); 2 (1 obrero and 1 empleado) on the State Bank (compared with 5 for other interest groups), and 1 on CORFO (compared with 5 for other private-interest groups and 10 from other banks). But the union appointments were till 1970 made by the President of the Republic; between 1947 and 1960, when the unions and executive were at odds, the President made no appointment to

[64] These were the National Society of Agriculture (SNA), the Society for Industrial Development (SFF), the Central Chamber of Commerce (CCC), and the National Mining Society (SNM) (see C. Menges, 'Public policy and organised business in Chile: a preliminary analysis', *J. Internat. Aff.* (Princeton), 22/2 (1966), pp. 343–65).

CORFO.[65] Naturally the appointments made by the President are more likely to please him than the unions. It seems that trade union representation on CORFO was of little benefit, as the union representative was largely inactive, ignoring issues that did not concern unions, and not strong enough to impose union interests on issues that did. Employers opposed increasing union representation on the grounds that they made no contributions to the discussion. The same picture was true of the provincial development committees. Trade unionists were not represented on the National Education Council, even though it had been agreed that provision ought to be made.

Even on the institutions more closely concerned with unionists' interests, such as their own social-security organizations, their desires are usually ignored. According to the law, unions can nominate representatives on the Conciliation Boards, wage-fixing bodies, and so on. But it is generally the government which nominates and removes them, tending to make this representation largely formal from the unions' point of view.

The unions did play a more direct role in the Popular Front government, when they participated in the organization of the Front and elected a number of deputies to Congress, and were also represented on the CORFO when it was formed. But they were never particularly influential in the Front; the political parties claimed the right to be speaking for the working class and the unions were expected to perform a more functional role. Further, the experiment resulted in bitter internal union rivalries and is a period that in many ways union leaders would prefer to forget.[66]

Government and unions until 1970, as if from mutual hostility, kept aloof. There was little real regular contact between them except in the area of industrial conflict, where the government was more likely to be seen as the ally of the employer than of the union. The hard-pressed labour inspectorate is so busy applying the law and investigating alleged violations that it has little time to play a more positive and constructive role towards the unions.[67]

[65] Barrera, 'Participation by occupational organisations in economic and social planning in Chile', *Internat. Lab. R.*, Aug. 1967, p. 158.

[66] See the discussion in ch. 5.

[67] Although they have manifold duties, they are given inadequate funds to carry them out; in 1966 the Inspection Dept had only one vehicle. They have little time for routine plant inspections (US Dept of Labor, *Labor Law*, p. 27). The situation has improved under the Frei administration, and presumably will improve further under Allende.

In a sense, though the unions were isolated from the decision-making process, they were always taken into account. In fixing incomes policies, for example, there must always be some estimate of what the reaction of the unions will be. Perhaps because this estimate was usually very inaccurate, the Frei administration broke with practice and actually consulted union leaders in the CUT for the first time in fixing the level of wage readjustments in the public sector for 1970, and the Chilean public was treated to the very rare spectacle of the leaders of the CUT and governmental ministers congratulating themselves on their mutual restraint and responsibility.[68] This was nevertheless exceptional in the period of PDC rule.

Unions were not normally consulted about their desires. One survey of union presidents showed very clearly how they estimated their own importance. Only 10% thought unions had much influence in issues of national importance; 33% thought they had some influence, and 57% thought they had none.[69] It is difficult to see this assessment, at least before the Allende government, as anything other than realistic.

[68] For details see *El Siglo*, 9 Nov. 1969, p. 5, and *Ercilla*, 10–16 Dec. 1969, pp. 8–9. But the agreements were for the public sector only; and no formal machinery for constant consultation was created.

[69] On the other hand 90% thought that employers had a great influence (Landsberger & others, *Pensiamento*, p. 26).

# PART 2

## 5. Socialism and Communism I

SINCE the 1930s Socialists and Communists have constituted the strongest political force in the Chilean labour movement. Leaving aside for the moment the question of whether they can be regarded as a combined force, it is a fact that most unionists support leaders who stand for election to union office as known Socialists or Communists.[1] As union elections are relatively free and frequent, this means that most unionists choose representatives of these two marxist parties.

The Communists and Socialists are strong in the union movement partly because they are strong national political forces. The firm institutional basis of each of these two parties does not lie only in an isolated union movement confronting a hostile political system. The Chilean labour movement, though strong by general Latin American standards, is not powerful or cohesive enough to impose its will on the political parties most closely associated with it. It is, of course, true that union backing provides the two marxist parties with important electoral and other support, and that the unions are an important influence inside the parties. But the core of party leadership lies outside the union movement, very largely in the parliamentary group, both in the Socialist party and, to a lesser extent, in the CP.

How strong socialism and communism would remain in the

[1] Thus one survey of 90% of presidents of plant unions in Santiago, Valparaíso and Concepción, conducted in 1962–3, found that 43% supported the FRAP parties (the uneasy electoral coalition of Socialist and Communist parties with the support of one or two minor parties), compared with 23% for the PDC, 6% for the Radicals, and 19% for no party (Landsberger & others, 'The Chilean labour union leader', *Industr. & Lab. Relations R.*, Apr. 1964, pp. 399–420).

labour movement if these two parties were not tolerated in the larger political system is a difficult question to answer. But while loss of political support would certainly have grave adverse effects, it is probable that marxist ideology, tradition, and organization are too deeply rooted in the unions to decay, as, for example, did communism in the Brazilian labour movement when faced with the assault of the state. The Chilean CP has been outlawed and persecuted, first under Ibáñez from 1927 to 1931, and again in 1948 under the Radical President González Videla. The persecution was relatively mild by Latin American standards, and the Socialist party and other left-wing groups were able to provide a resting place for Communists waiting for a change in the political climate.[2] Nevertheless, the Communists retained important support in the labour movement throughout the whole period of illegality from 1948 to 1957. If the unions do not provide the leadership of either marxist party, they do provide a very solid and loyal base.

The dominance of socialism and communism in the labour movement—especially in that sector of it that is politicized—is shown by their voting strength in the elections for the CUT executive. If we accept that most unionists are represented in the CUT congresses (something in excess of 60% is the usual estimate) it is interesting to look at the voting strength of Communists and Socialists since the first, founding congress in 1953.

*Votes cast for Communists and Socialists at CUT congresses* (%)

|           | 1953 | 1957 | 1959 | 1962 | 1965 | 1968 |
|-----------|------|------|------|------|------|------|
| Communist | 21   | 40   | 45   | 31   | 42   | 46   |
| Socialist | 25*  | 26†  | 28   | 28   | 33   | 25‡  |
| Total     | 46   | 66   | 73   | 59   | 75   | 71   |

* Three parties.        † Two parties.        ‡ Two parties.

Sources: 1953–62 from Barría, *Trayectoria*; later figures from newspapers. The figures given are the percentage share of the voting for party lists for election of the *directiva* or CUT executive. Complete voting figures are given on pp. 216 & 218 below.

These figures, though useful, certainly underestimate the strength of the Christian Democrats and the Radicals,[3] for in several con-

[2] E. Halperin, *Nationalism and Communism in Chile* (1965), p. 118.

[3] In 1962, at least, in the findings of a survey by Landsberger, a far smaller percentage of unions dominated by Christian Democrats (38%) were affiliated

gresses all or part of the PDC and Radical delegations withdrew from the proceedings. (The figures also—though less severely—overestimate the strength of the Communists relative to the Socialist party, whose lack of finance and organization limit the delegates it can send to the congresses.) As the Socialists and Communists place more emphasis on the role of the CUT than the other two parties, and as they largely dominate both its general operation and the specific task of arranging the conference and awarding the delegation rights, it is hardly surprising that their representation exaggerates their position relative to that of the Radicals and the Christian Democrats.

Socialists and Communists predominate in the 'older' unions, like copper, coal mining, and sectors of manufacturing where they have traditionally been dominant.[4] These unions and some public-sector ones tend to be more active in the CUT and hence once more to distort the representativeness of the relative party strengths in the unions. Even in these unions, however, the Christian Democrats and Radicals are represented in the leadership.[5]

In the rural areas and the services sector, both public and private, the Socialists and Communists are usually in a minority, though they dominate some public-sector unions. They control one rural confederation with perhaps a quarter to a third of organized labour, but the Christian Democrats and other Catholic groups predominate.[6] In the public sector the Radicals are in the majority in many unions, though the Christian Democrats are

---

to the CUT than those dominated by Socialists and Communists (68%) (Landsberger, 'Ideology and Labor Politics', in Zañartu & Kennedy, p. 129).

[4] Figures on the political composition of union leadership at the federation level are not readily available, though it is possible to find some by interview, and, less often, in newspaper reports. Thus in the CTC executive there are 7 Socialists, 4 Communists, 1 independent, and 1 Christian Democrat (1967). There used to be 4 Christian Democrats until the killing of a few copper workers and their families by troops in the El Salvador mine in 1966 led to a sharp fall in Christian Democrat support. In the FONACC there are 2 Communists, 1 Radical, 2 independents, 1 Christian Democrat, and 9 Socialists. In the Sindicato Industrial Obrero of Lota—in the coal-mining area—there are 4 Communists and 1 Socialist (1967). Other examples will be quoted later.

[5] On the executive of the Railway Workers' Union there are 4 Socialists, 2 Radicals, 2 Communists, and 3 Christian Democrats (1967). The overall federation of railway workers and employees (the FIFch) has a leadership of 4 Socialists, 3 Radicals, 3 Christian Democrats, and 1 Communist (1967).

[6] The 1969 figures for membership of the three major rural confederations are given on p. 259 below.

G

also strong. Unions like the ANEF or the CEPCH are well-known bastions of Radical strength, though they are not exclusively dominated by them.[7] As between the Christian Democrats and other Catholic groups in the countryside, since 1965 relations between Radicals and Christian Democrats in the labour movement have been hostile.[8]

The behaviour of any political party towards the labour movement—the tactics and objectives it recommends labour to pursue, the representation it allows to labour in its internal organization, are obviously conditioned by the nature of the party itself. A badly organized party is unlikely to have a well organized labour sector; a party whose objectives are basically electoral, rather than revolutionary will pursue a union policy consonant with these aims. To understand the party-union relationship in the Communist and Socialist parties it is necessary to look first at the development and main features of those parties.

## The Communist party

The Chilean CP has always been very orthodox in the sense of following the Moscow line faithfully, and—perhaps even more important—in closely modelling its action and organization on official Communist ideology.

The party has a strict sense of discipline and hierarchy. It is intolerant of deviation and demands submission from its intellectuals. It makes clear its belief in the need for objective conditions to precede action; so much so that this attitude has frequently aroused criticisms of over-cautiousness, of lack of confidence, of weak and uncertain organization. Thus in 1932 the South American Bureau of the Comintern, a frequent and severe critic, detected a wide gap between the development of the revolutionary situation in Chile and the ability of the party to direct it. It added that the level of ideological development was so weak that in

[7] On the executive of the ANEF, the major confederation of state employees, there are 9 Radicals, 3 Christian Democrats, 2 Communists, 3 Socialists, and 2 independents (1969).

[8] Indeed, the Radicals when moving to the left attack the Christian Democrats far more than they do either Socialists or Communists. Partly, of course, Radicals and Christian Democrats are competing for the same sort of clientele, and also the Radicals seem to regard such attacks as the best way of showing the commitment and solidarity of their party to the cause of working-class unity—a commitment which the Socialist party is always ready to doubt.

reality the majority of the regional organizations vacillated between proletarian ideology and bourgeois ideology; it criticized the party for playing safe in its selection policy by admitting only very few members; and felt that in the rising of the marines in 1931 the party had displayed complete passivity before and during the event, and yet after it had worked out the best policy for splitting the incipient revolutionary movement by proclaiming a slogan of 'All Power to the Soviets', and hence dividing the party from the masses.[9]

Yet in spite of these allegations, the CP arouses a degree of commitment in many of its militants which far surpasses the Socialist party; it is certainly more like the model of the 'totalitarian' or brotherhood party than its marxist rival. This has been expressed by Pablo Neruda:

You have given me brotherhood towards the man I do not know.
You have given me the added strength of all those living.
You have given my country back to me, as though in a new birth.
You have given me the freedom which the lone man lacks.
You taught me to kindle kindliness, like fire.
You gave me the straightness which a tree requires.
You taught me to see the unity and yet diversity of men.
You showed me how one person's pain could die in the victory of all.
You taught me to sleep in the hard bed of my brethren.
You made me build upon reality, as on a rock.
You made me an enemy to the evil-doer, a rampart for the frenzied.
You have made me see the world's clarity and the possibility of joy.
You have made me indestructible, for I no longer end in myself.[10]

In explaining the survival of the CP and its continuing influence in and on the trade union movement, its history is important. That the party and its associated unions were the major agents of

[9] Buró Sudamericano de la Internacional Comunista, *Las grandes luchas revolucionarias del proletariado chileno* (1932). The Bureau also criticized the lack of organization amongst copper workers; the scanty organization in the nitrate areas and coal mines in spite of the great support of the workers in those areas; and added that one of the greatest weaknesses was no influence at all in the countryside (pp. 24–33). Given that the party had been outlawed and persecuted for the previous four years, the Bureau seemed to be setting impossibly high standards.

[10] I am grateful to Robert Pring-Mill for allowing me to use his translation of this poem, the penultimate one of book 15 of Neruda's *Canto general* written, according to Pring-Mill, in 1949 when Neruda was in hiding and the CP outlawed. The translation appeared in the *Cambridge R.*, 20 Feb. 1970.

the working class in the isolated Northern nitrate areas and in the coal mines of the South gave it a firm proletarian base lacking in many other communist parties in Latin America. This solid mass base resisted and survived oppression during 1927–31 and 1948–57. Perhaps the experience of repression, with CP leaders isolated for long periods in remote places, aided rather than hindered the sense of solidarity and community. Though alternative ideologies were taken up by sectors of the labour movement, the roots of communism were deeper and more permanent—not until the 1930s did socialism constitute a real challenge.

Giovanni Sartori offers an interesting explanation of the emergence and persistence of communist strength which, though he is referring to European countries, is possibly even more applicable to Chile because communism there did not break away from an earlier socialist movement.

It is not the objective class (class conditions) that creates the party, but the party that creates the subjective class (class consciousness). . . . The party is not a consequence of class. Rather and before it is the class that receives its identity from the party. Hence, class behaviour presupposes a party that not only feeds incessantly the 'class image' but also a party that provides the structural cement of 'class reality'.[11]

If we are trying to explain why some 15% of the Chilean electorate regularly votes for the CP, and why it remains the majority party inside the labour movement, this explanation, in terms of what Sartori calls the organizational variable, seems very relevant, though it would be difficult to argue that the objective conditions of the Chilean working class were not also very important factors in explaining the origins and persistence of communist strength. The loyalty of party members and consistency of party voters can be explained not only in terms of developed class consciousness but also in terms of the persistent strength of organization and the behaviour and beliefs associated with it. In fact the brotherhood quality of the party is a real source of internal strength and cohesion.

The Chilean party has had to make frequent and violent

[11] 'Sociology of Politics and Political Sociology', in S. M. Lipset, ed., *Politics and the Social Sciences* (New York, 1969), p. 84. Kerr makes a relevant point when he writes: 'once a union movement gets a philosophy changes come slowly. . . . As in love, first sight tends to structure the lifeline of a relationship. An ideology or perspective has strong holding power and can even create the conditions for its own perpetuation' (*Labor and Management*, p. 259).

ideological swings in order to toe the Moscow line. In 1933, only shortly before the Popular Front, when the policy of the 'class against class' period was to be discarded completely, the party resolved that its task was 'to create a profound chasm between the Communist party and all the bourgeois and petty-bourgeois parties, above all *Grovismo* [Grove was the leader of the Socialist party] and *Hidalguismo* [Hidalgo was a leading Trotskyist who later entered the Socialist party]'. Repudiation of its past was another way in which the party demonstrated its loyalty to Moscow—'The ideological legacy of Recabarren must be rapidly overcome. Recabarren is ours. But his [liberal] ideas on patriotism, on revolution, on the building of the party are, at present, a serious obstacle in our way.' [12] It was all very well to declare, as the party did at the same time, that the only country it recognized was the Soviet Union; these sentiments may well have been to its credit as an expression of loyalty to the centre of world communism, but they were hardly an effective way to build up strength in Chile. If its leaders had made a serious effort to advance the party along such ultra-leftist lines, it is still doubtful, given the situation in Chile in the early 1930s and the party's size, that it would have advanced its cause much, but there is little evidence that the party followed up its strong words with action. This period of ultra-leftism showed little success. A communist attempt to assault an army barracks in Copiapó in December 1931 was defeated with relative ease but with some loss of life. Though the incident seems to have been the product of local party misunderstanding of the Comintern third-period strategy, it helped to discredit the party and provided further reason for government repression. [13] The party has rarely shown any apti-

[12] Resolutions of the CP National Congress, July 1933, *Hacia la formación de un verdadero partido de clase*, p. 5. The S. American Bureau of the Comintern also blamed Recabarren. Admitting his great virtues, it continued: 'His democratic illusions, his faith in universal suffrage, his bourgeois patriotism, his formation of the Party as a party of social reformism, with a structure and form as a federation of organizations with purely electoral ends, his ignorance and absolute lack of understanding of the worker–peasant revolution as a necessary stage imposed by development, his abstract idea of the 'social revolution' as a remote ideal, and finally his collaboration with the bourgeoisie excused away as a 'realistic policy' had prevented the party from getting on with its real task of making the revolution (ibid., pp. 51–2).

[13] Absent in Moscow when it happened, party leader Lafertte 'disclaimed any knowledge of or responsibility for this action and maintained that it was a

tude for violence or revolutionary attempts to overthrow the system.

Sent by the Comintern to Chile to organize the Popular Front, Eudocio Ravines, a Peruvian communist, judged the party leadership harshly. He recorded that his first meetings with the leaders were marked by 'inertia, incomprehension, and lack of faith in themselves. . . . Everywhere they saw dangers, obstacles, repression. . . . They voted resolutions that they had no intention of applying, they let time run by, hoping that it would bring them victory.' They reproached Ravines with thinking he was in France and not realizing the nature of the government in Chile.[14] The Chilean party's bewilderment at the abrupt change of line is understandable. Though Ravines's comments may perhaps be true of the party leaders when told to organize violent revolution in an unfavourable situation, they are not true of the leaders when told to carry out the Popular Front policy. This they did with skill and enthusiasm.

The Chilean Communists have always stressed their independence from the Comintern, but they have never shown unwillingness to follow its dictates; merely, from time to time, inability to do so, or to do so convincingly.[15] Lafertte wrote that 'to imagine anyone in Moscow even attempted to settle the internal problems of Chile is absurd'. According to him, relations were limited to an exchange of information and experience—not always satisfactorily either, for he added that some comrades from the Comintern 'did more harm than good on account of their overbearing character or because they enforced the line in a dog-

---

"police provocation". The truth seems to be that the Chilean Communists were at the time still so divided into factions and local branches acting independently that no effective control was exercised by the Central Committee or the Comintern' (Clissold, pp. 63–4). This was the time of the Ibáñez repressions and the Trotskyist–Stalinist splits in the Chilean party.

[14] Ravines, *La Gran estafa* (1954), p. 90. (He later became a professional anti-Communist.)

[15] Though the Chilean party was not so closely supervised as, for example, the British party—it was too remote and unimportant—its position with regard to Moscow was not dissimilar. Walter Kendall writes of the British cp that its position 'as a section of the Comintern was analogous to that of a constituency organization in a national party. As the local unit of a centralized organization the cpgb was bound by the constitutional principles and policy resolutions formulated by central congresses and between them by decisions of an elected central leadership' (*Revolutionary Movement in Britain 1900–21* (London, 1969,) p. 220).

matic way, thus bringing a negative influence to bear on militants of weak parties'.[16] Ravines, again according to Lafertte, was never accepted as a Comintern official, merely as a friendly Peruvian Communist—until he was 'discovered' to be an agent of Nazi Germany.[17] This question of the exact nature of the autonomy or dependence of the party on Moscow is important, for it has constantly bedevilled Socialist–Communist relations. Disputes over the Popular Front, the Nazi–Soviet pact, the Cold War, Yugoslavia, the Sino-Soviet dispute, Cuba—have all contributed to maintain the relationship of suspicion and mistrust between the two parties.

The development of the Chilean CP seems to have been marked as much by a struggle against the sectarians to the left, or rivals for control over the workers, as by a sustained struggle against the state or capitalism. Communist abuse has been as frequently directed to enemies on the left as on the right. Early on Recabarren argued strongly against the revolutionary tactics that the anarcho-syndicalists wished to apply in the unions. The Stalinist party leadership was constantly battling with the Trotskyists, who were unusually influential and difficult to expel owing to Chile's remoteness from Russia. The Trotskyists split the party during the Ibáñez dictatorship[18] and later made life increasingly difficult for the Communists by entering the Socialist party after its formation, contributing a strong strain of anti-communism to its ideological make-up. When driven underground in 1948, one section of the party leadership headed by Reinoso was in favour of armed struggle against the government;[19] but it was expelled by that section of the party still in control which favoured the tactics of lying low, working with the Socialist party, or at least a part of it, and letting the storm blow over.

[16] Quoted in Clissold, p. 63. These statements of Lafertte date from post-Stalinist 1961.

[17] Lafertte, pp. 325–6. Even if Ravines exaggerates his role in the formation of the Popular Front, it was certainly more important than Lafertte allows.

[18] This was one of the most difficult periods for the Stalinist party. Apart from the struggle with the Trotskyists, five of the party's parliamentary group (nearly all in fact) had to be expelled for advocating a policy of collaboration with the government of Ibáñez, and the then secretary-general, Isaias Iriate, was expelled when alleged to be a police agent (González Díaz, *Lucha por la formación del partido comunista* (1958), p. 8).

[19] Apparently Reinoso believed that setting up an illegal armaments factory rather than a party newspaper was the first priority—the leadership disagreed (Lafertte, p. 347).

The struggle against 'extremists' and 'adventurers' still continues, even though the threat to the party from such groups is negligible compared with that of the Trotskyists when the official party was much weaker. In the 1960s the president of the CUT, Clotario Blest, an independent radical Catholic influenced by Castroism, was ousted from the presidency when he advocated general strikes and criticized the interference of the parties in its organization and running. The Communists reacted sharply, not so much because, as in earlier years, they feared a real loss of authority and power, but rather because it was an embarrassing attack on their prestige and claim to be the true party of the masses.

There are some people with responsible posts in the workers' and peoples' movement who jump as if their corns had been trodden on every time that we communists alert the people against the adventurers and provocateurs who have the audacity to present us as engaged in doing a 'fire brigade's job' in the workers' movement. . . . We do not need to play at revolution and Sierra Maestra in order to affirm ourselves as revolutionaries.[20]

Latest of all, the battle was taken up with the small but vocal group of revolutionary youth, the MIR (the left Revolutionary Movement), which advocates armed struggle, though the two opponents came to an uneasy agreement after Allende's victory in 1970.

The CP has been persecutor and persecuted, and both processes have unified its organization and made it more homogeneous. For revolutionaries of the left have been driven out of the party or have left it in disgust; and those of social-democratic or liberal tendencies fled the party with the repressions of the first Ibáñez presidency and later of the cold-war period. Undoubtedly the party did attract in its earlier years (and later at the time of the Popular Front) a number of social democratic or liberal fellow-travellers, if not actual members; both of the other parties that could count on working-class and social democratic support, the Radical and the Democratic parties, by the 1920s had been fairly well identified with the corruptions and intrigues of Chile's parliamentary period. With the development of alternative left-wing parties (first the Socialist, later the Christian Democrats), radicals who could not accept either the ideological about-turns of the CP

[20] Luis Corvalán, quoted in Halperin, p. 71.

or its unquestioning subservience to Moscow, found more acceptable political affiliations. This again reinforced the homogeneity
of the party, at the cost of losing it support.

The exodus from the party of revolutionaries to the left and
social democrats to the right has left a tough, well-organized,
determined party working cautiously at all levels to protect and
consolidate itself. Its parliamentary group is by far the most
cohesive in Congress, observing the usual Communist practice of
paying congressional salaries to the party and receiving a small
proportion in return.[21] The extent and efficiency of the party
bureaucracy makes for an unusual institution in the normally in-
efficient and disorganized world of Chilean political parties (perhaps a unique one until the Christian Democrats started gaining
electoral support—and finance). The power and position of the
party bureaucracy was an object of attack from the expelled
Trotskyists, who criticized its isolation, conservatism, and demands for obedience.[22]

The Chilean CP always seems happiest—and best—at working
along the road of parliamentary democracy. It was much more
adept and successful in applying the Popular Front tactics than
the earlier ultra-left ones. Similarly the party was more successful
in its attempts to re-enter and work within the political system in
the early 1950s than it had been in attempting to oppose the
political system at the height of the cold war. In the 1950s,
according to Halperin, instead of allying with the left-wing PSP
which was supporting Ibáñez, who then was advocating a vague
brand of populism (and also the repeal of the law banning the
Communist party) it chose to align itself with the Partido Socialista de Chile, a more moderate socialist group which had earlier
supported the law banning the Communists (though it had
changed in composition and tactics). Halperin has made the
point that 'the Communists demonstrated that they preferred the
relative safety of parliamentary democracy to the hazards of an
anti-oligarchic, socially progressive experiment in authoritarian-

[21] Marcos Chamudes, a prominent Communist during the Popular Front
period, now a bitter anti-Communist, wrote that when he was a deputy in
1940, the party took 60% of his salary (*Libro blanco de mi leyenda negra* (Santiago,
1964), p. 10). In 1926 the S. American Secretariat of the Comintern ordered
the party to tighten control over its parliamentarians (Clissold, p. 121).
[22] PCCh *En defensa de la revolución* (1933), p. 104. This was the group that
later called itself the Izquierda Comunista, joining the 4th International.

ism. In choosing Allende . . . over Ibáñez [they] were evidently trying to work their way back into the democratic establishment. . . .'[23] Moreover, the CP was more likely to find a receptive ally in a minority Socialist party that had no other allies than in one linked to the powerful populist appeal of Ibáñez.

Since the early 1950s the CP has been one of the staunchest supporters of the representative and parliamentary Chilean political system—a logical enough position if the party held that the route to power lay through that system. For example, when a right-wing army coup was (most unsuccessfully) launched against Frei in 1969, the Communists leapt to the defence of the constitutional system, their union leaders declaring a general strike if the movement against the government went any further. The Socialist party was very critical of the Communists and offered no support at all to the government.[24]

Before Allende's presidency the CP had considerable political power—even governmental office, though briefly and unhappily, under González Videla. If little legislation favouring the working class resulted from the Popular Front period to 1946, if indeed the party acted as a restraining influence on the working class,[25] it could at least argue that no other tactics would have brought it power, that some positive legislation resulted, and that a good deal more adverse legislation would have resulted if it had let the right win. Further, its advocacy of the parliamentary and electoral road during the long period of the FRAP (formed in 1956) did end in the victory of the Popular Unity coalition headed by Allende in 1970. If, to revolutionaries of the left, the Communists' progress has been slow, the Communists can with some justice argue that it has been sure.

These tactics in the political sphere have been paralleled by union tactics which may well constitute the sin of 'economism', as the Socialists often argue, but this offends ideologists more than it does the rank and file of party and union membership.

[23] Halperin, p. 58. His evidence seems a little thin for his conclusions, but the main point—support for the parliamentary system—is clear enough.

[24] 'Chile en el filo de la espada', Ercilla, 22–8 Oct. 1969, p. 11.

[25] The party reproved the CTCH, then the major trade union confederation, for announcing that it would demand a socialist programme of the Popular Front candidate for the presidency—this was far too dangerous, as it could lead to the break-up of the Front and the isolation of the working class, which would be to play into the hands of the Trotskyists (Contreras Labarca, *Congreso de la victoria: X congreso nacional del PC*, Apr. 1938, p. 40).

Indeed, Communists realize that one way of holding on to and building up support in the unions is precisely by pursuing a successful 'economic' policy. If it may be difficult (though far from impossible) to see the connection between this and making the revolution, it is not difficult to see its relation to building the organization of and support for the party.

In the Chilean CP ideology is always subordinated to tactics, or at least, tactical considerations determine its particular ideological stand at any given moment. If the Popular Front tactic is collaboration with social democrats, then the necessary ideological justification is easily supplied.[26] Thus the party's prime objective becomes the creation of the organizational apparatus necessary to carry out current tactics, and at times it was so much concerned with the task of organization that the aims that organization was intended to serve took second place. In 1968 the theme of the CUT Congress was 'Unity in order to make change'. For the Communists present the theme of unity was as important as that of change; the Socialists present made it clear that in their view change was the important element to emphasize.

## The Socialist party

The Socialist party was, at its formation in April 1933 after the collapse of the short-lived 'Socialist Republic', a collection of various ideological groups previously organized in five parties. The historian of the party writes:

At its origin the party brought together great numbers of workers, artisans, peasants, white-collar workers, and students. . . . Many had no previous experience of party organization. But an important number came from other organizations; from the Radical party and the Democratic party; from anarchist groups and Communist cells; from masonic lodges and evangelical churches; ex-military men, popular agitators, professional co-operative members, and rebel intellectuals. It was a variegated, tumultuous, and impatient mass; although it lacked serious ideological formation it was resolved on action and combat.[27]

[26] Thus, against the wishes of the Socialist party, a left-wing policy was declared impossible in 1943 because it would hinder the fight against fascism (letter from the CPCh CC to the Socialist party secretary-general, *Una etapa de clarificación socialista* (1944), p. 152).

[27] Jobet, 'Tres semblanzas de socialistas chilenos', *Arauco*, Oct. 1965, p. 22.

Its various groups did have in common dissatisfaction with the
CP. The founders of the party were not former Communists, but
they were critical of that party for the unreality of its policies and
its current intransigence. But the Socialist party was not intended
to be a reformist alternative. Its first declaration of principles
made clear its acceptance of the main tenets of marxism and of the
class war; its basic organizational unit was to be the small
nucleus, not the 'irresponsible assembly'; and its guiding organizational principle was to be democratic centralism.[29]

However, the Socialist party did not develop a bureaucracy on
the lines of the CP. The personality and ideas of its leaders, not the
abstract dictates of its ideology, dominated the early party.
Grove, soon to emerge as the most popular leader, claimed to see
in Marx an excessive glorification of manual work and of the proletariat to the detriment of intellectual activity. For this reason he
always insisted that the Socialist party was an association of
manual and intellectual workers, of the working class, peasantry,
and petty bourgeoisie; it was not a purely proletarian movement, and he never spoke of the hegemony of the workers inside
it.[30]

Grove's ideas and style were of great importance in the party's
first decade. Chelén Rojas—well to his left in the party—admits
that its growth owed most to Grove, to the strong emotional
appeal he aroused, to his great human sympathy, and to his
tireless and combative work for the party.[31] Grove was a military
man, a romantic, and a nationalist, always ready to act—less
ready to see how his actions accorded with the ideas of the party.[32]
Moreover, his behaviour and leadership of the party led it into
contradictory positions; on the one hand it proclaimed itself a
revolutionary party, yet it participated fully in the parliamentary
and electoral process; it claimed to despise the bourgeois political
system, but grasped eagerly (at least at the leadership level—

[29] Jobet, *Socialismo chileno a traves de sus congresos* (1965), pp. 19–20.

[30] Jobet, *Arauco*, Oct. 1965, p. 22. Thus its first CC, nominated in 1933, consisted of '7 workers, 3 employees, and 5 professionals and intellectuals' (Jobet,
*Socialismo*, p. 24).

[31] Chelén, p. 85. The danger was that Grove developed messianic preten-
sions and debased the ideas of the party.

[32] He had been in the army for thirty years. There is no evidence that he
espoused socialism before the 'Socialist Republic' of 1932. But he did have a
deep concern for the plight of the poor in Chile (J. R. Thomas, 'The evolution
of a Chilean socialist: Marmaduke Grove', *HAHR*, Feb. 1967, pp. 22–37).

below this there was plenty of opposition) at the chance of ministerial office and bureaucratic positions. It has been criticized for its lack of real contact with Chilean problems; Raúl Ampuero, who became secretary-general shortly after the war, criticized it for making no effort to define the basic problems facing Chile. He argued that the party simply took over a whole portmanteau of foreign concepts, some of which were mutually contradictory, thus laying the seeds of future conflicts.[33] Reformists and revolutionaries fought out a battle for control which led, by the middle-1940s, to the near distintegration of the party.[34] The Socialist party was regarded by many political observers as almost as foreign or alien a political force to Chile as the Communist party, in the sense that its theory and ideology, and the fierce internal disputes about them, seemed to be derived from abstract concepts little related to Chilean politics.

Two important internal factions were the Trotskyists and the Social-Democrats, though this latter is a very approximate term.[35] Both were very hostile to the CP—the party was, after all, founded as a reply to the Communist tactics of the time, and after its foundation the Socialist party became the favourite target of the CP. Indeed, the personal attacks on the party leaders by the Communists, and also by the Chilean Nazi party, probably helped the growth of the *caudillo* tradition in the socialist movement, as its militants felt that defence of their leaders was a first priority against the bitter assaults from outside.[36]

The Trotskyists, organized in the Izquierda Comunista, asked for entry into the Socialist party in 1936, and they were admitted after a heated debate at the Socialist congress discussing the request.[37] The Trotskyists had been strong supporters of the Block de Izquierdas, an anti-fascist coalition formed in 1934 with the parties of the left, including the Socialist party but excluding the Communists. The entry of the Socialists into the Popular Front

[33] *Carácter de la revolución chilena*, p. 39.
[34] A. Pinto, *Chile: una economía difícil* (1964), p. 174.
[35] The party, for example, early decided to reject affiliation with any International—Communist, Trotskyist, or Social-Democratic—on the grounds that they were basically alien to Latin American problems (Jobet, *Socialismo*, p. 26).
[36] Certainly it led to the creation of the Socialist Defence Militias, which played an important role in the street battles first against the Communists, later against the Nazis and members of other right-wing groups (ibid., p. 30).
[37] The entry to the Socialist party was not acceptable to all Trotskyists; some stayed outside to form the Partido Obrero Revolucionario (Vitale, p. 78).

with the Trotskyists among them caused many problems with the Communists.

With this amalgam of diverse ideological groups and personal-ist leaders, it is hardly surprising that the history of the Socialist party should have been a turbulent one, with a long chain of splits, expulsions, changes of policy, divisions. From the entry of the party in the Popular Front until the unity of the two major socialist groups in 1957, there was seldom one socialist party in Chile. The first major break occurred even before the electoral triumph of the Popular Front when, in 1937, a group broke away from the party calling itself the Unión Socialista and supporting the candidature of General Ibáñez to return to the presidency. The deepest divisions in the party occurred over the performance of the Popular Front itself. In late 1939 an *inconformista* group left the party in disgust at the performance of the three Socialist ministers in the government and at their own inability to persuade the party to accept their view. César Godoy, their leader (who also opposed the alliance with the Communists, though he was later to become a leading Communist), wrote that one reason for the failure of the Socialist party in the Popular Front was 'the exaggerated emphasis on the person of the leader up to the point of creating a fetish or a myth that is the very antithesis of conscious and reasonable support'.[38]

Godoy's arguments that the Popular Front experience would discredit the party, demoralize the militants, and destroy the organization were to prove correct. Its ministers and bureaucrats proved timid in policy yet avid for office, even against the wishes of the party. When in 1943 the party Central Committee ordered all its provincial governors and *intendentes* to relinquish their offices so that the party could develop its new policy, practically none of them did so, most not even replying to the letters from the party which they were supposed to obey faithfully and thanks to whose support they had gained administrative office in the first place.[39] Jobet describes the action of the party as 'a conscious sell-out to the speculators, bourgeoisie, and reactionaries'.[40] Though his judgement of the Popular Front as little more than an electoral alliance to put the Radicals in power is too severe, it is certainly

[38] *Que es el inconformismo?* (1940), p. 20.
[39] *Una etapa*, p. 29. They were all expelled from the party.
[40] 'El Partido Socialista y el Frente Popular en Chile', *Arauco*, Feb. 1967, p. 29.

true that the ideas of the Socialist party were remote from the policies pursued by the government. The party seemed torn by the attraction of power on the one hand and the desire to maintain some revolutionary principles intact on the other. Thus in 1942 it was again deeply divided over whether to enter the new Radical government of Juan Antonio Ríos; when it did so, with little success, the dispute over whether to remain in office led to further splits and expulsions. Grove himself was expelled in 1944 for excessive *caudillismo* and set up yet another group, the Partido Socialista Auténtico.

The revolutionary nature of the Socialist party has often been overestimated. The anti-communism of many of its leaders was an attack from the right rather than from the left, and was associated—in men like Oscar Schnake, socialist Minister of the Economy in the Popular Front government, or Bernardo Ibáñez, presidential candidate of the party in 1946 and closely linked with the American Federation of Labor[41]—with a markedly pro-American standpoint. Left-wing, non-Trotskyist anti-communism had to wait for the development first of a strongly Leninist and later of a Castroist group.

Probably the worst two years of the Socialist party's history were 1946 and 1947 when, in addition to the bitter internal divisions, the Communists attacked from all angles, causing the split of the CTCH into a Socialist and Communist wing. A massacre of striking workers in a square in Santiago resulted in the short-lived entry of the Socialists once more into the government, even though they were partly responsible for calling the strike. These events, and the support of the Ibáñez Socialists for the Law for

[41] Bernardo Ibáñez was secretary-general of the CTCH as well as a Socialist deputy and a secretary-general of the party. At one time he had been a Communist and in 1943, as he was in favour of forming a Partido Unico of the Socialists and Communists, the latter backed him for secretary-general of the CTCH against the choice of the Socialist party, José Rodriguez Cortés (O. Waiss, *El drama socialista* (1948), p. 46). But his pro-communism soon changed. Apparently the Cuban Confederation of Labour newspaper, *Hoy*, printed in November 1946 a copy of a letter from Arévalo (an alleged American Federation of Labor agent inside the Cuban confederation) to Ibáñez on the need for splitting actions between free and communist unions (G. Morris, *The CIA and American Labor*, New York, 1967). That Ibáñez worked closely with the AFL is corroborated by the head of the Latin American department of the AFL (S. Romualdi, *Presidents and Peons* (1967), p. 323). Ibáñez's Socialist group later supported the decision to outlaw the CP in 1948; yet another occasion for splits and recriminations inside the Socialist movement.

the Defence of Democracy in 1948 (banning the CP), led to one of the most lasting splits in the party, between the Partido Socialista de Chile and the PSP.[42] This split was not healed for ten years and though the Communists were outlawed for the period, the electoral and popular advance of the Socialists was less than might be expected, partly because of their image of division and squabbling; party attention was turned inward rather than outward.

There would appear to be three major groups in contemporary Chilean socialism: the Leninists,[43] who stress the working-class party above all as the agent of the revolution and see the role of unions as creating and supporting working-class consciousness; the Castroists, who preach insurrection and expect to see the unions disrupting the existing system and supplying, with the rural workers, the troops of the revolution;[44] and the moderates or, perhaps, social democrats (for want of a better word, and always bearing in mind that they are much more left wing than European social democrats), who preach the road of economic gains and electoral strategies. Least vocal of the groups, this last may well be the most numerous at the rank-and-file level. Allende may be its unacknowledged leader, though it is even less organized than the other two groups—it lacks a separate organizational basis or a newspaper, though it has much support amongst unionists. It possibly differs more from the other two over tactics than over aims. It employs the vocabulary of Leninism as readily as the other groups, but is much more willing, for example, to make alliances with non-Socialist parties, like the Radicals, if this is electorally advantageous.

[42] Ibáñez's Socialistas de Chile even entered the government, again briefly. However, the split over Communism was superseded by a new division in 1952 over the candidacy, once more, of General Ibáñez, for the presidency. In one of those volte-face typical of the Socialist party at that time, the Socialistas de Chile collaborated with the Communists (whom they had helped to ban four years before) against General Ibáñez (and attracting to them for this purpose Salvador Allende who had been with the Popular Socialists). Drawn by his apparent populism and obvious popularity, the Popular Socialists entered the government of Ibáñez. But this caudillo was to disappoint them too, and a year later they left his cabinet (Chelén, p. 129).

[43] Strongest perhaps in the theory of the Unión Socialista Popular, the breakaway group led by Raúl Ampuero who was expelled from the party in 1967 for opposing its strategy based primarily on elections.

[44] Strong amongst the youth, and the magazine *Punto final*; a prominent spokesman of this group is Senator Carlos Altamirano, the present (1971) secretary-general.

The presidential campaign of 1964 was headed by partisans of this group, who judged it prudent to present a fairly moderate platform; thus the promises made to unionists during the campaign were hardly very revolutionary. Unions were to participate fully in the production committees of their enterprise, to have access to the books and documents of the managers, and were to have more representation on the state planning agencies.[45] This would certainly be advanced social legislation for Chile, but falls short of a revolutionary transformation. The general promise of the 1970 campaign were more radical. In an interview immediately following his victory, Allende declared: 'The workers will be permanently represented in the government of Popular Unity. I will seek all means of doing this. I will keep the president and secretary-general of the CUT informed of every step that the popular movement makes.'[46]

One of the weaknesses of the Socialist party in the trade union field has been personal and ideological factionalism in the leadership, which has affected the labour front. Often one group will try to use its influence in the unions to attack another group. This happened after World War II, when the Socialist group most powerful in the CTCH and led by Bernardo Ibáñez favoured collaborating with the government of the Radical President, González Videla. It was opposed by the party Central Committee and thus tried to use its influence in the unions to change the composition of the Central Committee, accusing it of being pro-Communist. On another occasion Grove's Partido Socialista Auténtico suggested joint pacts with the CP in the unions in order to oppose the majority Socialist party.[47] Even leaders regarded as organization men *par excellence*, such as Raúl Ampuero, are cap-

[45] From Allende's speech published in 'Los trabajadores en el gobierno popular', *Resoluciónes de la Asamblea Nacional de trabajadores Allendistas* (May 1964), p. 11. There was also to be widespread reform of union law—the *obrero/empleado* distinction was to be abolished, one federation per industry was to be established, union membership would be made obligatory, individual employment contracts would be replaced by collective ones, and the CUT would be legally recognized.

[46] From interview in *Ercilla*, 9–15 Sept. 1970. It seems clear that the labour code will be modernized if Allende can secure congressional approval—but how far the trade unions are to enter the state apparatus with any strength remains to be seen. Socialist–Communist rivalry in the unions is unlikely to decrease much.

[47] H. Portillo, 'Conclusiones del informe sindical del secretaria nacional sindical', *Pleno nacional del Partido Socialista Auténtico, Dic. 1945*, pp. 25–7.

H

able of trying to capture the party for their own ideological and personal purposes, and by grossly miscalculating their chance of success, ending up in the political wilderness.[48] These splits naturally affect and cause uncertainty in the Socialist sector of the labour movement. Ampuero took the secretary-general of the CUT and two of the members of its executive into a breakaway Socialist party with him, though he was unable to gain much rank-and-file support.

The theory of party-union relations in the Socialist party has not altered greatly since its first formulation over thirty years ago, as described by Jobet: 'Its union policy starts from a recognition of the decisive importance of the union as an instrument for the defence of the proletariat, and therefore, of its united and strong organization, to fight for its immediate aims and the improvement of the general standard of living'. But the Socialist party

does not accept the view of one sector of the working class that looks at the union as an end in itself, unconnected with the wider struggle of the proletariat, nor does it accept the view of the other sector which considers unions as subsidiary to the party, thereby excluding from their ranks the most numerous sectors of the working class.[49]

The party should aid the unions but not dictate to them; the party contains the revolutionary elite, the union the class-conscious mass; the union needs political and ideological support if it is not to become merely an 'economic' bargainer, but it must not be as inflexible as the party, or it will lose mass support, become sectarian, dogmatic, and isolated (as did the FOCH); there should be no strikes for the sake of strikes (which the Socialists saw as the position of the Trotskyists) but neither should strikes be merely for economic gains (which they saw as the position of the Communists at certain times—at other times it was the establishment of political control over the unions). Strikes should be

---

[48] His criticisms of the Socialist party sound like those made by the *inconformista* group some thirty years ago—'it has been incapable of widening and strengthening the social basis for a left-wing policy; it has been guilty of the virtual paralysis of the FRAP . . .; it is involved in an underhand internal campaign to eliminate ideological antagonisms . . .; it has failed in all the political and union tasks on which rest the life of the party; it has been handed over to a repugnant electioneering opportunism . . . with an alliance with the Radical Party' ('Llamado a la Asamblea Nacional Constituyente del PSP', *Punto final*, Sept. 1967).

[49] *Socialismo*, p. 30.

geared to a long-term strategy to undermine the capitalist system and increase the class consciousness of the workers.

These tactics demand a party that is supremely well organized and clear about strategy and tactics, ready to sacrifice temporary gain in the long-term interest—a description that does not apply to the Socialist party. A recent secretary-general of the party, Senator Aniceto Rodríguez, over twenty years ago criticized the party's role in the union movement. He argued that it very rarely made any effort to fulfil its intentions and intensify its activities in the unions; too often it was quite content to elect some members to a union *directiva* and then do nothing about it; it often failed even to do this, leaving the field clear to the Communists, when it should have been organizing a 'Democratic Union Opposition' against communism. Even those federations controlled by the Socialists failed to pay their dues to the CTCh.[50] Though Rodríguez wrote at the nadir of the party's history, other Socialists in more favourable periods have often endorsed his analysis. Lack of direction in the union movement results from confusion and division at the top, as has so often been the case in the Socialist party. Hence the division between union and party is greater in the Socialist party than in the CP, because of inability to organize matters otherwise.

## Socialist–Communist Relations in the Unions: from the CTCh to the CUT

The relations of these two parties inside the unions broadly follows those between the parties, varying from open, even violent, hostility[51] to open enthusiasm (on the part of the Communists) and cautious friendship (on the part of the Socialists). At the time of the dissolution of the Comintern, the Communists openly discussed the fusion of their party in a broad working-class movement. The objective of the proposed fusion was to further the struggle against fascism; the method was to be a new, strong, united organization, not just a federation of, or a formal unifica-

---

[50] *Tareas de un buen militante* (1947), pp. 22 & 24.

[51] As when the Socialist plenum resolved in February 1948 to 'continue the fight against the Communist bureaucracy and its corrupt interpretation of Marxism until it is completely eliminated from the working class' (Waiss, *Drama socialista*, p. 65).

tion of, various parties, but a new marxist party of the work-ing class. The Socialist party, however, never warmed to the idea.[52]

Although the Communists had been the major force in the labour movement since the early twentieth century, the Socialist party was able to win adherents after its formation. The Com-munists were still recovering from the repression of the Ibáñez dictatorship and, given their policy of 'extreme leftism', many more moderate unionists were willing to seek political allies in a party that did not reject the political and industrial system quite so categorically, or demand unions to follow party dictates so completely. The Socialists made gains amongst the unions which were prepared to accept legal recognition (at that time still opposed by the Communists, though they were shortly to accept it), for though registration did have drawbacks, it also brought legally recognized unions a share in the profits of their enterprise. A new organization set up in 1934, the CNSC (National Confedera-tion of Unions of Chile) adopted a platform broadly on the lines of that of the Socialist party, which had decided to capture the legal unions as a means of establishing their base in the labour movement. The CNSC even took the initiative in trying to set up a united labour confederation which, though it failed, helped to pave the way for the CTCH.[53]

The Socialists were later to gain support with the development of manufacturing industry and consequent growth of industrial employment during the period of the Popular Front and World War II. It was then that they controlled, on occasions, the Ministry of Labour. They made further gains when the Com-munists adopted an attitude of extreme hostility to the govern-ment with the onset of the cold war and the outlawing of the CP. This was when the powerful CTC was formed, as a socialist break-away from the Miners' Federation, which until then organized

[52] Contreras Labarca, *Unión nacional y partido único* (13th CPCH plen. sess., June 1943, Santiago), p. 28. The Socialist party, however, argued that a single party should come after all problems and differences had been resolved, not before. It agreed to continue talks at the top level but forbade its base groups to set up 'unity committees' (*Una etapa*, p. 15). The CP had first raised the idea of a *partido único* in 1936–7, and though the Socialist party rejected the idea in its Talca congress in 1937, several Socialists were expelled from the party for supporting the idea and several local branches also had to be disciplined. (I am indebted to Andrew Barnard for the last point.)

[53] Morris, pp. 259–60.

workers in coal, copper, and nitrate, and had been controlled by
the Communists. Though some Communists did enter the Socialist party when their own party was banned in 1948, they did not
remain in it for long. Halperin (p. 118) makes the point that even
though the Chilean CP is one of the strongest in Latin America, it
is still very short of cadres. The easing of restrictions and the final
restoration of legality meant that the cadres had to return to full-
time work in the party; there were not enough to spare to engage
in a full-scale infiltration of the Socialist party.

Hostility between Socialists and Communists in the unions is
not necessarily confined to the periods when the parties are at
odds. Given the factional nature of the Socialist party, the CP has
engaged in splitting tactics, working with the faction which supports the desired policy and combating the faction opposing it.
As an instance, this happened at the time of the Popular Front,
when the particular object of Communist attack were those Socialists who objected to the formation of such a Front. Ravines
describes the Communist tactics in some detail. They would first
of all attract to them all independent, or at least non-Communist,
union leaders whom they could win over by providing them with
assessors and experts, thus being exceedingly helpful to a hard-
pressed leader. Then they would create all sorts of obstacles for
the Socialist union leader unwilling to co-operate, with the aim of
breaking his nerve by isolation and persecution. Such a leader
would be slandered and rumours would indicate that he was in
the pay of the employer. Attempts were also made to undermine
the authority of a leader who would not co-operate. Ministry of
Labour officials would be informed of imaginary misdemeanours.
If, however, the position of the leader proved unshakeable, and if
he had the firm backing of his party, then the Communists would
have to come to an arrangement with him.[54] The Socialists were
quickly aware of these tactics, though prepared at that time to
excuse a great deal in the interests of the Popular Front. In 1938
the union department of the Socialist party declared that one of
the gravest problems for the left was the struggle between the
two parties for hegemony in the union movement. It added that
this lessened worker interest in the party outside, for it concentrated attention on party disputes inside the union. The Communists were condemned for their underhand guerrilla tactics,
yet the Socialists still resolved to attempt a pact with them on the

[54] Ravines, pp. 102–7.

basis of local agreements in order to take the struggle out of the unions; otherwise the Popular Front would be threatened.[55]

There have been three principal attempts to create a united labour movement in this century. The CP was strongly involved in the development of all three, and they offer interesting variations of party-union relationships. The FOCH has been examined in chapter 2, and the CUT will be examined in chapter 9. The CTCh, now to be examined, was founded in 1936 and dominated the political world of Chilean labour for ten years.

### The CTCh

With the overthrow of Ibáñez in 1931, one of the the first acts of the CP was to re-establish control over the largely moribund FOCH. An immediate purge of Trotskyists from its Construction Council[56] reasserted the FOCH's dependence on the CP. Rivalry with the Socialist unions (organized largely in the legal sector) meant, however, that the FOCH was far less predominant than it had been before the dictatorship, and CP sectarianism alienated many unionists. However, the change in Comintern tactics and CP control of the FOCH meant that it could pursue the Popular Front policy at the union as well as at the political level.

The FOCH issued its first call for a unity convention of all the forces of organized labour in 1934, but the Socialists, then organized in the Block de Izquierdas, did not respond.[57] It required the railway strike of 1935 and the resulting repressive action of the government before they would agree to co-operate with the Communists. Though this strike was basically about pay and conditions, the government was concerned about the growing power of the various railway federations, and the Minister of the Interior issued Governors and *Intendentes* with instructions to prevent the growth of similar federations, since their development could 'lead to the replacement of law and authority by the numerical

---

[55] Departamento Sindical Nacional del CC Ejecutivo del PS, *Política sindical del Partido Socialista* (Resolutions of the 5th Congress, Santiago, 1938), p. 31.

[56] PCCH, *En defensa de la revolución*, pp. 111–12.

[57] This call was, however, more in the nature of a command than an invitation. The agenda of the 1934 convention still reflected the preoccupations of the extreme leftist period—including fierce attacks on any rivals in the labour movement. Not until 1935 and the arrival of Ravines, did the Popular Front policy of collaboration become firmly established. (I am indebted to Andrew Barnard for this point.)

force of the workers'.[58] Several railway union leaders were arrested on the grounds of participating in a Communist plot to overthrow the government in conjunction with the Block de Izquierdas and foreign elements (including Carlos Prestes, the famous Brazilian Communist). With the declaration of solidarity by Communist, Socialist, and anarchist unions, the government declared a state of siege and placed the railways under state control. Subsequent reprisals against the strike leaders provided the impulse towards union unity.

On 24 December 1936 200 delegates from the FOCH, the Socialist CNSC, the anarcho-syndicalist CGT, and a number of non-aligned federations, including some *empleados*, met in a National Congress of Unity. The principal differences among the delegates concerned the right of participation of legal unions and the structure of the new organization.[59] The majority favoured uniting legal and 'free' unions, and a structure of national industrial unions, or federations (which were set up in nine designated sectors of the economy).[60] But the CGT opposed the inclusion of the legal unions and refused to merge with the new CTCH.[61]

That the CTCH was a political confederation, very much rooted in the circumstances of the Popular Front, is clear from its declaration of principles. Fascism was identified as the major enemy—the shock troops of reactionary capitalism. Stress was laid on supporting the Communist-dominated CTAL (the Confederation of Latin American Workers) in order to launch the continental fight against fascism. For this great task, the working class must ally with all progressive sectors of society, and must work together to perfect democracy and develop national industry by creating an Economic Council on which all sectors of the economy would be represented. Diplomatic relations should be established with the Soviet Union, and the property of fascists in Chile should be expropriated.[62] Reference was made to the need to replace the

[58] Quoted in M. Salem & J. Sandoval *Hacia una organización de los trabajadores: la CTCh* (*Memoria*, Univ. Chile, 1964), pp. 227–8.

[59] Morris, pp. 261–2.

[60] These were manufacturing industry, transport, construction, food supply, public services, education, mines, health, and the rural sector (Pereira & Torres, p. 246).

[61] Contreras Labarca, 'La gran experiencia del Frente Popular', *Principios*, July–Aug. 1967, p. 27.

[62] These principles are detailed in Poblete, 'El movimiento de asociación profesional obrera en Chile', *Jornadas* (Colegio de Mexico), 29 (1945), pp. 51–7.

existing unjust regime based on private property by a more just one, but this was mild compared with the ringing Marxism of the declarations of the FOCH.

The CTCH was silent on the destruction of capitalism and its replacement by a socialist order. The FOCH had not proclaimed the need to ally with the progressive bourgeoisie, and certainly would not have admitted that democracy existed at all, let alone that there was a need for perfecting it. The emphasis that the FOCH gave to imperialism was replaced in the CTCH by one on fascism.

Given the political support that the CTCH received initially from the Communists and Socialists, and the more or less benevolent eye of the Popular Front government after 1938, it is not surprising that the confederation grew rapidly. In 1938 it had 110,000 members grouped in 500 unions; by 1943 there were nearly 200,000 members in over 1,500 unions.[63] At its peak the CTCH brought together close on 90% of Chilean unionists,[64] but as with the CUT, few of them paid their dues.[65] The CTCH was a mass movement including Socialists, Democrats, Radicals, Communists, and other left-wing and centre groups. Though the Communists preserved their separate identity, there was, at least initially, to be no open struggle for hegemony. In line with party policy, Communist unionists were to appear primarily as unionists and not as party agents inside the unions; and, as the CP usually claims, were to be seen as working for the good of the working class as a whole. But if the administrative separation of union and party was apparently clearer than in the FOCH, the political separation was not. The CTCH, even more clearly than the FOCH, was a political creation aimed, in this case, at securing the victory of the Popular Front. The electoral victory of a Radical President was more important than the industrial struggle of the working

[63] The latter figure is made up of 561 plant unions with 122,645 members and 1,005 professional unions with 71,923 members (Bernardo Ibáñez, *Organo informativo* (CTCH, Santiago), 10 Sept. 1943; Poblete (n. 62, p. 48), gives a figure of 400,000 members for 1940 but this seems exaggerated (given the overall number of unionists). Vitale (p. 87) claims 300,000 members for 1941—again surely too many?

[64] J. Figueroa Araya, *Bosquejo y crítica de nuestro regimen sindical* (*Memoria*, Univ. Chile, 1945), p. 27.

[65] J. Diaz Martinez, 'Treinta meses de acción en favor del proletariado de Chile', *Memoria del consejo directivo nacional al 1° congreso ordinario del CTCh, 26–30 julio 1939*, p. 71.

class. Thus the party secretary-general urged: 'We must make every effort to solve political or economic conflicts by mutual accord. Strikes or other forms of violent struggle must be the exception.' Only when every possibility of conciliation had failed should strikes be undertaken. 'But before this there must be a public campaign to show the justice of the workers' demands.' [66] If peasant unionization was held to be a hindrance to increased food production for the city workers, then the peasantry would have to wait.

But it would be a mistake to write off the CTCh merely as the extension to the union field of the parties, and later the conflict between the parties. It did defend and extend some of the social gains of the unionists; it saw an expansion and, at least initially, a strengthening of the union movement; and the CTCh itself engaged in industrial conflict defending the workers' interests (though not so strenuously as to endanger CP aims). Though this was hardly planned by the CTCh, the *empleado* unions grew in power and strength because of government action favouring the white-collar sector by establishing minimum salaries and providing better social-security services. The efforts of the CTCh furthered economic development by attempting to curb excessive union demands and by trying to increase output (even if its efforts to deflect a greater share of the profits to the workers were not so successful). By collaborating with the government and employers, it gave many union leaders greater experience and maturity in dealing with questions of economic policy and industrial relations, although this valuable experience was largely to be lost in the fratricidal strife following the war.

Yet its failures, considering its relative acceptance by the government and its participation in the Popular Front and in such organizations as CORFO, are more striking.[67] It failed to get

---

[66] Contreras Labarca, *Unión nacional* (15th plen. sess. of the CP CC, Aug. 1944), p. 70.

[67] On the National Executive Committee of the Popular Front in 1937 sat 1 Radical-Socialist, 2 Communists, 2 Unified Democrats, 4 Socialists, 7 Radicals, and 3 representatives from the CTCh (*Reglamentos del Frente Popular* (1937)). Thus the CTCh was also represented in the congress called to select the presidential candidate of the Front in 1938. Half its delegation were Socialists— who on the first ballot voted for Grove; half were Communists, who on the first ballot voted blank, according to the party line. Both groups, following their party instructions, later voted for the Radical Pedro Aguirre Cerda (Jobet, *Socialismo*, pp. 38–9).

the labour code reformed and to prevent the gap between white-collar and blue collar-worker from widening; it failed to secure an increase in the standard of living of the workers relative to other groups and to make provision for forming unions amongst the peasantry and other unorganized groups; its eventual collapse left the labour movement gravely weakened for years. To serve the aims of the parties, it neglected the interests of its members; and as there was division about these aims, so there was division inside the labour movement. It was led by politicians rather than by union leaders, chiefly noted for their party militancy—its two most prominent figures, Bernardo Ibáñez, a Socialist, and Araya, a Communist, were both deputies who also held important party administrative posts. The CTCh singled out for strikes for higher pay and shorter hours not those concerns with high profits or below-average wage-scales, but rather those owned by alleged fascist sympathizers or those having trading relations with the Axis countries.[68]

The actions of the CTCh leaders followed the political line of their parties, at least until the Socialist party became so split that there was little central control or direction. Thus when this party left the Popular Front, the Socialists on the executive of the CTCh tried to secure the confederation's withdrawal too, only to be defeated by the combined efforts of Communists, Radicals, and Democrats.[69] The CP was so worried about publishing an 'extreme' CTCh newspaper or magazine that its representative declared that 'experience has shown us that the problems affecting the working class are essentially technical'.[70] When the Socialists and Communists entered the Alianza Democrática—a revived Popular Front—then so did the CTCh. When the CP was energetically pursuing its policy of a single party in 1943, then the CTCh also resolved that it would work for a single party of the workers.[71]

The Socialist party expressed concern over the subservient

[68] *La CTCh y el proletariado de América latina* (Publicaciones de la CTCh, 1938), p. 60. For the great emphasis of the CTCh on fighting fascism see also J. Vargas, 'Por un congreso de la CTCh que impulsa la unidad antinazi', *Intervención del secretariado sindical ante la 13º sesión plenaria del CC, Junio 1948* (1948).

[69] H. Abarca, 'Como organizar la victoria', *Informe al sesión plenaria del CCCP, Enero 1941* (1941), p. 20.

[70] Díaz Martinez, p. 91. No doubt the Communists were also unwilling to see competition for their party press.

[71] Ibáñez, *Memoria de la CTCh, 1943–6, al tercer conferencia nacional, 1946*, p. 14.

political role that the CTCh was playing; one of the resolutions of its 1940 Congress declared: 'The CTCh . . . has been . . . without life or independence because it has merely been an appendage to the Popular Front'.[72] Yet the party did little to strengthen CTCh independence. Its group in the CTCh worked with the Radicals, Democrats, and Falangists to try to combine against the Communists, and what little party finance was available was used to strengthen the Socialist party in the CTCh.[73] The Socialists argued that party rivalry was damaging to the interests of the labour movement, but, given the attitudes and actions of the Communists, that they had little alternative except to try to prevent Communist hegemony.[74] Nor did the Socialist party in this period put forward any radical alternatives in the union field; though they criticized the Communist tactics and expressed concern at the government's slowness in implementing the Popular Front policy, in practice their activity in the union field was confined to attempting to beat the Communists.

The situation became more and more bitter as the Socialist party split. The party had early asserted its aim to control the Socialist unionists on the CTCh when it demanded that those unionists who supported the breakaway Partido Socialista de Trabajadores should be removed from the executive,[75] irrespective of the support they might or might not have from the rank-and-file union members. The CTCh Socialists supported Bernardo Ibáñez and his militant anti-communism, against the other party group which, while also hostile to the Communists, disapproved of Ibáñez's attempt to take over the party and run it according to his dictates. Thus Ampuero, in opposition to Ibáñez, argued that the CTCh Democrática (the Socialist half of the divided CTCh in 1946) should work to establish the independence of the union movement, giving priority to economic problems. He wanted the Socialist unionists to work to unite democratic forces in the labour movement and to oppose the Communists on the basis of the unity of the working class; but he argued that the leaders of the CTCh Democrática, by following Ibáñez's policies,

[72] 'Resoluciones del 2⁰ congreso extraordinario del PS, Curicó, 1940', in *Rumbo*, July–Aug., 1940, p. 68.
[73] PS, *Una etapa*, pp. 11 & 22.
[74] Letter to the CP, published ibid., p. 145.
[75] *Resoluciónes del 3ª congreso general del PS de trabajadores*, Santiago, *1–3 marzo 1942*, p. 15.

merely led the unions along the path of extreme politicization. This attitude had led to the failure of the pact with the CGT, and to the failure to reach agreement with the Radical party in a mutual union alliance against the Communists.[76] As will be seen, Ampuero did not object to strong tactics against the Communists, but did object to the aims of the Ibáñez group in the fight against communism, to their choice of right-wing allies, and to the role they gave to the unions in that struggle.

Socialist–Communist hostility and intransigence, heightened by the first effects of the onset of the cold war and by the prevailing political uncertainty in Chile following the death of President Juan Antonio Ríos, caused the CTCh split in 1946.[77] According to Ibáñez, the Communists were determined to get representation in the cabinet, and strongly resented the Socialist refusal to allow them to use the CTCh for this end. The precipitate action of interim President Duhalde in cancelling the legal status of two unions on strike led to the call for a general strike, on Ibáñez's proposal. But before this could take place, demonstrating workers in the Plaza Bulnes were fired on by the police and army.[78] Though the subsequent general strike was a success, the Communists at first ignored the call to return to work and demanded an indefinite general strike to secure their particular demands; but Ibáñez, in independent conversations with the government, had secured the entry of the Socialist party into the cabinet, which, he asserted, meant that the demands made by the workers would be met. The Communists, furious because they wished to enter the cabinet of future President González Videla, assaulted the headquarters of the CTCh and, after occupying the place for a fortnight, removed records and files. Ibáñez also accused the 'red Nazis', as he labelled them, of assassinating Socialist coal miners in Lota.

The Communist version of these events by Araya differs on

[76] Ampuero, 'En defensa del partido y del socialismo', *Informe político del CC Ejecutivo al pleno nacional, 27–29 febr. 1948.*

[77] 'Into the Communist CTCh went the coal miners, the nitrate unions, the construction workers, the port workers, the bakers, and some industrial workers; into the Socialist CTCh went the public transport workers, the copper workers, railwaymen, the textile workers, chemical workers and some other industrial groups' (Poblete, 'Movimiento sindical chileno', *Combate*, 23 (1962), p. 31).

[78] This version is contained in *Memoria de la CTCh 1943–6*, and Ibáñez, *Socialismo y el porvenir de los pueblos, informe al Partido Socialista, 1946.* Frei, then Minister of Public Works, resigned in protest at the massacre in Plaza Bulnes.

every point,[79] and he accuses Ibáñez of advocating extreme action, and then capitulating to the lure of office. In Araya's version it is Ibáñez and the police who assaulted the headquarters of the CTCh, forcing the Communists to leave and set up office in the Miners' Federation, and Ibáñez was also accused of Trotskyism. The presence of the Ibáñez group in the government was short-lived. The electoral coalition that brought González Videla to power included the Communists, who then received their turn in office and the recognition by the government of their CTCh as the legal one. Their triumph was short-lived, for they were soon driven from the cabinet and subsequently outlawed and persecuted.

The period from the CTCh split in 1946 to the Law for the Defence of Democracy in 1948 was the most troubled, both in the relations between the two parties and in the internal affairs of the Socialist party.[80] An impeachment mounted by the Communists in 1946 against the then Socialist Minister of Labour, Lisandro Cruz Ponce, provides ample evidence of fraud, intrigue, corruption, and violence on both sides in the effort to gain control of the unions. Workers were taken away at their lunch breaks, plied with drink, and sent back, drunk, to vote the right way. The Communists were particularly bitter about the use by the Socialists of Ministry of Labour officials to rig union elections. The Minister of Labour, denying the charge that all labour inspectors were Socialists, retorted that the Communists were annoyed because loss of control over unions deprived them of their major source of finance at the time, union funds. He declared that the abuses of the Communists were so flagrant that he had had to take severe steps to curb them.[81]

Not long after this the Socialist party entered into negotiations

[79] B. Araya, 'Una CTCh unida, combatiendo en defensa de la clase obrera y del pueblo', *Informe a la 2º conferencia nacional de la CTCh, 29–31 Mayo 1946*. Ever ready to add political items to their demands, the Communists at the time of the general strike also called for a break in diplomatic relations with Spain and Argentina (*New York Times*, 30 Jan. 1946).

[80] This was a period of general strife in the Latin American and in some European labour movements. In Cuba, for example, the Auténticos and the Partido Socialista Popular (the CP) were engaged in a bitter struggle for control of the unions (B. Goldenberg, 'The rise and fall of a party, the Cuban CP 1925–59', *Problems of Communism*, July, 1970, p. 76).

[81] Cámara de Diputados, *Acusación constitucional contra el Ministro del Trabajo: Sr Lisandro Cruz Ponce* (12 sesión ordinaria, Santiago, 19 June 1946), pp. 487–92, 504, 581–6, 589–670.

with the Radicals to form an anti-Communist confederation. However, the insistence of the Radicals on equal representation on its executive was unacceptable, and the talks broke down.[82]

Hostility between Communists and Socialists reached its peak during the famous coal strike of 1947 in Lota, which also became a trial of strength between the government of Radical President González Videla and the CP. Both the then American ambassador and Ampuero, the secretary-general of the Socialist party (an unusual alliance), agreed that the workers' demands had eventually been met by the coal owners, partly because of presidential pressure, but that the Communists insisted on prolonging the strike against the wishes of the other workers. Ambassador Claude Bowers alleged that the Communists tried to provoke the soldiers into firing on them, thus creating martyrs, but the military disregarded the provocation.[83] Ampuero quickly seized the opportunity presented by the government's sending in the military. He organized some 1,500 Socialist workers to go in with the troops, help keep the mines running and hence destroy the basis of Communist union power there.[84] The army, however, was not particularly thankful for the offer of assistance and the expedition failed.[85] Though the military made some use of the new workers, they did so according to their own convenience and not according to the Socialist plan, which was to assure Socialist representation in all sectors of the mines; moreover, the military prevented union meetings and the solution of conflicts. The mine owners,

---

[82] Waiss, *Drama socialista*, pp. 64–5. As there would also have been Demo-cráticos on the executive, the Socialists would have been in the minority. Moreover the Radicals demanded the withdrawal of Ibáñez.

[83] *Chile through Embassy Windows* (1958), pp. 166–9.

[84] I. Araneda & X. Bulnes *Gobierno de González Videla* (*Memoria*, Univ. Chile, 1964), pp. 423–4.

[85] In his analysis of the situation Ampuero argued that the only reason for the strike was political and, given the critical state of the country at the time, that it could have led to civil war. This was also the charge made by the Chilean representative to the UN, Santa Cruz: 'The Communist ministers were . . . forced out of the Government, and very shortly, just as was the case in France, a wave of revolutionary strikes flared up in the mining and industrial centres where. . . the Communist Party had gained absolute domination due to a relentless trade union dictatorship. Even though the Government succeeded in having the economic conditions of the workers improved, the strike continued. To the amazement of the entire country, it was then shown that there existed a far-reaching plan for revolution and sabotage' (cited in Clissold, pp. 204–5).

once the original trouble-makers had been removed, had no wish to import Socialist trouble-makers, and so they were soon dismissed. As usual in the Socialist party, there were a number of internal disputes; the regional organization of the party felt it had been ignored by the Central Committee; the current ideological disputes continued bitterly amongst those sent to Lota; and the parliamentary group, when asked to send some of its members to the area, refused to do so because the whole group was too busy arguing about the rights and wrongs of the situation. In view of all this, the conclusions of a report by Ampuero seems a little unconvincing, to say the least. He writes: 'In spite of everything we continue to sustain the essential justice of our attitude, its political necessity, and the extraordinary richness of the experience obtained.' [86]

The third phase in the development of major labour confederations in Chile opened in the early 1950s when Communists, Socialists, and other left-wing groups came together to form the CUT. The Communists aimed at avoiding the mistakes of the FOCH and the CTCh—domination of the union by the party and exclusion of other groups from the labour movement. They hoped to make the union-party division even clearer than they had intended it to be (though without success) in the CTCh. Unity of the working class was to be the great theme, and now that they were in opposition to the government, this was much easier to achieve than when the working-class movement was directly involved with the government, as in the days of the Popular Front. Officially the party stressed the freedom of its union leaders from party surveillance and the political brief they were given was far less specific and demanding than in the previous confederations; at least it was not so difficult to carry out. Strict working-class unity against other sectors was no longer the policy; other social groups must be brought into the popular alliance. Even the national bourgeoisie must be given a chance to participate in the battle against the landed sectors and the foreign enterprises. Socialist objections to this policy must be treated with caution, to avoid offending the other great working-class party. Christian Democrats must be welcomed, for they too can serve the interests of the working-class movement. Partisan differences inside the union movement must be played down, not sharpened. The unions must fight for economic benefits; this will show the contradictions of capitalism,

[86] *En defensa del partido.*

strengthen the working-class consciousness, and earn their gratitude for the CP. In the political arena democratic elections rather than insurrections show the way; Communists should agitate for high electoral participation in their unions. Adventurism should be shown up objectively as a manoeuvre to discredit the working class.

The reconciliation between Socialists and Communists—both politically and in the union field—has been uneasy though not unsuccessful. The differences are to some extent ideological, though it might be more appropriate to call them differences of tactics or of general attitude towards politics. This was the view of a prominent Falange congressman when describing the response to the street demonstrations of April 1957:

The Communists are firmly inside orthodox Marxism concerning tactics, completely dominated by the idea that the leaders of proletariat must beware of any error that could hold back the final revolution. The Communist party would never embark on an unplanned revolution which would expose its militants. The Socialists, on the other hand, are revolutionaries *à outrance*—believers in taking advantage of all occasions for agitation, without discriminating between the levels of revolutionary consciousness of the masses. But their revolutionary spirit has never been important, because the verbal irresponsibility of their leaders is the dominating feature, as can be seen in union matters.[87]

The Socialist party does have, since the victory of Castro in Cuba, a group that preaches much more revolutionary (even guerrilla) tactics than the CP. But these ideas are not supported by many Socialists in unions, at least not by many who hold positions of responsibility. Socialist as well as Communist trade unionists helped to bring down Clotario Blest in 1962 when he preached the use of the strike as a revolutionary weapon. The Socialist party expects of its union leaders the creation of class consciousness amongst the rank-and-file unionists. While this is undoubtedly an indispensable task for any marxist group, it is a very wide and general brief, akin to a religious exhortation to be virtuous. It is hardly the issue that divides Socialists and Communists in the unions. The real disputes are much more obviously about hegemony, about larger political issues, about relationships with other political parties.

Behind all the rhetoric there is a struggle between the Socialists

[87] R. Gumucio, 'De la falange a la democracia cristiana', in R. Boizard, *Democracia cristiana* (1963), pp. 326–7.

and Communists for as much control over the union movement as they can secure,[88] though it has been a notable achievement of the alliance between the two parties that that struggle has been kept largely within the confines of a democratic and electoral process—in striking contrast to the period of the CTCh. This struggle has certain benefits for the union movement in that there is constant vigilance from members of the other party over the actions of a union leader; but it does tend also to polarize union matters into competition between the parties, leaving the non-party members who are, after all, the majority rather isolated from union affairs.[89] Only on one occasion have the Communists and Socialists presented a joint list of candidates for election to the executive of the CUT; otherwise they have competed. This is the general rule for elections to the executive of unions where there is party competition. Only rarely, and usually when they are in the minority, do the marxist parties come together to form an electoral alliance against the other parties or independents. Each party wishes to have as many union leaders attached to it as possible. The reasons for this are political, for there does not seem to be any substantial difference between the tactics or aims of the union leaders of the two parties in practice, whatever they may claim in theory. Both pursue economic objectives, and while this pursuit is clearly related to political considerations—for example the attempt to discredit the Frei government—it is less clearly related to 'revolutionary' tactics aimed at overthrowing the structure of state power. The Socialist party is not short of theoreticians who proclaim the need to follow just such revolutionary aims and who parade their theoretical differences from the Communists. In one party meeting it was resolved that the union fight must be national and that small-scale struggles were sterile and self-defeating. A general union movement, it was argued, cannot simply be the sum of a large number of small-scale unions; real success must lie in a total and global confrontation with the employers. This policy, it was stated, was contrary to that of the Communist party, which

[88] Even after the Socialists and Communists had agreed to join forces and found the CUT, Jobet who, though best known for his writings, was also for many years a member of the CC of the Socialist party, could still write: 'Communism has never given up its policy and practice of dominating in a totalitarian way unions and federations. In those where it did impose its will, immediately union democracy disappeared, minorities were crushed, and non-Communists eliminated' (*Socialismo y comunismo* (1952), p. 42).

[89] Ampuero, *Izquierda en punto muerto* (1969), p. 139.

I

opposes in practice any massive action against government policy.[90] Exhortation follows exhortation in the Socialist party, but in practice successful action takes place only when Socialists and Communists are in full agreement and the circumstances are genuinely favourable to the mobilization of massive union support against a particularly unpopular government policy, such as the forced-savings scheme in late 1967.[91] Both marxist parties were united in their opposition to the economic policies of the Christian Democratic government. It would have been strange if they were not so united, for these policies included a wage freeze. Opposition to this policy was successful in the sense that the government was not able to freeze wages at the levels it desired, and was therefore unable to implement its anti-inflationary policy, The failure to contain inflation was one of the biggest setbacks to the Christian Democratic government.

Socialists and Communists also disagree over the relationships with other parties, both in politics in general and in the unions in particular. Socialists are reluctant to admit Christian Democrats and Radicals into the working-class alliance, but the Communists were anxious to admit the Radicals and Christian Democrats critical of the policy of the Frei government.[92] This does not mean that Socialists do not work quite amicably and well with Christian Democrats and Radical union leaders inside a particular executive, for this they obviously do. But it does mean that they are unwilling to allow them the right to be considered as genuine repre-

[90] 'Tesis sobre política sindical aprobada por el 19° congreso del PS', *Arauco* Dec. 1961, p. 6. See also *Socialismo y la unidad: (cartas del PS al PC )* (1966), which refers to the different approach of Communists and Socialists in the copper unions.

[91] Thus Petras (pp. 176–7) argues that the left missed a chance to organize mass action when rioting broke out over a rise in bus fares in Santiago in March–April 1957. The labour unions played little or no role in the mass demonstrations which were basically a protest against the failure to halt inflation.

[92] Though these stances have been reversed in the past. 'Against their idea of the dictatorship of the proletariat we propose the idea of a government of manual and intellectual workers, a unity of middle and popular sectors inside the Socialist party. Against their idea of union sectarianism we propose the autonomy of the unions' (Allende, *Contradicción de Chile* (speech to the 4th PS congress, Valparaíso, 15 Aug., 1943), p. 3). Perhaps Allende at least has been more consistent than his party, for after taking presidential office in 1970 he still continued to refer to 'friendly' sectors of the PDC which should not be attacked.

sentatives of the working class. Thus the Socialists attack the
Christian Democrats and Radicals inside the CUT, though some of
the Christian Democratic unionists themselves were strong opponents of the government's economic policy.

The Socialists have mixed feelings towards the Communist
unionists. Because the CP is obviously a working-class movement
and larger and less heterogeneous than their own, it cannot be
ignored. In any policy of revolutionary unity the Communists
have to be considered, since their basis in the working class is so
strong. On the other hand the Socialists oppose in theory the
moderation and caution of the Communists and their attitude to
the so-called bourgeois parties.

The Communists are reluctant to air differences with the
socialists, at least openly, and will reply only if directly attacked.
They were instrumental in bringing the Christian Democrats and
Radicals into the 1968 CUT congress against the wishes of the
Socialists, but they did so in a way calculated to appease their
partners as much as possible. At the Congress itself, any remark
intended to draw attention to the party affiliation of the speaker
was drowned by the Communist chant of *Unidad*.[93]

Politicization is at one and the same time a strength and weakness of the Chilean labour movement. It is undoubtedly a strength
in that it provides leaders, organization, assistance, ideology.
But, as any survey of Socialist–Communist relations shows, it can
be a great weakness, for it introduces sectarianism into a movement whose primary strength must lie in its unity. The weaknesses
inherent in such politicization were shown most clearly in the
divisions causing the CTCh split. The strength of politicization was
shown in the CUT, especially in the late 1960s, for although both
parties continued to compete generally and in unions in particular, in this case the desire to remain united proved stronger
than the desire to impose hegemony. Co-operation between

[93] Indeed, Communist unionists can at times take the plea for unity too
seriously for the party leaders. One pointed out that the election of delegates
to the CUT must not be rigged. 'In congresses [of unions] where the immense
majority supported our party "to aid the cause of unity", in order "not to break
the congresses", executives were designated purely as a result of agreements in
which we Communists ceded positions that the masses had given us democratically with the highest majorities. This constitutes an abuse of union democracy and violates the most elementary norms of respect of the workers'
(O. Astudillo, *Pleno de abril de 1965*, p. 25). Perhaps this was also a subtle way
of publicly telling party members not to rig elections in their own favour.

Communists and Socialists in trade unions has not been easily achieved since World War II—as the cases of France and Italy clearly show. That in Chile the Communists and Socialists could co-operate, or at least compete democratically and peacefully in the unions, must have lent credibility to FRAP claims to be pursuing common policies.

# 6. Socialism and Communism II

THE fact that the Socialist and Communist parties claim to be predominantly working-class parties does not mean that trade union representatives dominate the internal power structure of those parties and decide their policies. Nor does it mean that the point of view of the unions is a crucial factor in the making of party policy, for the importance and influence of the unions inside the party largely depends on what the party considers to be its main concern. Although each party maintains the contrary, it would seem that the crucial arena for both is the parliamentary one, and they consequently accept parliamentary and presidential elections as their main mobilization process. Accordingly the power structure of the party comes down heavily in favour of the parliamentary group. The South American Bureau of the Comintern in 1926 criticized the independence of the Communist parliamentary group from party control.[1] If at the present time such tension between the Central Committee and the parliamentary group does not exist, this is because the party is much more disciplined and united. Now an electorally strong party, parliamentarians predominate in its hierarchy, and the party is firmly convinced that parliamentary and electoral methods are the best ones for achieving its purposes.

The Socialist party is more bothered about the tacit acceptance of the parliamentary road by many, perhaps a majority, of its members and leaders. Clodomiro Almeyda, a former Minister of Labour under Ibáñez and Allende's first Foreign Minister in 1970, declared at the Chillán party congress in 1967 that 'the Socialist party ought to reject electoral processes as a way of gaining power'.

This sentiment, and its corollary that 'the revolutionary armed struggle constitutes the fundamental revolutionary line in Latin

[1] For details see Clissold, pp. 121–2.

America', was accepted by that congress. In order to reduce the dominance of the parliamentary group inside the party the Central Committee went so far as to decide in 1968 that membership of the committee would be incompatible with parliamentary status—though the force of this was diluted when it was also decided that an exception should be made for the party secretary-general, Senator Aniceto Rodríguez.[2] Allende, speaking in a homage to Senator Salomón Corbalán, who died in a road accident, claimed that

the parliament of bourgeois democracy is not something that satisfies fully or even partly, our ideas and our aspirations. But a revolutionary can and should, when the party applies its discipline, stand out even in this battle ground—to be present at the debates to proclaim his revolutionary thought, without forgetting that his language should be the same as if he were on the barricades, on the popular tribunal, or writing in the party newspaper.[3]

This is a less radical view than that of Almeyda; the idea, expressed also by Régis Debray, is that it is not wrong to use parliament, but that it should not be used in a bourgeois way. However, if the idea of working not only for revolutionary ends but also to redress specific injustices by legislation is accepted, it is almost inevitable that the parliamentary and electoral road will be the main road for the party[3]—as the history of the Socialist party shows throughout the Popular Front period, at the start of the second Ibáñez presidency, and during the electoral campaign of 1970. This inevitably emphasizes the importance of the parliamentary group in the party power structure—a tendency that is even more accentuated when the party holds ministerial office as well as congressional seats, as both parties have done. Thus

[2] Reported in *Punto final*, Jan. 1968, p. 9.

[3] 'Homenaje a la memoria del ex-Senador Salomón Corbalón', *Arauco*, Apr. 1967, p. 6.

[3] 'All parties today,' wrote Michels in 1915, 'have a parliamentary aim. They pursue legal methods appealing to the electors, making it their first aim to acquire parliamentary influence, and having for their ultimate goal 'the conquest of political power'. 'Even the representatives of the revolutionary parties enter the legislature. Their parliamentary labours, undertaken at first with reluctance but subsequently with increasing satisfaction and increasing professional zeal, remove them further and further from their electors . . . and their comrades in the rank and file' (R. Michels, *Political Parties* (New York, 1959), pp. 82–3 & 136). Michels brought out very clearly the dangers for an allegedly revolutionary party in participating in the parliamentary game.

Chelén Rojas (p. 148) criticized the party (he was referring to the then PSP) for failing to create a socialist consciousness, for neglecting the political education of the militants, for not creating cadres at the local levels. Even though in 1953 the party counted on nineteen deputies and three senators (apart from the ministerial posts it then held under Ibáñez), he complained that they were only active in the legislature and neglected the extra-parliamentary party and the mass membership.

Petras, on the evidence of Almeyda, argues that, far from using parliamentary office to further the cause of the revolution, Socialist congressmen have used office to further their own careers. According to these data on the eighty-seven senators and deputies elected between 1932 to 1965, two-thirds rose in social position (whatever that may mean) through holding office. Of more concrete interest is the fact that a disproportionately large number of Socialist congressmen became politically more conservative, or left the party altogether, after their terms of office expired.[4] It cannot be inferred from this, however, that the present group of Socialist legislators will act in the same way.

Historically the relationship of authority between the party and its union wing has varied. During the Popular Front period the parties attempted to achieve a very close working link between a commanding party and an obedient union. The Socialist party declared that any 'member of the party judged and condemned by the disciplinary tribunal for errors or offences against the party political line' would 'automatically at the same time be punished by his respective union group; and vice versa'.[5] But the results were not successful, and in general at the present time the unionists of both parties enjoy a greater degree of independence from party directives.

[4] Of the 38 congressmen elected before 1953 only 21% continued to support the Socialist party after leaving office; 18% turned to moderate groups, another 18% to right-wing groups; 3% to other left-wing groups; and the remaining 40% either withdrew from politics, dropped out of sight or died. (Petras, p. 161. He somewhat unnecessarily uses percentages of such a small number as 38.)

[5] Departamento Sindical, *Organización sindical* (Cuadernos de Orientación, PS, 1937), p. 8.

## Communist and Socialist strength in the unions

Bare statistics of the estimated proportions of unionists supporting either of the marxist parties do not indicate how strong these parties are in the unions or how much control they have over their nominal adherents. The simple denunciation by the Chilean right of a labour movement completely obedient to the marxist parties is far from the case. Morris-Jones makes a useful fourfold division of union-party relations between dependent unions, sphere-of-influence unions, independent unions, and dominant unions. In practice, as he points out, most unions fall into the 'sphere-of-influence' category, tending to lean either towards dependence on or dominance of a party. [6] In Chile two additional factors influencing union-party relations are the existence of several political parties competing in the union field, and a varying degree of party influence over different levels of union organization—greater over the major confederation, less over the plant union. The 'sphere-of-influence' category is a wide one and certainly not a static one. Its usefulness lies in the emphasis it provokes on reciprocal party-union influences.

For a number of reasons the 'dependent union' model is inappropriate for Chile. There is first the problem of party control in a situation of party competition for influence over the unions. It is surely much easier for a party when it has a monopoly or near-monopoly in a labour movement to make use of its influence, unless that labour movement has independent sources of power and support. Strong rivalry between Socialists and Communists means that much time is spent in organizational, ideological, and tactical infighting. Competition for control within the unions, given that it has not decisively resulted in the victory of one party over the other, means overconcentration on internal union politics. [7] The Communists need to emphasize unity so much because it is so difficult to achieve and sustain.

There is secondly the constraint imposed by the structure of the Chilean labour movement. A union movement composed of a

[6] W. H. Morris-Jones, 'Trade Unions and Politics', in *Labour Unions and Political Organisations* (collected seminar papers, Inst. Commonwealth Stud., London Univ., no. 3, 1967), p. 7.

[7] For a list of CP tactics in winning control over unions see the right-wing pamphlet claimed to have been published by a trade union, *Comunismo en los sindicatos chilenos* (1967), pp. 6–12.

large number of small units is much more difficult to manipulate than one composed of a few large bureaucratic federations. Nominal control over the movement, measured by the number of union leaders affiliated to a political party, may not mean a great deal in terms of the ability of those leaders to mobilize the majority of the rank and file for party ends. It may be difficult enough to mobilize them for union ends. These factors obviously bear heavily on the nature of the leadership–follower relationship and the perception of a common interest by the various sectors of the movement. Only if the top leadership dominated extensive sectors of the union movement and if these sectors also co-operated could the structural obstacles to general union militancy and to unity in the political arena be overcome. In fact the particularism of different sectors is often more marked than unity of action, and the leader-follower relationship in Chilean unions tends to be unstable, conditional, and competitive.

Whatever their political beliefs, in practice most Chilean unionists behave as if their major concern was with pay and conditions; and surveys of union leaders clearly indicate that this is their stated major preoccupation. A survey by Landsberger in 1962 compares ideological differences with the personal and occupational characteristics of labour leaders. When asked about union goals, all three groups (FRAP, Christian Democrats, and non-committed) expressed a clear preference for economic betterment;[8] a mere 2% of FRAP leaders chose 'awakening political consciousness' as their first choice. Only at the level of second and third choice is there some ideological disparity; 15% of FRAP leaders—compared with 2% of non-committed and none of the Christian Democrats—believe in the union as an instrument of political activity.[9] This kind of distinction was maintained when they were asked about the amount of social change needed in Chile; 42% of FRAP leaders, compared with 28% of Christian Democrats and 22% of non-committed, wanted a 'total and immediate restructuring of society'.

The relationship between ideology and action, however, is

[8] It did not distinguish between Socialists and Communists but only between FRAP leaders and other groups, of which only the Christian Democrats were numerous enough to provide a contrast (Landsberger, 'Do ideological differences have personal correlates?', *Econ. Dev. & Cultural Change*, 16/2 (1968), p. 234).
[9] Ibid., p. 233.

surely more complex than in this presentation. The mere fact of the continuing strength of socialism and communism in the labour movement indicates that union leadership is not *only* concerned with economic betterment. In most collective-bargaining situations in Chile it is difficult to see marxist ideology as crucial; but collective bargaining is not, except in a very indirect sense, concerned with the political structure. Unions do not only engage in collective bargaining; the ideology professed by the leaders may be very important in determining the way they behave outside the bargaining situation. True, much time has to be spent on purely economic questions; it is difficult to see how this could be otherwise, given the very high rate of annual inflation in Chile and the average size and weakness of the plant unions. It is nevertheless true that party leaders would prefer unionists to engage more often in 'political' activities, or at least to pursue their economic policies in a way that would focus more on party political factors. Communist and Socialist political leaders continually deplore the kind of tactics that union leaders adopt in order to better the conditions of their members partly because such tactics might also result in union leaders being corrupted themselves. The Communist spokesman on union affairs, Astudillo, has insisted that 'we must reject the corrupting practice of some union leaders who spend all day lobbying in the Congress or waiting in the ministries instead of spending most of their time dedicated to their organization or carrying on with the struggle of the masses'.[10] Araya has also criticized the Communist trade union leaders in the CUT for acting in an individual, bureaucratic, and sectarian way, suggesting as remedy that all Communist union leaders should alternate one month of factory or production work with one of union work.[11]

Socialist party criticism of union leadership is a little different, stressing that the purity of the ideology rather than the solidarity of party organization suffers as a consequence of overconcentration on economic objectives. The party is often critical of the Socialist Brigades (the equivalent of the CP cells in the unions), on the

---

[10] *Más lucha popular para ganar el poder*, sesión plenaria del CC del PC (Santiago, Dec. 1963), p. 25. This he attributes in part to the fact that such leaders have only an irregular party life and underestimate the value of the party cells, which leads to depoliticization, *caudillismo*, and error.

[11] *Unidad sindical y lucha ideológica*, Informe al sesión plenaria del CC del PC, 11–13 Sept. 1959, pp. 26 & 36.

grounds that they do not in practice act to make the party the real vanguard of the masses or create class solidarity; they do not support or control the union leaders affiliated to them closely enough. Far too often they are content to elect a Socialist *directiva*, serving only personal ambitions and electoral ends.[12] Chelén Rojas, a Socialist senator and former union leader himself, accused the union leadership of the period 1958–64 of being 'old and spent leaders of the most repellent reformist opportunism who practised class collaboration to preserve their jobs' (p. 168).

It is true that Chilean union leaders are more inward looking than their parties desire. Most are understandably concerned with the problems of their own unions. Few plant or professional union leaders are in unions affiliated to powerful national organizations which could lend them support. Such national organizations as exist usually tend to work by themselves, co-operating with other national organizations sometimes for economic purposes but rarely for partisan activities of the sort desired by the political leaders. Politicians frequently criticize the particularism of the unions, though they have not helped greatly to overcome it. For the Communists the demand for unity is mostly for political unity of the different partisan tendencies inside the unions; a more fruitful effort might be made to overcome a different sort of particularism—that of the fragmented structure of the union movement, though it has to be acknowledged that the legal, economic, and structural obstacles to, say, setting up nation-wide unions with a national collective-bargaining system are very great. Even so, they have been overcome in some cases. The Socialist party recognizes the existing weakness of the unions and advocates a positive role for the party: 'These weaknesses can be neutralized only by the active intervention of the party which, via its brigades, can provide the national cohesion that is lacking, can help, by indirect means, to solve certain financial difficulties, and can play a decisive role gradually replacing the leadership.'[13] The party also perceives, however, that the state of organization of the brigades is very far from adequate to carry out those aims. If both union organization, and party organization inside the union movement, share similar faults of weakness and confusion of purpose, it is not surprising that the degree of control that the marxist

[12] PS, *Tesis política, sindical y organizativa* (July 1957), p. 22.
[13] Ampuero, '1964 año de prueba para la revolución chilena', *Arauco*, Feb. 1964, p. 20.

parties are supposed to exercise over the union movement is often exaggerated.

Party leaders often demand and expect too much of the union leaders (again not a Chilean pecularity). There is no reason to think that ideological loyalty precludes the rank and file from judging union leadership in Chile on its ability to secure the best possible pay and conditions, especially since not all of them share the same party loyalty. Though it is difficult for the rank and file to judge the achievements of the union leaders, the existence of competing parties in the union movement does mean that union leadership is more open in Chile than in many other countries to challenge on the grounds of inefficiency and incompetence. Union leaders could, and do, argue that it is hard to resolve specific union and economic functions with vague party and political ones. Frequently partisan commitment is an incentive to seek union office (though more at the national than local plant level), but immersion in the routine tasks of daily union administration often leads to a closer personal identification with the union than with the party, or at least an interpretation of function that tries to adjust party ideas to union activities rather than the other way round. This is more marked in the Socialist than in the Communist party.

## The unions and the parties

Before examining the role and importance of the unions in the internal workings of the two marxist parties, it is useful to consider why the link between union and party continues to exist, surviving even such periods of turbulence and strife as that following World War II.

One of the principal explanations must lie in the nature of union leadership. There are relatively few inducements in terms of finance, status, or power, except in the very few large unions. Dedicated party members seek union office, and this commitment of the union leader to his party is one of the strongest links between the two. In certain areas a very high degree of identification between party and union can occur; as in the coal-mining town of Lota, where the union and the municipality are largely run by members of the Communist party and where the social pressures to sympathize with the party must be great. But this is not the normal situation; it is no longer so to the same degree in the copper areas, where there is much more party competition and less isolation from the general political and social system. This commitment does not mean that Communist and Socialist union leaders are single-minded agents of the party, seeking by all possible methods to advance the party inside the union. Too often for the liking of party leaders, unionists tend to place union first and party second, acting inside the party as the defenders of the unions. Whether union or party takes preference in the commitment of the union leader, there is an attempt to reconcile the aims of both—usually by trying to interpret party policy in such a way as to harmonize it with union policy. The meaning and limits of this sort of party identification will be discussed more fully chapter 9—the essential point is that union leadership and membership of one of the marxist parties are seen as two complementary facets of the same tradition and system of belief, and are seen as normal and customary by most radical union leaders, in the same way as is membership of the Labour party for British trade union leaders. It is the absence of other advantages of union office— higher pay, power, prestige, except for few—that emphasizes the perceived unity of political and union activity.

A politically committed union leadership, and a rank and file accepting such commitment, are the obvious bases of a close relationship between party and union. There are also a number of other more practical factors that help to explain why unions value the connection, specifically the aid that the parties can supply to the unions.

Given the all-embracing role of the law in the Chilean system of industrial relations, the lawyer is correspondingly important. Few unions can afford to retain a permanent legal staff or fee legal advisers. Here the parties play an important role in supplying lawyers, often themselves party members, to offer advice or act as union agents in disputes with the government or employers.

Mediation at the political level is another recurrent need of unions in Chile. Because so much that happens in the area of industrial conflict is legal or political, the parliamentarian has an important role to play in supporting and assisting unions in conflict.[14] The Socialist party at one time insisted that every

[14] See e.g. the details of Socialist party help to and frequent contacts with the copper workers striking in 1967 (Rodríguez, *1966*, pp. 35–7): 'Comrade Tomás Chadwick (a senator) with special dedication has also been in the mining centres and assumed the judicial defence of the numerous prisoners before the Appeal Court in La Serena'.

deputy and senator should be assigned to a particular union sector to look after the interests of the unions therein.[15] Unions frequently need parliamentary help in order to introduce legislation favourable to their interests, such as special social-security treatment, or upgrading of status from *obrero* to *empleado*. More, since incomes policy has become so important in economic planning, mediation is necessary at the ministerial and departmental level. Parliamentarians knowledgeable in the byways of the complex Chilean administrative structure, and sophisticated enough not to be afraid of challenging it, once more become indispensable allies of the unions. This was certainly the case during pre-Allende administrations, and even under the new government this relationship is likely to continue.

Unions are usually poor in Chile. Revenues are hardly sufficient to cover the costs of collective bargaining or strike funds, let alone for luxuries such as the expenses of delegates, e.g. to CUT congresses. The parties certainly help to finance the more obviously political activities and may help the unions to finance their industrial activities as well. It is fairly widely accepted that the CP pays the expenses of some delegates to the CUT (and this is also true for the Christian Democrats). This position is something of a reversal of its position immediately after World War II, when a penniless party relied on unions to help the party's finances.[16] The poverty of the Socialist party probably prevents much aid of this sort, but certainly when the opportunities permit, it subsidizes union activities.[17]

Party newspapers and pamphlets are important communica-

[15] 'Conclusiones de la conferencia de parlamentarios socialistas', *Arauco*, June 1961, p. 40.

[16] Alexander alleges that Communist unionists made a special assessment on the workers of the Chuquicamata copper mine, supposedly to construct a union hall, but in fact to finance the party's organization for the presidential campaign of González Videla ('The Industrial Labour Leader', in W. Form & A. Blum, *Industrial Relations and Social Change in Latin America* (Florida, 1965), p. 81).

[17] 'We [the party] had to finance the 3rd National Congress of the CTCH, set up many provincial councils, train leaders . . .' (Ampuero, *En defensa del partido*). Alexander (p. 80) claims that the salary Ibáñez was receiving as a deputy not only made it unnecessary for the CTCH to pay him a salary as its secretary-general, but also meant that he could assist it financially. The Socialist party in 1943 lamented that a sharp decline in funds—due to non-payment of quotas from party members holding political and administrative office— meant that they could not help union leaders as before (*Una etapa*, pp. 22–8).

tions media for the unions. There are few union newspapers in Chile; apart from the rather technical publications of the very large federations little is published. Even the CUT does not publish regularly, according to the Socialists, because the Communists do not want any rival to the official party press.[18] No union newspaper exists with a circulation remotely comparable to that of the communist and socialist press. The links between union and party are, obviously enough, emphasized in these newspapers, and this form of publicity strengthens unionists' attachments to their parties.

### 1. The Socialist party

The formal party statutes refer at several points to the role of unions and unionists.[19] It is the duty of a party militant to be active in his union, or to press for the formation of a union where one does not exist. The base organization of the party is the nucleus of 5–15 members and, like the CP cell, it can be organized by neighbourhood or enterprise. This nucleus controls the activities of the rank and file, 'maintains revolutionary discipline,' and 'exercises fraternal vigilance over private conduct', and for these purposes it meets at least weekly. The executive body of the party between congresses (which meet every two years) is the Central Committee, whose thirteen members are elected at the party congress. Although the head of the parliamentary brigade, of the youth federation, and the women's federation are ex-officio members, the national secretary of the party union department is not, though he is normally one of the thirteen elected members.[20] In

[18] A. Rodríguez, *Forjando la unidad popular* (report to the general congress of the PSP, 1956), p. 30.

[19] *Estatutos del Partido Socialista* (1962). References occur on the following pages: 6, 11, 22, 24 f., 33, 35–6, 39, 41.

[20] Thus to the CC elected by the 235 delegates to the 1965 congress was chosen, as eleventh preference, the then president of the CUT, Oscar Nuñez, who had been elected to the CC in 1961 as head of the union department, and as twelfth, Waldo Iriate, a railway union leader who was head of the union department. Fifteenth preference (and so not a full member of the CC—i.e. lacking the right to vote) was the secretary-general of FONACC, Armando Aguirre (Jobet, *Socialismo*, p. 118). At the 1967 congress were elected the new head of the union department, Armando Aguirre, and the most prominent Socialist *campesino* union leader, Rolando Calderón (*Punto final*, 5 Dec. 1967, p. 46). If the head of the union department should not be elected by the Congress to the CC, he has the right to attend and speak in the meetings, but not to vote (*Estatutos*, p. 24).

any case, it is the Central Committee that formally chooses the secretary. Among the committee's powers are those of making pacts and alliances or taking common action with other parties of a political, parliamentary, electoral and/or union character, 'in conformity with the prevailing political line of the party'.[21]

The union department, created at the 4th congress in 1937, is empowered to guide, direct and control the activity of the party members in the unions. This is performed by the union brigades which are set up in the workplace. Only the Central Committee can authorize the creation of national brigades. The union department can propose to the committee the replacement of any leader of any national brigade who does not perform his allotted role correctly.

The party statutes are by no means unambiguous, nor does reality match the statutes, but this formal outline does indicate the theory of the party on the relationship with the unions. The authoritative body is clearly the Central Committee, and this stands in the same sort of relationship of democratic centralism to the union department as does the executive of this department to its affiliates regionally and in different economic sectors. Thus it is not unusual, for example, to find the party ordering its union leaders to ensure that their unions pay their affiliation fees to the CUT; or ordering the regional sections and the local parliamentary member to carry out a local census of socialist strength amongst the unions and ensure that the local branches of the union department are fully operative; or demanding from all union leaders when elected to office an undated letter of resignation to the national union department to be used if necessary.[22] (There is, however, no evidence that any census was carried out or letter sent by union leaders.)

The whole structure of the party separates ideological and political work, from (in a subordinate position), the 'mass' organizations—the youth department, the women's organization, the union department, the *campesino* department, and the *pobladores* (or shanty-town dwellers, the so-called marginals) department. This conveys an impression of the primacy of the political and ideological party line, largely made by politicians

[21] *Estatutos*, p. 24. The party congress is also supposed to discuss and resolve union and organizational questions.

[22] 'Resoluciónes del 21° congreso general ordinario del PS', *Arauco*, July 1965, pp. 28–30.

and ideologues, and of subordination of the mass auxiliary movements to the application of that line. One former member of the
Central Committee held that it was responsible for the development of three distinct types of the party members: the intellectual
theorist, the practical politician, and the unionist, and argued
for a reorganization of the party that would put ideological and
political roles on the same level as mass activities, so that the party
line would evolve from interaction between them.[23] The more
usual solution to observed defects of this sort is to call for another
restatement of ideology and for greater effort to diffuse it amongst
the workers to persuade them of its essential correctness.[24] This
democratic–centralist emphasis on the crucial role of hierarchical
organization which decides policies which the mass membership
must accept tends to exclude consideration of reorganizing the
party, in such a way as to give greater weight to the point of view
of unionists, or to changing the relationship of authority between
party and union.

It is hardly surprising that the union groups fail to meet the
demanding requirements of the political leaders in politicizing the
workers and converting them to the revolutionary standpoint of
the party ideologists, though in terms of building support for the
Socialist party in the unions, their achievements are not so inconsiderable. It is possibly true that the Socialist union brigades
in practice confine their efforts to electing the largest number of
members to the union executives, and so do not, as the Central
Committee complained, act in such a way as to create class solidarity, or take advantage of the union struggle to further the
political consciousness of the workers. It may even be true, as
the Central Committee further complained, that too often the
desire for leadership is based on personal ambitions rather than on
real revolutionary feeling.[25] But for a hard-pressed Socialist
brigade with probably few dedicated activists and normally little
money, ideological training, or time, elections to the executive of

---

[23] M. Garay, *La crisis política y el PSP* (1969), p. 21. (Garay wrote this when
a member of Ampuero's breakaway group, the Unión Socialista Popular.)
In 1961 the party congress had resolved that 'our union leaders must understand that the application of the political line of the party has first priority'.
The congress felt that the divorce between the political and union wing of the
party was due particularly to the lack of doctrinal training of the great majority
of members ('Tesis sobre política sindical aprobada por el 19° congreso del
PS', *Arauco*, Dec. 1961, p. 7).

[24] Ibid., p. 9.                                   [25] Ibid., p. 22.

K

the union are a concrete situation where success can be measured; class consciousness is a less substantial target, and it is not self-evident that the two aims are contradictory; indeed they seem complementary.

Socialist union brigades are in general far from vigorous. Apart from a few large federations where the Socialists are traditionally strong, like the copper workers and railway workers (and where, in a sense, there is less need for a strong brigade because the party already enjoys wide support) the brigades are generally weak and inactive except during union and national elections. Thus Ampuero commented that the brigades did not supervise and control 'our comrades who hold prominent union posts', and as a result the misappropriation or misuse of union funds 'has been held to be the responsibility of the party as well as individual members'.[26] He added that because of poor co-ordination, many Socialists regarded union activity and political action as if they were entirely different worlds, even with contradictory objectives; and he criticized the unionists' notorious apathy about creating combative nuclei.[27]

The structure of the union department has not changed to any marked extent.[28] The department is still composed of one representative from each large union or federation, a total in the late 1960s of twenty-six members. This larger group meets monthly, with smaller groups meeting fortnightly and weekly. The secretary holds the most important post, and besides being a member of the Central Committee, he participates in relevant meetings of the Political Commission, the small politbureau which is the most powerful body in the party. The secretary receives no pay and in this sense can hardly be regarded as a party bureaucrat. Indeed, it is clear that he has little enough time to perform the minimal duties of his office (especially as he usually also holds union office elsewhere). Most of his time, and that of the executive members of the department, is spent on economic and social matters concerning unions; directly political issues are important only at the time of national elections. The department aids

---

[26] Ampuero '1964, año de prueba', *Arauco*, Feb. 1964.

[27] Ibid., p. 32.

[28] The description of the union department and its activities is largely based on an interview with the national union secretary in April 1967. The incumbent at that time was also president of the Railway Workers' FOF—the blue-collar section of the FIFch; his successor was also a railway union leader.

striking unions with advice on tactics and on legal matters, but it has no funds to help them. Its members practically never hold congressional posts, but contacts between union leaders and congressmen are said to be strong.

What is the real importance of the union department? The usual response of its members is to refer to its role in fostering class consciousness, but quite how the department as such does this, or how effective it is, remains uncertain. It represents the unions' point of view inside the party, with the secretary of the department in particular undertaking this role. When interviewed, the secretary himself regarded the department as fairly influential in the party, and certainly more so than the other comparable departments (such as the *pobladores* or *campesino* departments). But the more general verdict is that its role is relatively unimportant in the overall making of party policy and tactics.[29] One Socialist senator described it as 'not so much a policy-making department as a department that exists to carry out the policy of the party. It is essentially under the control of the Political Commission.'[30] The political importance of the department naturally depends on the circumstances of the time. In a period of internal struggle, it can expect a role of some importance, as happened in 1945–8, when politicians struggled to control it.

The union department takes an active interest in the choice of candidates for union posts. According to its secretary, it plays a very active role in the selection of candidates in some unions. In the FOF, of which in 1967 the union department secretary was president, a large list of candidates is sent by the Socialist delegation elected to the FOF congress for approval and final selection by the union department and the Central Committee. The department plays a similar role in the selection of the party list for the CUT executive though, given the importance of certain persons and unions, much of the choice is fairly automatic. The department is supposed to play a similar role in the selection and approval of candidates for union office at the local and regional level, but outside Santiago the local or regional union department frequently exists only on paper. In practice, it seems that most socialist brigades in unions enjoy very real freedom from control and supervision.

[29] Thus the president of the FIFch described it to me as 'pretty marginal' (interview, Apr. 1967).
[30] Interview, Senator Tomás Chadwick, Apr. 1967.

The role of the union department in the choice of candidates for the FOF may well be the exception rather than the rule, explained because the secretary of the union department was president of the FOF. In FONACC, for example, where the Socialists predominate, the Socialist group does not consult the union department on the choice of candidates for office. On the other hand in the CTC the party does play a role in assessing and advising on the choice of candidates—but in view of the crucial importance of the copper workers, it seems that this comes directly from members of the Political Commission rather than the union department.[31]

The role of the union department in the Socialist party is limited; by no means all union-party relations are channelled through it. It seems to have only limited influence over party policy, and given its small size and lack of funds, it is unlikely to exert a powerful influence over unions, especially in their conduct of economic policy. But it does act as a means of information, of help, of persuasion; it does help to represent the point of view of the unions in the party; and it is important in transmitting the party message to the unions. The verdict of Oscar Waiss, expelled from the party for Trotskyism, was that the department 'does not unify, co-ordinate, lead or even have influence'.[32] This is too severe. Waiss was thinking primarily in terms of its success in developing a revolutionary consciousness amongst workers, and at this level it is easier to point to its defects rather than its achievements, but its role is more influential in binding workers to the party and in building up support for the party in the unions.

### 2. The Communist party

There is officially no union department in the CP organized like that of the Socialist party; here the unity of political and union action is taken to preclude the necessity of a separate department of unionists for union affairs,[33] though in practice a member of the secretariat is in charge of union matters, heading a Union Commission. As in the Socialist party, it is a duty of a party member to be active in the affairs of his union, or to work to create one

---

[31] Interview, president of CTC, May 1967. The socialist group on the CTC did acknowledge the union department role in helping training and educating union leaders and in acting as a co-ordinator between union and party.

[32] *Socialismo sin gerentes* (1961).

[33] PCCH *Estatutos* (1965).

if a union does not exist. The base organ of the party is the cell, organized in the workplace as well as in the community.[34]

Between party congresses, the executive body is the Central Committee, elected by the National Congress which meets every four years. The committee organizes and controls the various commissions and auxiliary organs, directs the political work of the party, and also that of the party's parliamentarians. The Central Committee elects a secretariat, which supervises the implementation of its decisions, and also the small and powerful Political Commission. The secretariat is the smallest body of the party, and the party secretary-general heads it and the Political Commission. One of the six named secretariat members is the Encargado Nacional Sindical (literally national union manager or representative, hereafter national union secretary). He heads a National Union Commission of nine members, mostly unionists, designated by the Political Commission. This Commission advises the Central Committee on union matters and is also supposed to control, direct, and plan the work of the co-ordinating teams. These teams, which group together factory cells, are organized vertically up to the level of federation, national union, and the CUT, and are designated by their immediate superior body. In the case of the CUT the co-ordinating team is the National Union Commission itself. The CUT team is the chief one in the Communist union movement; it takes decisions on a variety of policy matters and transmits them to the other teams.[35]

The real workings of the party do not precisely conform to the smooth outlines of the party statutes. Year after year Communist leaders stress the need, following correct agitational theory, to set up factory cells rather than community ones; just as regularly they lament their inability to do so. Astudillo in the 1962 party congress estimated that only 30% of the party cells were factory ones. His explanation was that the organization of community cells was the easy way out, and that the ideological message to

[34] References to unions occur on pp. 16, 25, 36, & 44. Each cell has five or more members and the leadership is elected annually. Different cells are linked together by a co-ordinating team. The leadership of the cell must ensure that party members are regular in their attendance and active in performance of their duties.

[35] This information comes partly from a students' investigation, P. Ricci & others, *Movimiento sindical del partido comunista*, Dec. 1964 (kindly lent by Prof. E. Morgado).

party militants had been defective, leading to an underestimation of the importance of the proletariat as the motor of the revolution.[36]

It is not just at the cell level that the party organization falls short of its objectives. The majority of the regional and local committees do not have Union Commissions. They leave the work in the unions to 'comrades of goodwill', who may not be the most capable, and who are not subject to party discipline.[37] Even the party National Union Commission, complained the party union secretary in 1961, had worked without co-ordination and drive. Many of these repeated declarations of failure may simply represent the Communist penchant for self-criticism as a method of inducing even greater efforts. But any examination of the Communist organization in the unions, though it confirms that it is more efficient and disciplined than that of the Socialists, also discloses local and regional weaknesses. One remedy proposed from time to time is to create a training school for local union leaders, on the argument that if only a handful of local leaders can be trained to perceive their ideological duties, the organization will be transformed.[38] This is doubtful, and has never been tested in practice, for such schools have been shortlived and largely based on unionists from the Santiago region; even the CP finds it difficult to draw hard-pressed local leaders away from their duties, for the problems of compensating for lost earnings, let alone of getting permission from employers, have been very real obstacles.

The need to raise ideological levels is not just the cry of party spokesmen with no union experience. Luis Figueroa, the CUT president active in union affairs for many years, has written that 'the tendency to isolationism, to live for the union alone, unconnected with the rest of the union movement or the working-class struggle, has its origins in the lack of politicization of the leaders

[36] *Fortalecer la lucha y la organización de la clase obrera* (report to 12th CP congress, 1962, Santiago), p. 18. O. Millas argued that even in the few factory cells that existed membership for most was a formality and led to no real activity (*Pleno de abril de 1965*, p. 54). Twenty-five years earlier Galo González was making the same point, and saying that even in the cells that did exist, little more was discussed than routine union matters, so that the cells were superfluous and often ceased to exist (*Por el fortalecimiento de partido* (9th plen. sess. of the CC, Oct., 1940, Santiago), p. 18).

[37] Astudillo, *Fortalecer la lucha*, p. 23.

[38] Araya, *Unidad sindical*, p. 37.

and their low ideological level'.[39] To overcome this weakness, or at least the consequences attributed to it, the party tries to exercise close control over its leaders. Nearly all Communist union leaders also have posts inside the party, in order to help the party supervise them and to communicate the union point of view to the party. The party theory is that this is also useful if pressure needs to be brought on the government in the interests of a particular union. It can then be done so via the party, and this is often more effective, and it also avoids possible splits in the union movement, since union leaders do not have to take a direct stand against the government but can let the party do this. During the Frei administration this was intended to help avoid clashes with Christian Democratic unionists who might have resented attacks on the government.

The CP plays a more active role than the Socialist party in supervising the choice of candidates for union office.[40] It has more funds and bureaucrats than the Socialists. Thus, though its objectives and tactics in the union field do not necessarily differ from those of the Socialists, the CP is able to perform them better; for example by providing more help for its candidates in the electoral campaigns, or more money to help delegates attend conferences. The number of Communist delegates to the CUT congresses reflects their true strength in the unions more truly than the Socialist representation, because the Communists are richer and have a better party machine.

The Communists have two main problems in their relations with the unions. The first one is the relatively weak organization of the party at most levels outside the CUT, which is especially marked at the local and regional level. The party proposes to remedy this by making a greater propaganda effort, but it is difficult to believe that a party which has been active in unions for nearly half a century and has in recent years been completely free to propagate its ideas, and which produces daily, weekly, and monthly publications, can hope to extend its influence by the

[39] 'La clase obrera y la elección presidencial', *Principios*, Jan.–Feb., 1964, pp. 96–7.
[40] Interview, secretary-general, FIFch (Santiago, Apr. 1967). (The secretary-general at that time was a Communist, a member of the National Union Commission, and on the CUT executive.) Interview with two Communist members of the executive of the Sindicato Industrial de Obreros, Lota, May 1967.

sudden awakening of new interest in its ideology. The Communists are weak in local unions because local unions are weak, and because their leadership is weak and unstable. To explain failure in terms of lack of grasp of its ideology is perhaps inevitable in a party which claims the essential correctness and validity of its ideology. This explanation also conveniently deflects blame from the national leadership to the local leaders. But it may be wondered if such explanations are necessary. The Communists are certainly the most powerful group in the unions, command loyalty from a not inconsiderable group of tough and dedicated union leaders, and help to deliver a large vote to the party at election time. At another level, they are dissatisfied at their inability to monopolize the political commitment of the labour movement or to woo the workers away from the false doctrines of the Christian Democrats and—though they would now not admit it openly—from the embrace of the Socialists too.

The second main problem is the conflict between a desire to allow some autonomy to the union sphere and yet to maintain control over it. In Communist theory, the union and the party serve distinct, if related, ends. If they come to be too closely identified, then both suffer, as in the last years of the FOCH. The Communists want the union movement to be a mass movement of unionists of all persuasions; it must not be seen simply as an appendage to the party. Communist union leaders must therefore be responsive to the mass feelings of the unionists. But what if these do not happen to coincide with the party line? It is all very well for the party to tell the union leader he must convert the masses to the party point of view. In practice this is extremely difficult, especially when several parties are competing for the workers' allegiance. The Communist union leader may find that he is being pulled in two directions, that party commands may conflict with what he sees as union needs; and he may well perceive union needs as more pressing, more specific, and more important, at least in the short run, than those of the party. In this case he is likely to act for the union rather than the party, not because of a low ideological level, but because the situation presses him in a direction of 'economic' unionism rather than ideological work. But contradictory pressures of this kind are common to any partisan union leadership, and by relative standards, the CP and its unionists manage to reconcile them remarkably well. The party has experienced relatively little of the divisive role that unionists have played in the Socialist party splits. Communist union leaders have not been prominent in deviations to the left or in splitting tactics generally. They do not trouble the party by opposing its line; and if they do trouble the party because they tend to give primacy to the more pressing problems of their unions, this may be held to reflect more on the party's unrealistic expectations than on the disloyalty or incapacity of the union leadership.

## The parties and the unions

It would be strange if parties regarding themselves as the van-guard of the working class did not make every effort to maintain close links with that class. As well as the imperatives of ideology and class, however, there are other, and perhaps more practical, reasons which explain those links and their nature. In fact, it has been argued that the links that do exist militate against the ideological imperative to create a revolutionary class consciousness in favour of building up a privileged, if loyal, sector of the working class. Petras, for example, argues that the marxist parties 'have abdicated their role as spokesmen for the working class as a whole . . . In its role as defender of the unionised industrial workers the Left has raised the standard of living of that group, preserved its electoral base and access of office, and widened the gap between different strata of the working class'. The result has been that the 'only means available for political action have been an occasional general strike, the dubious proposition of voting every six years, and a periodic street battle with the police'.[41]

This point of view would be consistent with arguing that the two marxist parties are largely electoral and parliamentary in orientation, that power is concentrated in the hands of a leader-ship in which the parliamentarians carry great weight, and that unions have a subordinate though vital role in the party. That role, moreover, is seen by the party mostly in terms of what electoral advantages the unions can bring it.

It is in the electoral contests that union leaders attempt to mobilize support for party candidates by, for example, making campaign speeches for them (though they have to do so in their capacity as individuals, not as spokesmen for their unions—a legal necessity that deceives no one). Union leaders can also set up

[41] Petras, *Politics & Social Forces*, pp. 163–4. After the electoral victory of 1970, voting is perhaps not such a 'dubious' proposition after all.

organizations inside their establishments to work for the candidates of their party; Communists and Socialists collaborated in the Comités pro Allende that were set up in 1964, and again in 1970, to win over workers to his cause. These committees are in theory separate from the union organization, but in practice personnel at least overlap. Unions, then, provide some sort of organization which can be mobilized for the candidates at election time. An example of this in the 1964 campaign was the state petroleum workers who formed an electoral committee. Besides the usual electioneering activities, the committee produced a series of technical studies on the industry which they then discussed with Allende, announcing with maximum publicity that they had agreed upon a series of measures to further the interests of the industry and the nation.[42] The cp insists that these electoral committees should not be the same as the union leadership—they should not commit the union as such to support a particular candidate. On the other hand, as well as activities in propaganda, in registering electors who were not inscribed on the official lists, and so on, Figueroa, the chief Communist spokesman on union matters, also advised that they should head the union struggles for betterment (*combates reivindicativos*).[43] It is difficult to see how they could do this without either acting as the union leadership or largely replacing it. Unions are forbidden by law to engage in politics; the creation of the electoral committees is one way of getting round this obstacle, and of engaging in partisan in-fighting in a union without dividing its formal leadership. These electoral committees are very numerous and very active, especially during presidential campaigns.

Unions are also important to the parties in their general socialization role. This is a universal phenomenon; members of the working class who are also unionists are more likely to support candidates of working-class parties than members of that class who are not unionists. Particularly in a place like Lota, for instance, convention and social pressure to conform must work strongly in favour of the cp.[44] Unions are fairly important agents of communi-

---

[42] Astudillo, *Más lucha popular*, p. 28.

[43] *Principios*, Jan.–Feb. 1964, p. 92.

[44] Butler & Stokes found for Britain that in industries with compulsory unionism and geographical separation (especially mining) the worker's environment encourages high activism and strong Labour partisanship. They also found, however, that elsewhere Labour partisanship tended to *precede* union

cation in Chile, and while their message is sometimes rather confused, in essentials it is directed to making the members aware of their class and the political consequences that flow from it. This would be correspondingly easier in a single rather than a multi-party situation; but even pressure from several parties brings home the importance or the relevance of politics, if not a clear idea which particular party is the right one. This point will be dealt with more fully in chapter 9, but surveys of election results show that the vote for the marxist parties is highest where the unions are strongest—and even more markedly so where the unions are an important social as well as political reference group, traditionally in the mining areas.

The larger the number of union leaders who are attached to any party, then, the greater the party prestige. It makes claims to speak in the name of the working class more realistic. Defections of prominent unionists from one camp to the other are greeted with much publicity by the receiving party and usually exaggerated out of all proportion to their true relevance to the general shift in union opinion. Parties, especially the marxist ones, compete for the largest possible number of union leadership posts, and though both party leaderships criticize this effort to demonstrate numerical superiority, posts on the union *directiva* represent for unionists a true sign of the importance and power of a party. This is also true of the largest union confederation in Chile, the CUT. The rise or fall in voting for party lists at the CUT congresses receives considerable publicity. One reason why Christian Democrats and Radicals are anxious not to be permanently excluded from the CUT—even though they are from time to time driven to resignation—is that the electoral contest there serves as a kind of public trial of strength between the different parties, and that participation in the contest is an index of the claim any party makes to be speaking in the name of organized labour.

It does not seem at present that the parties rely on unions for any large measure of financial support. Certain regional and union differences no doubt exist, but broadly speaking the situa-

---

activism, especially where union membership was not compulsory. They found little evidence that the ethos of the workplace, and still less the persuasive efforts of the unions themselves, had much impact on the direction of the worker's party allegiance (D. Butler & D. Stokes, *Political Change in Britain* (London, 1969), p. 166).

tion of the early postwar period when the CP relied on union funds (given the critical financial shortage of the party in Chile and the preoccupation of the Soviet Union with other matters and other areas) no longer exists. Few unions with any financial resources are controlled completely by one party alone, so that grants to a party are always likely to be discovered by members of another party, who, it may be presumed, would have no hesitation in denouncing it to the members at large and to the Labour Inspectorate.

For the marxist parties the unions do have a useful political role to play when, as usually has been the case, these parties are in the opposition. The unions can embarrass the government and create obstacles to its economic policy, especially when that policy is based on a wage-freeze. Not only can the parties claim credit for helping to break the freeze, by the support they give to the unions, but it also helps them in their attempt to show how much the government sides with capital rather than labour. The constant harassment of the government on the economic front, combined with some political insult, is all useful grist to the mill of opposition policy.

The unions can serve the politicians of the marxist parties, too, in trying to divide from governments those of its supporters who are in the unions; this was especially true of the Christian Democratic administration, which had a large popular following. The Communists have been more successful at this than the Socialists, as they were continually trying to win over Christian Democrat unionists to oppose the government's economic policy. Hence the great emphasis that the Communists placed on bringing back to the Christian Democratic union movement into the CUT. Communists are also more ready to be persuasive with Radical unionists in order to ensure that the Radicals play the correct role assigned to them in the political alliance against the government and the right. This policy has been rather less successful because of the greater conservatism of the Radical unionists and more especially of the Radical party, at least when the Radicals were in government. When in opposition, it was easier to win over the Radicals —first in the Popular Front, and then in the Popular Unity Alliance of 1970.

When the marxist parties are in government, as in the Popular Front period and at the present time, then the party support they enjoyed in the unions can be mobilized to support the government. This can take a number of forms: threatening mass action if the right provokes a coup; holding down wage claims; stopping strikes; trying to increase productivity. But there are dangers here for the parties. Too stringent curbing of union demands may well lead to disaffection amongst unionists, as happened in the Popular Front era. And if short-term sacrifices do not result in long-term gains, then unions and unionists are likely to be even more hostile to attempts to control them in the interests of the politicians. Though formally united, the parties continued to struggle for hegemony in the unions during the Popular Front period. The struggle today is likely to be far less open and less visibly bitter, but no party will enjoy surrendering, or losing an opportunity to extend, influence in the unions.

The foreign-policy aims of the parties can also be served by the action of the unions. Both parties are anxious to detach Chile as much as possible from the influence of the United States. Beyond that their aims differ, as the Socialist party is wary of any step that would seem to attach them to the Soviet orbit, but they both welcomed the decision in 1958 of several important trade union federations to withdraw from the ICFTU, the heavily American-influenced international based in Amsterdam. The CP secretary-general attributed this to the party's work in the mass organizations.[45] The presence at the CUT congresses of fraternal delegations from a host of Communist countries makes it plain that, although the CUT is not affiliated directly to any International, its sympathies lie with the Communist WFTU. This was symbolized by the Soviet presentation to the CUT of a car, the first such vehicle ever possessed by its executive.

These advantages to the parties of influence in the unions would exist for any party, whether mildly reformist or ultra leftist. Both marxist parties, however—especially the Socialist one—have frequently criticized the unions for failing to further the revolution. There is no lack of theoretical statements of what a revolutionary union policy ought to be. Waiss writes of the tradition of strikes in the labour movement, and these, he argues, should at some appropriate moment, spread like a wave, accompanied by factory seizures and nation-wide solidarity strikes and demonstrations; this movement would then move from economic to political action and would be the Chilean version of the Sierra Maestra

[45] L. Corvalán, 'Strengthening the National Liberation Front', *World Marxist R.*, Apr. 1959, p. 40.

(where Castro organized his guerrilla movement).[46] Presumably this sort of action has to wait for the right level of revolutionary consciousness of the workers. Union leaders have been constantly reminded of their duty in this field. The Socialist party insisted that their union leaders must 'fight the reactionary tendency towards apoliticism. The union department must set to work immediately to elaborate a programme to put these ideas into practice.'[47] Congress after congress, the errors attributed to the unionists are mechanically repetitive: lack of doctrinal preparation, neglect of party work, tendency to apoliticism and *caudillismo*. The solutions are somewhat mechanical too: a new programme, a massive effort to elect delegates to the CUT congress, more obedience to party orders, perhaps a training school, better communications between party and union. These solutions tend to overlook the reality of the actual structure of the labour movement in Chile, and the kinds of action that that structure permits.

The very division of the left into two marxist parties is a standing contradiction to the appeals for unity of the working class, especially as it is a division marked by a long history of hostility, competition, and disagreement. The unionists incorporated into the Socialist and Communist parties are organized as two rival camps, identified very strongly with their political collectivity. It is somehow appropriate that one of the strongest critics of this disunity is a leader who did so much to bring it about. Ampuero blamed this division in the unions on the decline of the left: 'It has inculcated insuperable hatreds amongst its members, but above all has virtually suspended the scientific Marxist effort to examine, interpret and change the structure of the country.'[48] This statement may reflect more on the politicians than the unionists, for if unity of action is an objective of both parties, then it could be argued that, at least since the late 1950s, the basis of that unity was found in the labour movement. If parliamentarians and ideologists disagreed and, frequently, insulted each other's party, unionists co-operated. If unionists did

---

[46] 'Hacia adónde va Chile?', *Arauco*, Nov. 1960, p. 10. Rodríguez expressed similar sentiments when he wrote that 'each conflict ought to surpass the purely economic stage and should be extended and transformed into real insurgent movements directed at the transformation of the regime' (*Forjando la unidad popular*, p. 32).

[47] 'Tesis sobre política sindical . . .', *Arauco*, Dec. 1961, p. 7.

[48] *Izquierda en punto muerto*, p. 179.

not develop a level of revolutionary consciousness such that they overwhelmingly favoured a mass general strike and recourse to arms to overthrow the political system, they did develop a level of political consciousness strong enough to help keep the FRAP alliance together and to lay the basis for the Popular Unity electoral victory in 1970.

# 7. The Radicals and the White-Collar Workers

THE phenomenon of white-collar unionism is not an easy one to fit into a neat model of the relationship between social class and ideology. On the one hand the adoption by white-collar workers of union organization and methods could be seen as the entry of this group into the working class, completing the polarization of society into two rival camps, as white-collar workers throw off their petty bourgeois ideology and mentality. On the other hand it is possible to argue that the adoption by white-collar groups of unionization is simply a more determined attempt to maintain differentials compared with the blue-collar groups. If the use of similar tactics seems to put the two groups in the same camp from some points of view, nevertheless the important distinction, that of relative wage differentials and work situation, is better maintained. The mere fact of membership of a union alone cannot be taken as evidence of convergence of the perceived interests of the white- and blue-collar workers; a study of the 'affluent' worker in Britain found that a particular affluent group of working-class unionists was not undergoing a process of embourgeoisement, and neither were the white-collar unionists in their sample becoming proletarian. There were significant differences in the situation at work (hours, conditions, pensions, status differences), in their patterns of sociability, and in their aspirations and social perspectives.[1] As J. A. Banks writes, 'in strict Marxist terms, of course, clerks are not distinguishable from each other, or indeed from manual workers, when they are considered from the angle of their relationship vis-à-vis employers'. They have no control over the means of

[1] Goldthorpe & others, *The Affluent Worker*. Their study was of three factory groups in Luton—an area of high wages, recent immigration, and little traditional pattern of class behaviour such as might be found in a mining community.

production. 'Like manual workers they are obliged to sell their labour power in order to live'.[2] However, as Lockwood has pointed out, the clerk's market situation 'is not identical with that of the manual worker. He still enjoys a higher income than all except craftsmen.' He has greater security and less fear of possible unemployment, i.e. a relative immunity from the hazards of the labour market, better chances of rising to supervisory and managerial posts, and more favourable pension rights, holidays, and conditions of work.[3]

To assess the significance of white-collar unionism, it is necessary to look at the numbers in unions and the economic sectors in which they are organized, and also at the way their unions act and the objectives they pursue. In Chile's case one needs to look also at the party through which the white-collar workers have traditionally expressed their political aims, the Radical Party.

## The white-collar unions

There are many reasons why the *empleado* or white-collar workers should think of themselves as a separate group. They have a more privileged legal status and enjoy better salaries and social-security provisions; their situation in industrial establishments tends to make them identify more with the managers than the workers on the shop floor. Their level of unionization is much lower than the blue-collar workers, except in the public sector, which is a special case. Their unions are rather weaker than the blue-collar unions because they enjoy neither the advantages of compulsory unionization nor of profit-sharing.

Nevertheless there are militant white-collar unions in Chile, mostly, it is true, in the public sector, where the various school-teacher unions, the public health employees, and the postal workers have been very vigorous in pressing for wage claims. But the white-collar workers of the private sector also are organized in unions, and a number of federations are grouped in the CEPch, which organizes employees in commerce and the services sector.

Another feature which distinguishes white-collar from manual unions is that they lack the traditions and early political involvement of the manual-workers' movement in Chile. The *empleado*

[2] *Marxist Sociology in Action*, p. 161. Banks is writing of the British case, but his remarks can be applied to Chile.
[3] Cited ibid.

L

movement owes little to the radicalism of the Northern mining sectors or the anarchism of the port workers. It is true that the former leading figure of the white-collar unions, Francisco Hinojosa Robles, a Radical, has claimed to share in that tradition: 'I soon realized that for us white-collar workers [Recabarren] was more than a teacher, he was a disinterested friend. . . . He imbued me with clear ideas, especially on the best way to organize the white-collar workers. So it must be made clear that the organization of the CEPch is the offspring of the FOCH.'[4] This is really a sort of 'praise by association'. If Hinojosa was influenced by Recabarren, few other white-collar workers, apart from some in the railways, demonstrated any of the radicalism of the movement led by Recabarren; nor did Hinojosa abandon his membership of the Radical party, which at that time had little contact with or the desire to help the union movement.

Hinojosa himself emphasizes that it was very difficult to convince the white-collar workers of the need to organize, for 'they were fully convinced that they constituted a class very superior to the workers, to such a point that they would mock and despise the acts and street demonstrations of the workers'. He thus saw the mentality of the white-collar workers themselves as the main obstacle to organization.[5] The other chief reason (apart from employer and government resistance) is the fact that unlike the manual workers, the white-collar workers had no party to help them organize. Though Hinojosa was a Radical, as were many of his white-collar colleagues, the Radical party itself was relatively indifferent to the small group of white-collar unionists other than the schoolteachers. The party leadership showed real interest only after World War II, when white-collar unionists had become

[4] W. Mayorga, 'Luis Emilo Recabarren, el amigo', Ercilla, Nov. 1968, p. 42. Hinojosa at the age of 18 entered the Radical party on the side of Letelier in the great MacIver–Letelier debate on the so-called 'Social Question' and the way to deal with it, an early debate between laissez-faire and (moderate) intervention in the Radical party in 1906. His book, Libro de oro de los empleados particulares (1967), is indispensable for understanding the movement he was associated with throughout his life. It is also very revealing of the man—far from revolutionary, deeply concerned with the status and economic position of the white-collar workers, and anxious to exclude parties (other than the Radical) from the white-collar unions. A photograph shows him with his 'favourite instruments'—a telephone and a typewriter. Though he also claims inspiration from the Russian Revolution (p. 68).

[5] Libro de oro, p. 9.

more numerous and powerful. The politician who captured the imagination of this group, as he did of the working class in general, was Alessandri in his 1920 presidential campaign, but this was a personal appeal that transcended parties.

The example of the growth of the manual workers' unions, and the depressed economic circumstances of Chile after World War I seem to account for the first flickerings of interest in white-collar unionism. A precursor in the public sector were the teachers, who formed their first rudimentary union, the Primary Schoolteacher's Society in 1915. According to Hinojosa, the primary school-teacher was considered an object of social ridicule. 'In the "social" world he was looked on with contempt, and it was usual to say that anybody could teach reading and writing. They were at the very bottom of the queue when it came to fixing their salaries in the public administration.'[6] Perhaps this explains their militancy; they organized one of the first white-collar strikes in 1918 and were instrumental in leading other teachers' organizations into a united General Teachers' Association in 1922.

One of the reasons why the white-collar workers supported Alessandri so strongly in 1920 was that he had promised legislation that would deal with some of their grievances.[7] This promise was redeemed in 1924 when a special social-security organization was set up, and a legally-regulated contract of employment for white-collar workers was drawn up. The promulgation of this statute and the subsequent challenge to it by the military regime which succeeded Alessandri gave great impetus to the movement, culminating in the UECh, founded in 1925 and bringing together white-collar unions which had largely performed mutualist functions.[8] Though local groups of the UECh did co-operate with manual unions for specific ends, the UECh was not prepared to lose its separate identity, either by joining local unions or by entering the FOCH. Recabarren, in one UECh congress, proposed uniting the two sectors, but this was rejected, as the white-collar workers saw little benefit in such a merger.[9]

The UECh, echoing the general sentiments on the left at the time, endorsed a programme of nationalization, social reform and

---

[6] Ibid., p. 27.                                    [7] Ibid., p. 89.

[8] Barría, *Breve hist.*, p. 30. The statutes of the UECh are reproduced in Poblete, *Organización*, pp. 117–26. Echoing the FOCH, it declared that the emancipation of the *empleados* must be the work of the *empleados* themselves.

[9] Lafertte, pp. 165–6.

equal rights for women; and proclaimed the desirability of co-operating with the blue-collar unions. But its main activity was largely economic or *gremialista* (i.e. concerned with their own union affairs only), especially the fight for the eight-hour day and the minimum salary. Its composition was heterogeneous. It drew on employees from many commercial and banking establishments and some industries, journalists, printers, and some government employees, especially the teachers.[10] Although the Radical party gave verbal support to it when the legislative reforms were threatened by the Ibáñez government, the UECH never achieved the same working relationship with that party as did the FOCH with the CP. Indeed, the Radical party limited itself largely to pronouncements; it rarely acted to support the UECH, though one or two left-wing Radical parliamentarians did so. When Ibáñez was persecuting manual union leaders, the UECH was quite pre-pared to come to an agreement with him if he would respect the pro-white-collar legislation, and it issued in anticipation, several declarations proclaiming Ibáñez as the saviour of the nation.[11] Given the weakness of the movement, their lack of allies, and the fact that many white-collar employees worked for the government, it is not surprising that they should have felt very much at the mercy of the state; certainly in the intransigent FOCH and CP of that epoch they could have looked for little support.

The UECH suffered with the unions in general under Ibáñez when he attacked the leadership of the labour movement and tried, unsuccessfully, to replace existing organizations with a state-sponsored union federation. Nor was the white collar-worker movement free from the partisan struggles in the whole union movement which succeeded the formation of the Socialist party.[12] After the fall of the dictatorship the remnants of the unions in the UECH were regrouped in 1934. However, it seems that the core

[10] Poblete, in *Jornadas*, 29 (1945), pp. 68–9.

[11] Hinojosa, pp. 132 & 222–4.

[12] Even earlier the CP tried to split several of the white-collar organizations. Ricardo Fonseca, a Communist and a schoolteacher and a secretary-general of the party, formed a marxist Teachers' Federation in opposition to the Teachers' Association and even inside this breakaway union he formed a Union Opposition Group attached to the FOCH (Frente Democrático de Latino-america, *Hist. del Partido Comunista en Chile*, n.d.). This anonymous publication, allegedly by a 'former leading communist', was distributed by the Propaganda Dept of the Radical Youth probably during the early 1950s. Fonseca's group published a newsletter regularly in FOCH's journal in the late 1920s.

group of the old UECh, nearly all Radicals, in the new federation became alarmed at the way that it was being used in the politics of the Popular Front at the time, especially by the CP, and in 1939 they withdrew to form yet another confederation.[13]

Until then the central government employees had largely been organized in mutualist societies. Certain groups like the school-teachers had a militant record, partly because of anarchist influence and also because many schoolteachers were Radical party activists, sharing the anti-clericalism of the party. The employees of the central government joined together in 1943 to form the increasingly powerful ANEF.

In 1946–8 the labour movement split. Many manual unions deserted the CTCh and concentrated on internal activities. But this period witnessed the growth of white-collar militancy and unity, which reached its highest point from 1949 to 1951. There are several reasons for this. First, the banning of the Communists removed one potential source of division, for they now became anxious to support any union movement that attacked the government of González Videla and that encouraged the growth of white-collar militancy. Had they not been banned, the Communists might well have tried to capture white-collar militancy for their own ends. Secondly, the government's economic policies had encouraged the growth of the white-collar sector, especially in government service. Most important of all, postwar inflation hit the white-collar sector hard and the white-collar workers felt that their government had largely left them to their fate. While Radical rank and file support had been very strong for the first Popular Front President, Aguirre Cerda (and had been rewarded by several important legislative benefits for white-collar workers), and was still strong for the second one, Ríos (whose portrait adorns the office of the president of ANEF today),[14] the third President, González Videla, lost that support through his inability to contain inflation (in 1946 it reached 30%, in 1947 23%) and through his reliance on the right wing Liberal and Conservative parties in his campaign against communism.

[13] This in its turn in 1948 became the basis of the present-day CEPCh, the largest confederation of white-collar employees in the private sector. A further politically motivated breakaway in 1943 led to the formation of the third national confederation, the Confederación de Sindicatos de Empleados Particulares (Barría, *Breve hist.*, p. 37; Hinojosa, pp. 269–74).

[14] Or at least did in 1969. Ríos was President when ANEF was founded; and the president of ANEF in 1969, Tucapel Jiménez, was a prominent Radical.

The white-collar militancy in this period was not due to support from the Radical party. Rather, it was a non-party movement, arising partly out of the political desertion of the white-collar rank and file by the leadership of the Radical party, and by the failure of the Radical government to deal with the problems inflation was causing to the growing numbers of public-sector employees.

### 1. The CEPCh

In 1948 the major confederations in the private sector formed the CEPCh. In August 1949 a public protest at an increase in the fares on public transport in which, as usual, the students were active, led to the formation of a Comando Contra las Alzas (Command against Price Increases), which included CEPCh, the employees of the central and municipal government, and the autonomous agencies grouped in the JUNECH.

This newly found unity was demonstrated in the strike of February 1950. The immediate cause was the refusal of the government to pay the usual December bonus to state workers, the general cause was the government's attempt to pursue a strict wage-freeze policy. The normal ranks of the white-collar unions were swollen by the decision of the FIFCh to join in the strike, thus paralysing the railway network, at first partially and then completely. The bank workers' union also joined in a twenty-four-hour solidarity strike. The only group refusing to support the movement were the members loyal to the Partido Socialista de Chile and Bernardo Ibáñez's CTCh, which still had some support amongst the bus drivers' union.[15] The unity and determination of the movement, which held out for twelve days, was striking. It impressed the government, partly because it was obviously non-political and it did not seek political ends as had the blue-collar confederations in their rival Communist and Socialist sectors. González Videla was at first very hostile to the strike. The Radical party itself was not favourably inclined to the movement, even though the strikers sought support from it; only one Radical Senator gave them encouragement. However, the Radical attitude changed when the strikers received support from the Falange party, the PSP, and from the Partido Social Cristiano and the

---

[15] G. Vidal & G. Barría, *Doce días que estremecieron al país* (1950) is an important source for the 1950 strike. Also useful is E. Pizarro Novea, *Victoria al amanecer* (1950).

PAL (which became the party base of General Ibáñez's successful presidential campaign in 1952). González Videla, though now he had lost the backing of his party, continued to accuse the strikers of trying to undermine public order, led by well-known Communists (three leaders were even accused under the Law for the Defence of Democracy, but the judges found no evidence against them). The copper workers in Chuquicamata seized the opportunity to embarrass the government and declared their solidarity with the strikers. The Radical party began to move away from the political formula of a coalition with the right, and the President was forced to remove two right-wing members of his cabinet and to form a new government of Radicals, Social Christians, and Falangists.[16] A congressional majority now emerged for the demands of the CEPCh and JUNECh and they achieved most of their economic objectives, including the abandonment of the proposed wage-freeze, recognition of the economic claims of the public-sector unions, and the rapid solution of many *pliegos* that had been kept waiting indefinitely in ministerial offices. There was also an amnesty for many union leaders arrested for their part in this and previous strikes.[17]

However, in retrospect the movement must be seen as a temporary and rather spontaneous outburst of white-collar militancy. The two main agents, CEPCh and JUNECh, soon disagreed, as the public employees sought the repeal of the Law of the Defence of Democracy as part of their demands, while the private-sector unionists were not prepared to make an issue out of it, though they too opposed the law. Nor did the white-collar unions maintain any influence with the government after the cabinet reshuffle; it was almost as if the parties used the strike to solve some outstanding party problems, and when these had been solved continued to ignore the white-collar unions. The energies of the public employees were soon to be taken up with the move to form the new labour confederation which eventually resulted in the CUT. The private sector was less enthusiastic, and though it welcomed the move in public did not join the CUT, but later came to work with it. Some unions in the CEPCh left it to affiliate to the CUT, and some became members of both confederations. But the formation and growth of the CUT weakened the CEPCh and it never recovered the

[16] R. Abbott, 'The role of contemporary political parties in Chile', *Amer. Pol. Sci. R.*, June 1951, p. 460.
[17] Barría, *Trayectoria*, p. 26.

brief moment of power and unity of 1950. The CEPch itself, in a publication celebrating its ten years of existence, stated that one of the reasons why it was unable to secure many of its demands was the 'suicidal indifference' of its members who consistently refused to back up the leadership by supporting its calls for strikes, demonstrations, and increasing the membership.[18]

The membership of the present-day CEPch is difficult to estimate accurately, though it certainly falls short of the possible number of white-collar workers who could form unions. Its president claims something like 70,000,[19] which is approximately the total number of white-collar workers in their professional unions organized by establishment and independently (see table p. 51 above). Another source states that the membership in 1966 was generally estimated at about 20,000, which was a decline from the approximate 40,000 of the early 1960s.[20] Given the increase in union numbers since the mid-1960s, it is likely that the number is near the president's estimate. These members are grouped in ten large federations, though it seems that where no union exists, the CEPch accepts individual members.

Officially the CEPch is opposed to the distinction made in Chilean law between *obrero* and *empleado*. It does not, however, wish to surrender the advantages of white collar-status, but would prefer to see a uniform system of social-security benefits at a high level (which may well be a rather unrealistic demand on the Chilean economy). The CEPch has never felt particularly close to government employees simply because they share white-collar status. In fact they rarely work together because they operate in different economic sectors (though the public and private-sector employees did co-operate in the great strike of 1950). However, the CEPch does share common interests and employers with many manual unions, and it has generally preferred to try to work with them.

[18] Cited in Hinojosa, p. 308.

[19] Interview, president of CEPch, Santiago, Dec. 1968. Much of this section is based on the interview. The major federations in the CEPch are the employees in the Caja or social security bank of the *empleado particulares*, Federation of Copper Employees (which is also in the Confederación de Trabajadores de Cobre), the Federations of Commercial Employees, of Employees of Electrical Enterprises, of Retired Employees, of Employees of the Pharmaceutical Industry, of Employees of Saavedra Benard, of Employees of Insurance Companies, of Employees of Travel Agents, and of Hairdressers.

[20] US Dept of Labor, *Labor Law*, p. 33.

Relations at first between the CUT and the CEPch were not friendly. In 1960 one leading Communist blamed the white-collar unions for the defeat of the workers in their battle against the government's economic policy, castigating their 'apoliticism, economism, and legalism', which let them be manipulated by bourgeois parties. He quoted the party secretary-general, who warned the workers that the entry of white-collar groups into the CUT was good in that it exposed these workers to the proletarian tradition, but it was also dangerous in that it exposed the workers to the petty-bourgeois mentality of the white-collar unions.[21] However, the CEPch feels that its salary levels have been dropping behind those of skilled manual workers, and this accounts in part for the increasingly radical tone of its pronouncements in the late 1960s. In 1967 the CEPch and the CUT for the first time agreed upon a common platform of economic proposals and joint action against the government in pursuit of those proposals.[22] Recent years have seen even closer contacts between the two partly because the political parties powerful in the two confederations (Radical, Socialist, and Communist) drew together in opposition to the Christian Democratic government, and then worked successfully together in the Popular Unity campaign of 1970. But it is also clear that inflation and falling real incomes of white-collar unionists increased their militancy, gave them a stronger desire to co-operate with the CUT, and therefore exerted pressure on the Radical party to move to the left. In the 10th CEPch congress in December 1968, the confederation decided unanimously to join the CUT. This was not so momentous a decision as it might seem, for several of its constituent unions were individually affiliated to the CUT, though the proposal had several times failed at earlier congresses.[23] The 10th congress, as if to demonstrate its authentic radicalism, denounced the ORIT as an agent of imperialism and the ILO as an organization contrary to the interests of the working class. In the election to the executive the Radicals, Socialists, Communists, and PADENA (the Partido Democrático Nacional) presented a joint list against the Christian Democrats, who presented another, and the independents who presented a third. The combined list took about three-fifths of the votes, and was headed by Ernesto

---

[21] Astudillo, 'Luchas reivindicativas del primer semestre de 1960', *Principios*, Aug. 1960, p. 9.

[22] *Memoria del consejo directivo al CUT*, 1968, pp. 14–15.

[23] Press reports in *Ultima hora*, 2 Dec. 1968; *El Siglo* 29 Nov.–3 Dec.

Lennon, a Radical. The four parties making up the alliance have roughly equal representation on the CEPch executive. As a gesture of solidarity, the Communist president of the CUT, Luis Figueroa, was elected to the executive.

In spite of a shift to the left in pronouncements, the major aims of the CEPch are still firmly rooted in the differential status of the white-collar workers. In contrast to the CUT conference of 1968, where the slogan was 'Unity to make change', that of the CEPch was 'For the defence of social security and salary readjustments'. Their debates were almost exclusively about these issues, and given the maze of tangled provisions that makes up the white-collar social security system, this is hardly surprising. The CEPch is a very legalistic confederation, largely involved with issues of pensions and bonuses.[24] Its entry into the CUT is hardly likely to make it emerge as a new revolutionary element in itself, though it might help to influence white-collar unionists to support, and vote for, candidates like Allende rather than candidates of the centre or right.

## 2. The ANEF

One of the largest of the union confederations in the public sector is the ANEF, which brings together 50,000 members from all the central organs of government (which are defined as those run by a director-general and not by a board) in 38 different associations, ranging in size from 20,000 in the postal services to 26 in the Tourist Department.[25] Though it never joined the CTch, it was active in the 1950 strike and in the formation of the CUT. The first president of the CUT was the president of ANEF, Clotario Blest, and for many years until it had a building of its own, the CUT had its headquarters in ANEF's building. Although legally the ANEF should not perform union functions, in fact many of its various activities have been recognized in law. Its leaders, for example, enjoy the legal immunity of leaders of a recognized union, and its system of financing, by direct membership dues to ANEF, rather

---

[24] It now appears to be reasonably efficient in dealing with the issues. Certainly its organization has improved since 1955, when the copper workers asked CEPch to send them representatives from time to time—and to answer letters! (CTC, *Estatutos e informes del 2⁰ Congreso*, 1955, p. 23).

[25] Much of this section was based on interviews with leaders of ANEF in December 1968. ANEF also invited me to sit in on one of the meetings of their executive—an unusual opportunity to see a union 'from the inside'.

than an indirect one through a federation, has also been recognized in law. Nearly all central government employees are members of their union. An additional source of strength is that most public-sector unionists are classified as *empleados*, so that the weakening division between *obrero* and *empleado* does not apply to the public sector (other than the Ministry of Public Works, which employs a large number of manual labourers).

All members of ANEF's executive are also leaders of their base unions. At one time the two functions were separated, but it was felt that the union leadership was losing contact with the rank and file. Several ANEF leaders are also on the CUT executive—a fairly formidable load of assignments.

The ANEF executive elected at the 1967 congress consisted of 9 Radicals, 3 Socialists, 2 Communists, 3 Christian Democrats, and 2 independents. One member of the executive, Carlos Morales, who heads ANEF's disciplinary tribunal, is also a leading Radical parliamentarian. Since the late 1960s party differences have not been a source of internal strife in the executive, for there exists common agreement to try to find working solutions to problems that divide the parties, though this has led to trouble for executive members with their parties. The three Christian Democratic members of the ANEF executive were obviously in a rather exposed position inside their party when the public-sector union strenuously opposed the wages policy of the Frei government.

The ANEF usually acts as the leading public-sector union in joint meetings with the CUT, and the two have worked closely in opposition to government limitation on wage increases. Government unions like ANEF are always more ready than the private-sector unions in CEPch to take to the streets and demonstrate against the government, even though many of the interests of the two white-collar confederations—salaries and social-security benefits—seem perhaps to have more in common with each other than either does with the general industrial unions in the CUT. ANEF and other government unions are much stronger than the unions in CEPch, both in terms of membership and funds. The government, in order to try to set an example to the private sector, does try to establish and apply fairly strict norms of annual salary readjustments in the public sector, though with far from complete success. The ANEF was formed at a time when the government was trying to squeeze salaries of public employees. It permanently opposes such wage policies. Part of its continuing militancy was

also due to the influence of its first and long-serving president, the
Catholic radical Blest, who, while avoiding identification with
any of the political parties, was in many ways more revolutionary
than the Communist union leaders. (Later, predictably, the
Communists branded him as a Trotskyist, even though he wrote
and still writes articles praising the unions and the living standards
of working class in the Soviet Union in terms which would be
rank heresy for any Trotskyist.)

### The Radical party

If it is true that political groups other than the Radicals are strong
amongst sectors of the white-collar workers—the Socialists in
the Bank Employees' Federation, the Communists in CEPch,
the Christian Democrats among the Public Works Ministry
employees—it is nevertheless the case that nearly all Radical
unionists are found in the white-collar occupations, especially in
those of the public and tertiary sector.

The Chilean Radical party has long been considered a typical
'centre' party in politics. But the 'centre' is not a stable position
and the Radical party has been far from consistent in its long
political development.[26] Nor has it ever been a party with comparable organization and discipline to that of the CP or the
Christian Democrats. Opposing groups have fought for its control,
and it has witnessed quite as many splits and divisions as have the
Socialists. Its rhetoric tends to lie on the left but its action in
government inclines to the right. The revolutionary rhetoric dates
from the 1931 Convention, when the party adopted a socialist
platform, declaring that the existing capitalist system was in
crisis and must be replaced by a regime in which the means of
production were owned by the community and based on social
solidarity instead of individualism. The convention also declared
that the Radical party recognized the class struggle and sided with
the workers. Liberty without economic liberty was held to be
meaningless; the wage-earning classes were deprived of economic

---

[26] For such an important participant in the Chilean political process there
is relatively little on the Radical party apart from rather anecdotal accounts
by party members themselves. Two of the most useful of these are L. Palma,
*Historia del partido radical* (1967) and Florencio Durán, *Partido radical* (1958).
There is more on the Popular Front; see especially Andrés Bande, *The Chilean
Radical Party and the Popular Front* (B. Litt. thesis, Oxford, 1969).

liberty in the present system, and as union activity was a way of fighting for economic liberty, the party would fight with and in the unions. It also added that the party opposed all type of dictatorship whether military, capitalist, or proletarian.[27]

The 1931 convention appears to have been a rather unusual one in that the youth section dominated the formal proceedings while the leadership was more occupied in planning future political tactics.[28] In any case party conference declarations seldom reflect party policy, as was the case this time, for the party was soon to enter the government of Alessandri, now considerably more conservative than he had been when elected to his first term of office in 1920. Even the policy pursued by the Radical party in the Popular Front government, while it might be described, at least initially, as developmental, can hardly be described as socialist.

The party has always been a rather loose coalition of different social groups. Prominent in the early days were some of the Northern mine owners and landowners. The party was created here in the mid-nineteenth century and has always retained a provincial strength in Coquimbo and Atacama, even though mines are now mostly run by the state rather than by small entrepreneurs. It was not only a movement of the incipient bourgeoisie, for it gained, and retained, some popular support in these provinces and in the farming areas of the South. It has much support amongst the petty-bourgeoisie of the small towns, and among white-collar and professional workers, especially those employed by the government; teachers strongly supported it because the Radicals were the champions of popular lay education. A typical and not inaccurate description of the party is that 'it brings together, essentially professional and bureaucratic middle sectors, ideologically represented by Free Masonry, and with strong links with the public sector. . . . [It] does not exclude sectors of the agrarian oligarchy and entrepreneurial groups linked with the economic activities developed in the 1940s.'[29] The close resemblance to the French Radical party is striking.

Votes for the party in the Congressional elections of 1969 showed that its support was scattered fairly evenly throughout the various provinces. There was no positive correlation with any particular

[27] G. Urzúa Valenzuela, *Partido radical* (1961), p. 20.
[28] Bande.
[29] E. Faletto & E. Ruiz, 'Conflicto político y estructura social', in *Chile, Hoy* (Centro de Estudios Socio-Económicos, Univ. Chile, 1970), p. 214.

form of economic activity, but there was a negative correlation between voting for the party and the large urban concentrations. This is the reverse of the situation for the Christian Democrats, for whom Santiago is the area of maximum support, whereas for the Radicals it is one of the lowest.[30]

The party is so composed that it can incline either to the right or to the left without violating its basic principles—by common party agreement these principles are those of a lay, social democratic, progressive movement, and are all vague enough to permit considerable tactical flexibility. A marxist critic points out that in times of crisis it has been the sectors most compromised with the status quo that have controlled the party.[31] This was clearly the case in the Popular Front era and even more so during the last years of Radical domination when the right of the party was easily able to impose itself.

Yet there has always been an identifiable left in the party which sometimes is strong enough to persuade it to adopt its point of view, as in the acceptance of the coalition with the marxist parties in the Popular Unity Alliance of 1970. Though this left wing usually has the support of the Radical unionists, its leadership comes from parliament or the party bureaucracy, and not from the party 'mass' organizations such as the unions. One of the defining characteristics of this left element is that it sees the fortunes of the middle class, which it claims are bound up with the party, linked to those of the working class. Thus Senator Alberto Baltra, a leading exponent of this wing, wrote in a lecture on the Popular Front President Aguirre Cerda: 'In 1938 the middle class was not between capital and labour; it was not an intermediate group but, just like the working class, lived from the sale of its labour. It occupied exactly the same class position as the manual workers.'[32] Yet the leaders of this party were to end their period of office in coalition with the Conservatives and Liberals,

[30] The absolute vote is high, for Santiago concentrates about a third of the total electorate, but in percentages of total votes cast, the Radicals do disproportionately well in small towns (ibid., pp. 219–20). A survey investigating party identification by social group found that the Radicals had most support amongst the group classified as non-managerial white collar (G. Briones, 'Estructura social y la participación política', *R. Interamerica de Ciencias Sociales*, 1963, p. 394. See also R. Cruz-Coke, *Geografía electoral* (1952)).

[31] 'Lautaro', 'Critica de una tésis tradicional', *Punto final*, Feb. 1968, pp. 3–7.

[32] A. Baltra, *Pedro Aguirre Cerda* (1960), p. 66.

having outlawed and persecuted the CP, having refused to contemplate the need for agrarian reform, and opposed in the white-collar strikes of 1950 by precisely the social group that they made so much fuss about representing. The contractions in the party may even be embodied in a single leader. The Radical President who moved so much to the right, González Videla, had been one of the most outspoken proponents of the Popular Front and leader of the left sector.[33]

The move of the party into the Popular Unity alliance in 1970, though obviously a victory for the left, does not necessarily signify the final defeat of the more conservative elements. The party divided over the attitude to adopt to the invasion of Czechoslovakia in 1968. A Senator and a deputy (brother and sister in fact) both resigned from their future senatorial candidatures because they felt that the party leadership was so eager to revive the Popular Front that it was unwilling to criticize or condemn the invasion, thereby violating fundamental party principles. A handful of party congressmen later joined them to form the breakaway Radical party which supported Alessandri in the 1970 campaign.[34] In the party which outlawed the CP in 1948 there is still a strong element of anti-communism.

This anti-communism has brought upon the Radicals the hostility of the Socialists rather than the Communists. The Socialists frequently denounced the Radicals as the instrument of the bourgeoisie and argued, not without justification, that they were totally unreliable as political allies. Though the Radicals pledged their support for the Socialist candidate in the 1967 by-election in the provinces of O'Higgins and Colchagua, this offer was indignantly repudiated by the Socialists, with the temporary excep-

[33] In 1944 he had declared that if the Radical party had anything to be proud of, it was precisely that its highest leaders after having occupied the leading positions in the affairs of state had died poor. (González Videla, *Informe a la convención: política internacional y económica*, XV Convención del Partido Radical, 1944, p. 141.)

[34] Reported in *El Mercurio*, 24 Aug. 1968. A group of 50 Radical women staged a sit-in at the party headquarters in support of the resigning parliamentarians. They successfully repelled a group of the Radical youth bent on dislodging them (ibid., 4 Sept. 1968). The resigning Senator Humberto Enríquez said, 'I am a Socialist and a man of the left, but language such as the Radical party has employed before the crushing of a people by a new form of imperialism and colonialism—I cannot tolerate it'. The Asamblea Pedro Aguirre Cerda, of Santiago, supported Enríquez and called for the breaking of relations with the Chilean CP.

tion of Allende, who had always been more ready than the majority of his party to work with the Radicals. The Socialists accuse the Radical leaders of having identified themselves with (when they have not come from) the oligarchy; of having used office to enrich themselves and to identify socially with the aristocracy in the Conservative and Liberal parties; of betraying their election pledges in office; and of having betrayed their rank and file support, the white-collar workers. These are not merely polemical accusations.[35]

Yet if these accusations were the whole truth, it would be difficult to explain the persistence of the Radical party in the Chilean scene. While the party, in contrast with its over 20% poll in the peak days of the Popular Front, rose at the most to 13% in recent years, it still maintains a great deal of popular support among white-collar employees. Habit and tradition to some extent explain this, and if the activity of white-collar unions is aimed at maintaining differentials over manual workers, support for the Radical party may be a way of maintaining a political differential. The party is in theory, and largely in practice, a social-democratic party, a member of the Socialist International. For the relatively sophisticated white-collar worker attracted neither by the dogmatism of the CP nor by the verbal revolutionary postures of the Socialist party, and who was either politicized before the PDC became important or who is suspicious of their allegedly clerical and confessional characteristics (hotly denied as they are) in theory at least, the Radical party, with its long commitment to democratic reform, is a perfectly understandable choice.

[35] The Socialists were very critical of the party during the strike of the health service employees in 1963. As Burnett (pp. 234–45) writes: 'Of all parties the Radicals found themselves in the most enigmatic position. From one standpoint they should have supported the health workers fully, since government workers in large measure adhered to the Radical party. On the other side, the Radicals still formed part of Alessandri's coalition and thus were obliged to stick with the chief executive.' Faced with a situation where the FRAP parties and the PDC strongly backed the health workers, the Radical congressmen abandoned their cabinet colleagues to support the proposals of the left. The Radical ministers strongly condemned the desertion of the congressmen; but the National Executive Committee in its turn denounced the ministers for attacking the congressmen, and took the party out of the Alessandri coalition.

## The Radical unionists

On 24 January 1960 the Radical party held a public meeting to pay tribute to its union leaders. Forty-nine of them were singled out for specific mention, and of these no fewer than thirty-two worked for the central or local government; the rest were largely from the white-collar private sector.[36] The political base of the party in the unions lies overwhelmingly in the government bureaucracy.

It is hardly surprising, then, that representatives of these white-collar unions dominate the party's union department, which is not known as the *departamento sindical* but as the *departamento gremial*, an expression which can include associations of a professional sort not normally regarded as trade unions.[37]

The party statutes refer to the unions at various points.[38] The important base unit in the party is the assembly, a larger, more public body than the CP cell. But these assemblies can set up smaller nuclei, organized on a union or industrial basis or on a neighbourhood basis. Between National Conventions[39] the ruling body in the party is the Comité Ejecutivo Nacional (CEN). The union department has one ex-officio representative on this body. Of the seven-man Political Commission in 1969 three white-collar unionists were members.

The first national congress of Radical unionists was held in 1949 and this created the national union department.[40] The party and its unionists were obviously weary of the political infighting characterizing relations between the Socialists and Com-

---

[36] Reports in *El Siglo*, 23 Jan. & *Ultima hora*, 17 Jan. 1969. Radicals preside over the executives of the Primary and Secondary School Teachers' Unions, over the post office workers, the railway white-collar union, the Health Workers' Union, the union of workers in the Contraloría General, the union of labour inspectors, the Confederation of Municipal Workers, and several other unions of public servants.

[37] Rather like the difference between 'guild' and 'union' in English. Though the president of the union department felt that 'gremial' was rather old-fashioned, reflecting the right-wing mood in the party when it was created, and he hoped to get the party to change the name to *sindical* (interview, Santiago, Dec. 1968).

[38] *Estatutos del Partido Radical* (1967), on pp. 8–9, 14, 20, 22–3, & 29.

[39] At meetings of the National Convention, which is, according to the statutes the supreme authority in the party, those Radical unionists who head national federations or unions have the right to attend.

[40] 1º *congreso sindical nacional radical, 28 Apr.–1 May* (1949).

M

munists in the unions, and wished to create a rival national organization under its control. Earlier talks with the Socialist party to this end had broken down. In 1951 the party, impressed by white-collar militancy during the 1950 strikes, raised the status of the union group from a department to a national organization giving the Radical unionists more influence in the party.

The union department is described in the statutes as a dependent organ of the CEN. All members of the twenty-five man executive are full-time unionists, mostly from the white-collar public sector; for example in 1968 the president was an income-tax inspector. These leaders are fully occupied with their jobs and can spend relatively little time on the departments' affairs. The department president lamented the absence of a technical commission, because there were no funds for such assistance. This tends to give a good deal of influence to the department's assessor, who is appointed by the CEN and is usually a labour lawyer.

The Radical union department is not important in deciding party tactics and strategy. Perhaps more than any other Chilean party the Radical party is essentially a parliamentary one; decisions are made by the parliamentarians, and divisions occur inside the parliamentary bloc rather than between the parliamentarians and any other group. The parliamentarians are the only full-time party functionaries; the party has less of an organized bureaucracy than the Socialist party, and in some ways resembles a federation of provincial clubs rather than a modern political party. It is only in recent years that the department has been run by unionists alone instead of under the guidance of a politician. In theory the department is supposed to organize Radical groups in factories and regionally but, given its scarce resources and manpower, it does very little and there are few Radical organizations in unions outside the white-collar sectors. Even these white-collar unions are largely autonomous in their activities; they certainly do not take orders from the party's union department. The only time when the department does have some authority, though largely of a coordinating sort, is at the CUT congresses, when it issues instructions on how to vote and influences the composition of the Radical list for election to the executive. In this sense, however, it is difficult to distinguish the department from merely a small circle of prominent Radical union leaders. The department does sometimes indicate preferences between possible candidates for election to the executive of a particular union, but not systematically, nor are they invariably followed.[41] Even in compiling the list of Radical candidates to the CUT executive the union department tends to make a rough allocation to various union groups and allows them to make their own nominations. It is unable to pay delegates' expenses to the CUT congresses and therefore cannot mobilize its true support. The department realizes too that Radical white-collar workers are less inclined than a dedicated Communist to accept instructions.

Inside the party the union department adopts a left-wing stance, especially as it has become more independent from control by politicians. It opposed the alliance in 1964 with parties of the right to support the presidential candidature of Julio Durán. In the division over the invasion of Czechoslovakia it firmly supported the CEN and accused Senator Enríquez of using this to try to divide the Radical party from its left-wing allies.[42] It supported the CEN in its attack on the right-wing Minister of the Interior, Pérez Zújovic, during the Frei administration, accusing him of being responsible for several outbreaks of violence that the government had been blaming on the left.[43] In the union conference held in August 1968, the department sponsored a motion favouring re-entry into the CUT.[44] The 1968 conference strongly denounced the UTRACh a right-wing union confederation formed with some support from the right wing of the PDC, and with the backing of the American Institute for Free Labour Development. The conference, which spent most of its time discussing salaries and social-security provisions, called for the abolition of the distinction between *obrero* and *empleado*, for full consultation with public-sector unions in the fixing of salary increases, for a general extension of industrial democracy and a revision of the labour code to remove the obstacles to union action and unity.[45]

When the party is moving politically to the left, the union department is active in supporting the move. When, however, the party is moving to the right, the department is obviously torn between the demands of party loyalty and its perception of the

[41] Interview with the president of the provincial organization of CEPCh in Concepción (May 1967).

[42] *El Siglo*, 27 Aug. 1968.

[43] *Ultima hora*, 16 Aug. 1968.

[44] The Radicals had left the CUT in 1965 in disagreement over the policy that the CUT was then pursuing, and because they felt they were being denied adequate representation at the conference and on the executive.

[45] Organización Nacional Gremial, *Acuerdos de la conferencia sindical realizada el 30 y 31 de agosto de 1968* (typescript).

interests of the labour movement, Radical unionists do not seem to have protested to any marked extent when the party lauched its policy of repressing Communists.[46] This ambivalence has been frequently attacked by the Socialists, who alleged in 1961 that the Radical union department advocated the division of the CUT and desired to take Chilean unions into alliance with the ICFTU and the ORIT.[47]

Radical unionists are not particularly ideological. When the party is pursuing policies distasteful to them, the unionists seem to retreat into union concerns and avoid the major issues. The white-collar unions have never had a sustained tradition of militant political action, or placed a great deal of emphasis on the virtues of solidarity. Even if they did, they have not enough power inside the party to give them much influence over policy decisions; they prefer left-wing policies, but they are not so committed to trade-union solidarity with the Socialist and Communist parties that they desert the Radical party in large numbers when they disagree with party policy.

In one aspect, however, they almost equalled the Socialist party in intransigence, and that was in hostility to the PDC government—a hostility that spilled over into resentment against that party's union leaders. For the Radicals felt their position as the natural centre of Chilean politics was being undermined by the Christian Democrats—hence they were intransigent not because the two parties were poles apart in the Chilean political spectrum, but because they were so close, resembling the hostility in France between the MRP and the French Radicals. They refused, for example, to participate in the arrangements for the CUT congress in 1968 if the Christian Democrats were allowed to participate. They hotly opposed the Frei government's wage policies on the ground that they fell particularly hard on the white-collar sector, especially in public service. In so far as there was a struggle for party hegemony in the public sector it was probably between Radicals and Christian Democrats. The Radicals resented the sudden intrusion of the Christian Democrats into an area that they had long regarded as their special preserve.

Predicting the final demise of the Radical party is a long-stand-

---

[46] It is true that JUNECh asked for the repeal of the law, but the CEPch never took any particularly strong stand against it, though expressing opposition.

[47] S. Corbalán, 'Las bases técnicas de la revolución chilena en la política de frente de trabajadores', *Arauco*, Nov. 1961, p. 8.

ing habit in Chilean politics. Among union leaders one often encounters the opinion that the Radicals only have influence over an older generation of union leaders, in ever diminishing sectors of the government service, and that they are progressively declining. But if this is so the party, and the support it receives in unions, continues to demonstrate a stubborn capacity for political survival. The pace of social change under the Allende government may hasten the process of decline—but the life of a party is not determined by social factors alone. If the Radicals continue to play a pivotal part in the Popular Unity coalition—bringing in middle-class sectors that would otherwise remain outside—then it may continue to confound predictions.

# 8. The Christian Democrats and the Challenge to Marxism

## The origins of the party

THE PDC grew out of the Falange, which failed in its intention to arouse the social conscience of the parent Conservative party and so was forced to split off.[1] The Falange was a movement of Christian inspiration, headed by a group of young Catholic intellectuals, many of them law students in the Catholic university, under the spiritual guidance of a small number of radical Catholic priests.[2] It deplored the laissez-faire attitude that dominated the practice, if not the theory, of the Conservative party, and was equally hostile to Marxism, rejecting the idea of the class struggle in favour of the communitarian or corporate society, a concept that could appear utopian or authoritarian, depending on the particular interpretation of this rather vague philosophy given by individual spokesmen.

[1] The divisions in Christian Democracy are reflected in its literature. Boizard, *Democracia cristiana en Chile* (1963) deals with the early years in an anecdotal but useful fashion; there are several volumes of speeches and writings by Frei, e.g. *Pensamiento y acción* (1958), *Verdad tiene su hora* (1955); A. Silva Bascuñán, *Una experiencia social cristiana* (1949) deals with the early years. The ideas of the radical wing (now separated into another party) are outlined in J. S. Solar & J. Chonchol, *Desarrollo de la nueva sociedad en América Latina* (1965). The ideas of the 'orthdox' wing are contained in the numerous volumes of Jaime Castillo, among them *Fuentes de la democracia cristiana* (1963) and the influential monthly he edits, *Política y espíritu*.

[2] While acknowledging the inspiration that the early movement received from priests like Manuel Larraín and another Jesuit, F. Vines Solar (who incurred the hostility of the clerical hierarchy for organizing trade unions), the party leadership plays down their organizational role. The party was sharply rebuked by Father O. Larson in his *ANEC y la democracia cristiana* (1967). Larson wrote his book in anger at an interview in which Frei gave the impression that ANEC was taken over by a group of already politicized young Catholic radicals, thus reducing the role of Larson and ANEC to insignificance.

The effect of the devastation of World War I in what for many Chileans was the 'cradle of civilization', the severe impact of the economic depression and the indifference of the ruling groups in Chile to the suffering it brought, the dictatorship of Ibáñez, the impact of the revived interest of at least part of the church in 'social Catholicism', the tensions in Spain that were soon to break out in civil war,—all these factors were felt by the young Falangists to demand a reappraisal of the political, social, and economic system and its reorganization in the light of a new set of ideas.

The ideas were not so new in themselves, though they were original in the Chilean setting. Many were derived from Jacques Maritain, with his emphasis on humanism, pluralism, and democracy.[3] Frei, who attended Maritain's lectures in Paris, felt that his philosophy closely linked democratic ideas with the evangelical message. Enthusiasm was also expressed for the corporate state, but this was not so much the corporatism of fascism (even if some leaders used the notion in a very similar way to the Spanish Falange leader José Antonio Primo de Rivera) as the organic community of Christian society, better expressed perhaps in the later use of the word 'communitarianism'. It is certainly true that the early Falange considered itself an elite, possessed of the ideals and abilities necessary to transform Chilean society; indeed, without a very strong commitment to that belief, it is difficult to see how the party could have survived the long period of semi-obscurity. While it is also true that the faith in the movement led some leaders to adopt intransigent attitudes, intransigence was a fairly common political attitude in Chile in the late 1930s and early 1940s; nor are all beliefs in a hierarchically organized society are necessarily fascist.[4]

The movement expressed its belief in the need for social reform in a way that criticized the Conservatives and also demonstrated the hostility of the Falange to communism and socialism, between

---

[3] For a discussion of these ideas see E. J. de Kadt, *Catholic Radicals in Brazil* (London, 1970), pp. 51–8.

[4] Frei's first book, published in 1937, showed a 'preoccupation with the dignity of the common man that is the exact opposite of the fascists' disdain for the weak and glorification of brute strength' (Halperin, p. 187). See P. E. Sigmund, 'Christian Democracy: Chile', *J. Internat. Affairs*, 20/2 (1966), pp. 332–42 for a discussion of Maritain's influence. On the other side F. Gil points to the early influence of Rexism, the Belgian Catholic movement tainted with Nazism, though its influence did not last long (*Political System of Chile* (1966), p. 267).

which it seemed to make little theoretical distinction. The roots of the party's social doctrines lie in the Papal Encyclicals, which for all their concern with social justice nevertheless constitute a strong attack on the materialism of atheistic socialism.[5] In a Declaration of Principles, the Latin American Christian Democratic parties even blamed the old order for creating marxism, condemning 'the exaggerated and irreligious liberalism which has directly engendered individualism, jacobinism, individualistic capitalism and anarchy, and in reaction has spawned Marxist collectivism'.[6] This anti-marxism helps to explain why a movement apparently so radical as the early Falange could join forces, even temporarily, with the Conservative party. The point is that the Falangists rejected not conservatism but laissez-faire liberalism. There was in the 1930s little to distinguish the Conservative party from the Liberal party, but there had always been among the Conservatives a minor wing of reformist Catholics, and the Falangists agreed with the Conservative emphasis on the family, religion, social responsibility, and the obligations of authority. Where they differed was over the application of these principles in politics. The Falangists wished to put them at the forefront of action [7]— according to Frei, 'it is absurd to present a political programme without the underpinning of a conception of man, society and the state' [8]—but if the then Conservative party was acting in accord with some principles, they were certainly not those of the Falange. The Falange agreed with the early Catholic reformists' stress on the importance of union organization as a defence against the liberal system, though not as a means towards socialism, for the Catholic unions were also intended to protect workers from the appeal of marxism. The FOCH itself developed out of an earlier mutualist society founded by a Catholic and Conservative lawyer. The 'social' Catholics were an important element in drawing up

[5] Castillo, cited in E. J. Williams, *Latin American Christian Democratic Parties* (Tennessee, 1967), p. 27.

[6] Ibid., p. 44.

[7] Writing of European Christian Democracy M. Fogarty remarks that 'one cannot circulate among the Christian Democrat movements . . . without being impressed with this sense of apostolate; and not only among younger people or leaders of youth or educational movements' (*Christian Democracy in Western Europe 1820–1953* (London, 1957), p. 31).

[8] Williams, p. 52. Though it might well be argued that the Christian Democrats' general philosophical statements are so general as to allow for almost any kind of political programme.

the first proposals for a labour code, admittedly of a rather authoritarian nature.[9] However, outside the official Conservative party, with its small group which had an ethical view of industrial relations, there were other, and more radical, manifestations of Catholicism in this field. In 1920 a group of Catholics, including Blest, founded the Casas del Pueblo in an attempt to practise Christian poverty and redeem the working class by example. This movement was stopped by the ecclesiastical authorities when the group wished to call one of their branches 'Christ the Worker', but they resumed activities in 1922 with the formation of a short lived Partido Popular, influenced by the ideas of the Italian, Luigi Sturzo and his party. Even if short-lived, these movements recurred. In 1928 the Catholic radicals formed a party called 'Germen'[10] and in 1932 a Partido Corporativo Popular, in which several leaders of the later Falange were active.

Thus the Falange drew on an already existing, if minor, tradition of activity of Catholics, both priests and laymen, concerned with the condition of the mass of the population, although it did not arouse much response among the working class, because it was directed by a paternalist elite. Elements of imposition from above in the interests of the working class, without much consultation, have persisted in the present-day PDC, notably in its unsuccessful attempt to reform the labour code in 1965.

The formation of the Falange was preceded by a long debate over the most appropriate name. On the one hand it was thought inconvenient to use the word 'Christian', as the party wished to remain non-confessional, even though it made no secret of drawing its inspiration from Christianity. On the other hand, it was also felt important that the party should make clear where it stood in the political combat between the two world philosophies of communism and Christianity; hence it decided on the name Falange

[9] Morris (pp. 122–3), writes of J. E. Concha, the leading figure in making these proposals, that he and other Chileans 'analysed labor-employer relations . . . from the broad vista of morality and with a kind of cataclysmic philosophy of the downfall of modern industrial man, support for which they found in contemporary Chilean literature and in papal doctrine'. For them it was not essentially an economic or legal matter, but, as Concha explained, it was 'fundamentally a psychological, moral and religious question, whose solution will be found, the world willing, only in the teaching of Christ, practiced by the individual and respected and supported by the state in its laws'.

[10] Which means 'seed' or 'genesis'. The emblem of the party was a cross, a hammer and a sickle (Boizard, p. 201).

Nacional in the spirit of international solidarity. Though it formed a party of the Youth Section of the Conservative party in 1935, it was always a rather independent and autonomous entity inside it, setting up a para-military wing, following the example of the Socialist and Communist parties and of the extreme right.[11] However, the connection with the Conservative party was soon to be severed. When the Falange opposed the nomination of Gustavo Ross—Alessandri's unpopular Finance Minister and champion of the right—as presidential candidate for the 1938 election, the Conservatives ordered a purge and reorganization of their Youth and the Falange, which led to the Falange breakaway in 1938.

The party maintained a fairly independent stance in politics. It supported some measures of the Popular Front government; it voted for the Radical presidential candidate Juan Antonio Ríos in 1942 in opposition to the candidature of Ibáñez; it occupied, briefly, a few ministerial posts, withdrawing when it disagreed with policies such as the labour policy that led to the massacre of Plaza Bulnes in 1946, which caused Frei to resign from his post as Minister of Public Works. It opposed the suppression of the CP in 1948 (and as early as 1954, United States involvement in Vietnam). In short, the party moved to the left, shedding its early ambiguous connections with Fascism of the Spanish variety. It preserved a reputation for integrity and deep attachment to its ideals—unusual qualities in Chilean politics at that time. It did not make a notable impact in the labour world, though it elected one member to the executive of the CTCh.[12]

The party remained small though not unimportant until 1957, after it had been joined by members of the Social Christian Party of Eduardo Cruz Coke—another Conservative splinter group— and had renamed itself the PDC. Not until this fusion did it begin to get considerable electoral support, gaining 9·4% in the congressional elections, when it attracted the votes (many of them from the recently enfranchised women) of disillusioned supporters of Ibáñez.

[11] This militarized section, not particularly important, is a little disingenuously explained away on the ground that it was not an imitation of fascist methods but the opposite—the creation of a strong force to fight fascism (ibid., pp. 189–90).

[12] Yet as if to indicate that the Falange was not very concerned with union matters, Bernardo Leighton reporting to the Fourth Congress of the Falange in 1946, lamented that the work of Lorca (the Falangist on the CTCh) was almost unnoticed, even in the Falange itself (ibid., p. 272).

The party also gained a considerable influx of members with the collapse of the populist coalition that had supported Ibáñez in his victorious 1952 electoral campaign, notably in the PAL. Members of this party, with the end of Ibáñez' mild attempts at populist reform, moved to the party that they had least to object to—the Christian Democrats. Members of the PAL were far from being marxist, felt that the Radical party, ousted from power in 1952 was discredited, wanted to advocate more changes than seemed acceptable to the Conservative and Liberal parties—and were anxious to get back to power.

## Party doctrine and party divisions

The PDC is part of an international movement which, if less demanding than the international Communist movement, nevertheless helped to shape the doctrine, organization and aims of Chilean Christian Democracy (and to provide it with funds at times of crucial elections, notably that of 1964).[13] The Chilean party reflects the general ideas, and contradictions, of the international movement. Possibly even more than the Communists, the Christian Democrats are fond of debating or parading their fundamental ideas. The importance of the family is extolled, basic human rights are defended, the evils of unrestrained capitalism and totalitarian communism are attacked.[14] Against these systems the alternative proposed is that of the communitarian society, though the tension between this form of social pluralism on the one hand and the need to control a powerful and bureautic state in the interests of economic development on the other provoked debate inside the party, especially after 1964.

One basic element in the pluralist doctrine of Christian Democracy is the idea that individuals or groups have a legitimate sphere of their own, which should be free from interference by those on the same level or on a higher level. In keeping with this a union is seen as a natural entity that should be free from political interference, state domination, or employer control. The justification is not economic. As Fogarty writes, 'in the field of work, as

[13] Though this is not admitted by the leaders of the party it is generally regarded as one of the most public secrets in Chilean politics—especially in view of the enormous amount of costly propaganda used in that campaign.

[14] See, e.g., PDC, *Declaración de principios y el ABC de la democracia cristiana* (1963).

everywhere, they [Christian Democrats] are chiefly interested in human personality, and so in building up the co-operative, self-governing industrial communities, which seem to them most likely to favour its development'.[15] If capital has functions and responsibilities, so does labour, and the logic of this joint responsibility is joint control of industry. Here arise practical problems, for a union may not be controlled by Christian Democrats, but by communists or socialists who (according to the views of the ortho-dox theorists), by importing false notions of class conflict and political control will distort the 'true' function of unions. In prac-tice, moreover, Chilean Christian Democratic employers, like their European counterparts, are far less interested in sharing real power with the unions than their Christian Democrat employees.[16]

Christian Democracy has little difficulty in devising models of the future communitarian society, including the future role and structure of entities like unions. But it is far more difficult to devise a model of how Christian Democrats ought to behave in the im-perfect real world—in a situation where, for example, Marxists have very different ideas on the role of unions and are equally sure that they are right. Should Christian Democrats co-operate with them and thereby appear to accept the idea of class conflict—or oppose them and thereby look just like any other political group trying to carve out a sphere of influence in the labour movement? This became a real dilemma for the Christian Democrats in power.

The party 'ABC', devoted to exploring the implications of pluralism, argues that unions must be free from state, employer, or party domination. Though the union may act as an instrument of class warfare in liberal–capitalist society, this function will have been superseded in Christian Democratic society, when it will become the agent for transforming the enterprise or firm, moving from profit-sharing to joint management, joint ownership, and finally to a fully communitarian enterprise. Though strikes are justified in liberal capitalist society, they will not be justifiable in a

---

[15] Though writing of European Christian Democracy, Fogarty's outline of doctrine, though not of political practice, can be applied to Chile (p. 59).

[16] This kind of dilemma between theory and the world of politics recurs frequently. Thus Fogarty explains that the Italian Christian Democrats, while keen on the ideal of regionalism and local self-government in theory, for many years did little to advance these ideals—for some regions were controlled by Communists! (p. 88).

fully operating Christian Democratic society, for here the interests of the workers will be those of the nation as a whole and the means of production will be owned by the workers[17]—an argument whose similarities with Communist doctrine are obvious.

From the idea of pluralism also tends to follow the advocacy of *libertad sindical*, or the right of the worker to join the union of his own choosing—the doctrine that was used to justify the proposed reform of the labour code which would have ended the present system of compulsory membership of the one plant union, and which also would have reduced Socialist–Communist influence. These ideas had been put forward earlier, by Father Alberto Hurtado the priest responsible for creating the ASICH, the Catholic Action union movement. Hurtado argued that there must be freedom to form and join unions, as this is more democratic, avoids forcing people into associations, keeps the leadership of the union active in service of the unions rather than creating posts of privilege, frees unions from outside control, helps to create consent, not obligation, as the basis of union action, and allows more unionists to have leadership experience.[18] His ideas were generally accepted in the party.

The subject of trade unions was not the most important issue for the Christian Democrats. Agrarian reform, the problem of the 'marginals', education, the copper issue were all topics of more pressing concern. In fact there seems to have been something of a conflict between concern with the marginal sectors and with the unions. Landsberger writes that 'labor policy in the narrow sense of what to do about *organised* labor is therefore best visualised either as a subordinate part or indeed as a competitor with the government's program of aid to the previously unorganised poor'.[19] The Christian Democrats regarded unionized labour as a sector relatively privileged already; their more pressing concern, not devoid of interest in building a wide electoral base, was with rural labour, where there were hardly any unions, and with the poor, who were scarcely in employment, let alone in unions.

The Christian Democrat concentration on the marginals was

---

[17] Ibid.

[18] *Sindicalismo: historia, teoría, práctica* (1950), pp. 56–65.

[19] 'Ideology and Practical Labor Politics', in Zañartu & Kennedy, p. 117. While the goals of labour policy were the usual ones of full employment, stable prices, minimum incomes, etc., they also included greater economic equality inside the worker sector—a notoriously difficult objective for any government.

distinct from that of traditional European Christian Democracy. The party was much influenced by a group of Jesuits led by the Belgian Father Roger Vekemans of DESAL, a study centre for social and economic problems publishing an influential journal, *Mensaje*.[20] Vekemans defines marginals as the group at the bottom of the social scale and which is really outside the social framework altogether.[21] They are essentially passive concerning their own welfare, and they have no power to alter their situation: they cannot exert influence because they cannot organize and they lack any internal cohesion. Because they constitute such a large part of society, their existence tends to restrain revolutionary change. Vekemans differs from the marxists, who see a solution in the development among these groups of class consciousness and the will to change the situation of exploitation. Marginality is a total condition; it does not apply merely to employment but to all aspects of political, social, and cultural participation. Hence change can only come about by external pressures, by Promoción Popular (or popular promotion). This work cannot be done by a single governmental agency; it must represent an approach shared by all ministries, for the marginals amount to no less than 50% of the total population of Chile—including all rural labour, the third of the urban population living in the shanty towns, and the sub-proletariat which is underemployed.[22] The integration of this huge section of the population can be performed only through massive general social change. Promoción Popular will assist the marginals to organize themselves; the pressures thus set up will be irresistible, and they will be integrated into the total society.

This analysis was very important in the development of Christian Democratic doctrine. The solution to the problem of marginality could be put forward as the peaceful road to dramatic social change, avoiding the class war and conflict of marxism. It

[20] For a discussion of Vekemans and his ideas on Promoción Popular see de Kadt, 'Paternalism and Populism: Catholicism in Latin America', *J. Contemp. Hist.*, Oct. 1967, pp. 96–7.

[21] 'Marginalidad, incorporación e integración', *Boletin* (Inst. Estud. Soc., Centro de Documentación), no. 37, pp. 29–41.

[22] Ibid., p. 35. And if his calculations were correct it was a potentially enormous electoral base which the Christian Democrats could mobilize, for according to Halperin (p. 210) they had one great advantage over European social democracy—'they are not hampered by the historical tradition of nineteenth century socialism', i.e. belief that only the working class strictly defined can be a party base.

was convenient, too, for it meant that the Christian Democrats did not have to challenge the marxists on their own ground in the unions, but could build up mass support outside the union framework. Hence, in practice, the secondary role that union matters assumed in the early period of the Christian Democratic government—that is, when optimism surrounding Promoción Popular had not yet been dispelled. But as de Kadt points out, there is an important contradiction here: 'What the masses come to want, *their* kind of revolution, may well have little in common with the plans of the government for the running of the state and society'.[23] However, because of financial shortages, political opposition, and party disenchantment, Promoción Popular, far from being the keystone of governmental policy, was relegated to a subsidiary role, and it never looked like providing the secure alternative mass base to the unions.

Promoción Popular, in spite of its radical-sounding nature in the writings of Vekemans, was really a paternalist and manipulative concept. It became the policy of the right wing of the Christian Democrats. The left wing advocated the opposite policy of working with other groups including marxists, in trade unions against the employers and capitalists. This doctrinal division in the party was to lead to a split, when in May 1969 the rebel wing broke away to form the MAPU and join forces with Allende in the presidential campaign, later to participate in his first cabinet.

The PDC is by Chilean standards a reasonably united party, but there have always been internal divisions of opinion. Petras divides them into corporatists and populists. Corporatists he defines as those who support the existing hierarchical structure of society and its economic organization. This hierarchical structure allows for little participation of the base. Elites control and manipulate; policy is made by bargaining between elites who share common values and assumptions: the old Christian Democratic leaders and those who came to the party from Ibáñez's PAL fall into this group. The populists stress popular participation (though not Promoción

---

[23] De Kadt, *J. Contemp. Hist.*, Oct. 1967, p. 97. He adds: 'This is a real problem, and it is reflected in the hostility to Promoción Popular of those to the left of government, both within the PDC and outside it. They regard the organization as an attempt to smother the revolutionary potential of the sub-proletariat. . . . To their opponents, then, Promoción Popular is intentionally or unintentionally being made into an instrument of the PDC, into a political organization which provides jobs for supporters and votes at elections.'

Popular). They can be radical egalitarians and opponents of all forms of hierarchy. Their strength lies in the unions, especially among the rural unions created by party action, though they also have support amongst the Christian Democratic youth and in what was the rebel section of the party.[24] All groups share a common vocabulary, but whereas one group may mean by communitarianism a system close to socialism, where there is fully collective ownership, another means little more than workers having some share in the function of management.

The left wing of the party headed by the rebel faction gained a narrow majority in the party Junta Nacional, briefly, and embarrassingly for the government, in July 1967. The rebel deputy Julio Silva Solar was elected secretary-general and the executive was composed predominantly of the left of the party. The Junta unanimously approved a report of a commission headed by the party agrarian reform expert, Jacques Chonchol (later Allende's Minister of Agriculture), entitled a 'Plan for the Non-Capitalist Development of the Country'. This envisaged a widespread policy of nationalization and social reform, and was taken to imply criticism of the slow pace of reforms under the Frei administration. The party Junta also approved the establishment of a branch of the Havana-based OLAS, so long as the branch did not advocate or support insurrection in Chile, though the aim of the organization was precisely to spread Castroist ideas throughout Latin America.

The victory of the left in the party was short-lived. By great effort the government secured the calling of a Junta Nacional Extraordinaria in January 1968, when the rebels were defeated and a pro-government executive was elected. With this defeat the rebel faction lost its platform from which to attack the government in general, and in particular William Thayer, the Labour Minister, whose policies they completely opposed. In May 1969 some but not all of the rebel faction quit the party to form the MAPU. Senator Rafael Gumucio, one of the leaders of the rebels (along with a small number of deputies, including the acknowledged leaders of the faction in the Chamber of Deputies) summarized their feelings in his letter of resignation.

The ideal which always united us [in the party] was the struggle against the injustices of the capitalist structure. . . . Now things are different. . . . We are less an instrument for the revolutionary trans-

[24] Petras, *Chilean Christian Democracy*, pp. 2 & 12–16.

formation of society than a force administering the system, guaranteeing the established order.[25]

At the January 1968 congress when the rebel faction was defeated, the supporters of the government passed a defensive resolution claiming that 'only the unity of the government, the unity of the party and a strong unity between the government and the party' will bring into being the revolution in liberty.[26]

The debate in the party ending with the schism of 1969 brought to the forefront all the differences that had split the party into factions—and the Christian Democratic trade unionists were not indifferent to the debate and its implications. On the one side were ranged the supporters of the government, those who feared the challenge on the left more than compromise with the right, those who saw as an essential part of government strategy the need to impose strict limits on the trade unions' wage demands, those whose approach to the key issues of agrarian reform and the copper proposals was cautious, more concerned with a smooth transition than with a drastic change, those who placed great emphasis on

[25] 'Chile: schism among Christian Democrats', *Latin America*, 9 May 1969. He added that 'In the course of 35 years of political activity I never thought before now that the moment could arrive when for motives of political honesty I should have to leave the party. . . . The experience of government had the effect, in my judgement, of radicalizing political positions, some to the right, some to the left. This brought about a series of clashes and grave disagreements impossible to hide.' This was not the first division in the party since 1964, but it was by far the most serious. In August 1965 deputy Emilio Lorenzini, a lifelong Falangist and active in the famous rural strike in Molina in 1953, resigned in protest at the slow pace of agrarian reform. He wrote: 'there is a real machine that has taken control of the party, displacing the old militants. And nothing is being done for the workers. There is a great loss of faith among the campesinos.' However, party persuasion secured his return after twenty-four hours (A. Olavarría Bravo, *Chile bajo la Democracia Cristiana* (1966), p. 303). In 1966 deputy Patricio Hurtado was expelled for too much public sympathizing with Cuba; and in 1967 deputy Rudolfo Werner suffered the same fate for stating that his colleagues had betrayed their promise to make a revolution in liberty and accusing the Christian Democrats of building up a new elite without popular support (*Punto final*, June 1966, pp. 8–9). Apart from the rebel faction of the party there was also a *tercerista* group—less radical but still critical of the government, and still arguing that there must be a decisive confrontation with the oligarchy.

[26] 'Chile: Frei turns the table on the rebels', *Latin America*, 12 Jan. 1968. The meeting praised the government for its considerable achievements; though it also passed (by a tiny majority of four) a motion opposing the partial restriction on the right to strike tabled by the government in Congress.

N

the need to be loyal to the government. On the other side were those impatient with the progress of the government, who advocated seeking alliances on the left in order to undermine the power of the right, those who preferred structural reforms in the economic system to simple limitations on wage demands and who pressed for urgent action in the rural sector and tougher terms with the American copper companies. The division was by no means clear-cut, and there were groups sharing some of the points of view of both camps, such as the *terceristas*. The unionists in the party, or at least those in its union department, gradually came to adopt the point of view of the rebel faction, though they remained loyal to the party in the division of 1969.

Before examining the relations of the Christian Democratic unionists with the labour movement before and during Frei's administration, it is necessary to glance at the social composition of the party, and the sectors where it has union support.

### The social base of the party

As the party was founded by middle- and upper-class Catholic intellectuals, for many years they constituted its essential core; even today the continuity of such leaders in posts of authority is striking, though the social base of the membership and of the electorate is much wider. The party's founders, Frei, Radomiro Tomic, Bernardo Leighton, and others have continued to command the authority and prestige natural to leaders who remained active in the party for many years when its electoral and political future was very doubtful, very much as in the French MRP.

The party has continued to be, at least in the social composition of the membership, overwhelmingly middle class, though to some extent a middle class of more recent formation than the Radical supporters: the 'typical' Christian Democratic member is not the old-style government bureaucrat or school teacher or provincial lawyer who make up the core of the Radical party membership. He is more likely to be a member of the urban professional middle class or a skilled worker or manager—groups that have developed with the diversification of the economy in the last twenty years.[27] The party attracted support from industrialists and commercial and banking sectors with the great Christian Democratic electoral

[27] 'Lautaro', *Crítica de una tesis tradicional*, p. 7.

triumphs of 1964 and 1965, but many members of these groups switched their support to Alessandri in 1970.

The parliamentary party reflects the continuity of former Falangists in the political hierarchy. Though the figures are not exact, it seems that in 1967 of the 81 deputies, 30 were former Falangists, 32 served their political apprenticeship after the party had renamed itself, 9 had moved over from the PAL, 5 from the Conservative party, 2 from the Liberals, and 2 were of undetermined political background. In the Senate the predominance of the Falangists was more marked; 7 had belonged to that party, 1 moved over from the Partido Democrático Nacional, 2 from Socialist groups, 1 from an Ibañista group, and 1 from the Conservatives.[28] Nearly all came from middle-class backgrounds, lawyers being the largest single group.

The electoral base of the party has greatly widened since the early 1950s when it received less than 5 per cent of the poll. This does not simply represent a shift from other parties, for this increased vote has taken place at the same time as a big expansion of the electorate. In the Congressional elections of 1953, for example, about three-quarters of a million votes were cast; in the municipal elections of 1963 (when the PDC had 22% of the vote) the electorate had risen to just over 2 m.; by 1965 (when the party had 44%) it had gone up to close on 2,300,000; and in the congressional elections of 1969 (when its share fell to 31%) the total number of votes cast had risen to over 2,400,000. The spectacular rise in the PDC share of the poll took place between 1961 and 1964–5; after that the party share fell to about a third of the total, and in the municipal elections of 1971 to a quarter.

The party does particularly well at election time in the larger towns, among the shanty-town dwellers (at least in 1964 and 1965), and among women—of whom 63% voted for Frei in 1964 compared with 49% of the male vote. Even in the highest vote for

[28] 'Ficha de los 81 diputados del PDC', *Punto final*, 19 Dec. 1967, pp. 4–6. A survey following the 1958 presidential election confirmed the impression that, at least at that time, the party was supported by middle-class sectors. Thus almost 40% of those surveyed who had voted for Frei in 1958 described themselves as holding a 'centre' political position; and in the occupational grade 2 (described as 'managerial employees' and 'university professionals'), the highest preference (22% of the total) was for Frei, as it was also (19%) in occupational group 4 (described as non-managerial employees and non-university professionals) (Briones, in *R. interamerica ci. soc.*, 2/3 (1963), pp. 390 & 394).

the PDC, when Frei took 56% of the total in the presidential election of 1964, the areas where unionists were most numerous were those where Allende held out best against the PDC challenge. Though the index is not a perfect guide to union strength, Zeitlin and Petras found that in those municipalities where 40% or more of the labour force was occupied in manufacturing, mining, or construction, Allende's vote was on average higher than Frei's. Frei's electoral support increased directly as the percentage of the labour force in manual occupations decreased. In Gran Santiago itself they found that in the seven municipalities with 40% or more employed in the secondary sector, five recorded slight majorities for Allende.[29] The presidential election of that year was in many ways exceptional, for it was a polarized contest with many sectors of the right voting for Frei as the lesser of two evils. Careful analysis, however, shows that Frei made less headway amongst the working class.

The congressional election of 1969 may lend itself better to analysis for all parties were standing. The PDC ran strongest in the two major cities, Santiago and Valparaíso, and least well in the older mining areas. There is a clear link between a high level of economic development and support for the party and a negative association between voting for the PDC and voting for the Radical party, which did best in smaller towns and less developed areas.[30] Those provinces with most industry and high employment in commerce and the service sectors are those where PDC support is highest. On this basis Faletto and Ruiz argue that 'Christian Democracy represents the modern industrial bourgeoisie . . . backed up by state financing, given that 70% of total investment comes from the public sector.' And this has generated a modernised bureaucracy, located in the great urban industrial centres which support the PDC.[31] If it was true that the 'modern industrial

---

[29] M. Zeitlin & J. Petras, 'The working class vote in Chile: Christian Democracy versus Marxism', *Brit. J. Sociol.*, Mar. 1970, pp. 21 & 26. They also found that taking the male vote alone in the nine largest Chilean towns, apart from Santiago, Frei had a majority 4 times compared with 5 for Allende. In 1970 too the higher the proportion of workers in mining and secondary occupations, the higher the vote for Allende (Petras, 'Clase obrera chilena', *Punto final*, Jan. 1971, pp. 2–5).

[30] The association was −0·5 (Faletto & Ruiz, in *Chile, Hoy*, p. 218). The information in this paragraph is taken from this article.

[31] And they also refer to the support that the PDC enjoys in those areas where the agrarian reform has had some positive benefit for the rural labourers, and

bourgeoisie' supported Frei in 1964, this surely was more from fear of Allende than liking for the Christian Democrats. Presented with an acceptable, and popular, right-wing candidate in 1970, industrialists' support returned to Alessandri.

The support of trade unionists enjoyed by the Christian Democrats has to be set in the context of the growth of support for them nationally. Though the Socialists, Communists, and Radicals have well-entrenched positions in the union world, they far from monopolize the political sentiments of union labour, and there is no reason to suppose that trade unionists were immune from the wave of popular enthusiasm for the Christian Democrats in the early 1960s or that there was not some drift from other parties, and from those who had not previously held any strong partisan commitment, into the Christian Democratic camp. At first at least the PDC government held strong attractions for right-wing union leaders like Wenceslao Moreno of COMACh, or Ruben Hurtado of the Viña Sugar Refinery Workers, or Carlos Ibáñez King of the Santiago Choferes union, who hoped that membership of the party would not only be beneficial for themselves and their unions, but would also be compatible with continued association with ORIT and the ICFTU, a course that was taboo for the Socialist and Communist unionists and was to become so even for the Radicals.

It is certainly true that PDC enjoys considerable support among the white-collar workers, especially in the public sector, but there is also support for it in the industrial plant unions. The survey conducted by Landsberger as early as 1962 found that 23% of the sample of union presidents admitted to supporting the PDC.[32] The differences between the Christian Democratic union presidents and the others were not dramatic, though Christian Democratic presidents had had a slightly better education in terms of years of schooling and of attempts to continue with some sort of adult education. There were few differences in social origin or in present occupational status (both FRAP supporters and Christian Democrats were spread along the occupational scale from unskilled to skilled

amongst the marginal sectors, brought in through Promoción Popular (ibid., pp. 224–5).

[32] The figures were 32% in Valparaíso, 18% in Concepción, and 23% in Santiago. Altogether 230 presidents were interviewed in Santiago—including 18 out of a possible 21 presidents of unions with more than 500 members (Landsberger, in *Econ. Dev. & Cult. Change*, Jan. 1968, p. 222).

with supervisory responsibilities). There was a mild tendency for Christian Democrats to be more satisfied with their jobs and they had slightly better relations with employers (though this need have nothing to do with their ideology), but there was practically no difference in their conceptions of the goals of the union. There was little difference in the length of time served as union officials[33] or in the distribution by type of industry or enterprise, but FRAP-presided unions were much more likely to be affiliated with the CUT. On the question of the amount of social change needed in Chile 28% of Christian Democrats compared with 42% of FRAP supporters wanted a 'total and immediate restructuring of society'.

At the national level the strength of the Christian Democrats lies in the public-sector and rural unions, though there are few major confederations or unions that do not have some Christian Democratic representatives on their executive. At the 1968 CUT congress, for example, of the 21 members proposed by the Christian Democrats for election to the executive, at least 10 worked for state or municipal enterprises and of the others at least 5 were white-collar workers.[34] Two recent presidents of the party union department were members of the executive of the railworkers' union (the Christian Democratic Railway Workers' Front kept an office in the department's old headquarters) and the department's executive is heavily weighted with state employees.[35] The Christian Democrats themselves claim that their strongholds are in the public sector, especially in the railway workers' union, in the Ministry of Public Works, and among the postal employees and

[33] 19% of Christian Democratic unionists (compared with 21% of FRAP) had served for ten years or more; 39% (compared with 27%) however had only had three or fewer years experience (ibid., p. 235).

[34] This information is taken from a sheet circulated at the Congress, entitled 'Lista de Acción Unitaria', which gives the union affiliation of the candidates, though it is not always possible to determine their occupational grade. The sheet is headed: 'Comrades: when the economic right is uniting, when the underdeveloped countries are oppressed by international imperialism, when the bourgeoisie is uniting to divide us, our reply is a confederation of united action'. The sheet nowhere refers to the PDC as such, but no one doubted that it was the party list.

[35] Interviews with the president of the PDC union dept (Santiago) May 1967 & Dec. 1968. On the executive of the departmental in 1965, of the 14 signatories to a departmental document, 10 were from unions in the state sector, 1 represented the copper unions, 1 the CEPCH, 1 a taxi drivers' union, and 1 a campesino union (Política y espíritu, May–June 1965, p. 62).

the teachers. They are also strong in certain modern and large industrial establishments like the Huachipato steel refinery and the Bata shoe factory, which is not a member of the FONACC, though it is by far the largest single firm in the industry. In industry generally and in mining, especially in the copper mines after the incidents at El Salvador in 1966 (see p. 200) they are weaker.

## The party structure and union department

The party structure is hierarchical and disciplined. In this it is possible to see imitation of the democratic centralism of the marxist parties and also of the corporatist ideas of Catholic theory; certainly the unusually large number of affiliated organizations (which exist also in other Chilean parties but rarely with the life and activity that they have in the PDC) point to the influence of corporative theory.

The reorganization of the party in 1957 centralized great authority in the National Council, which has power to direct and discipline the party's congressional representatives. Apart from the formal powers that are vested in the National Council, a great deal of cohesion results from the fact that many members of that body were the original founders or early members of the Falange. Although the position has changed to some extent with the growth of the party and corresponding growth of party-government tensions, nevertheless, as Gil writes (p. 273),

the homogeneous nature of membership makes the Christian Democrats a party in which . . . the bonds of friendship are extremely strong. . . . A remarkable community of interest and purpose has existed in the party leadership . . . probably due . . . to the intimate friendships in the small group of national leaders, and it contributes to the immense prestige that these leaders enjoy.

There are two basic types of party organ; the political ones which function at the communal, provincial, and national level, and under their supervision, special or technical departments, such as, for example, the union department or the *campesino* department.[36]

The National Junta is the permanent organ in which authority resides between National Congresses. The national director of the union department is ex-officio a member, and a representative of

[36] PDC *Estatutos*, p. 1963.

each of the national federations, confederations, or unions has the right to attend. The Junta elects the 12-man National Council, the most powerful body, which has two union leaders on it. The party has a Political Commission to supervise and report on the departments. As Gil writes (p. 275), the 'Christian Democratic party is a highly centralised national political organisation in which the influence of the top leaders is paramount'. The influence of those top leaders was shaken in 1967 by a combination of skilful manoeuvring by the rebel faction and some rank-and-file disillusionment inside the party. The challenge to the top leaders' authority was short-lived, though its defeat was at a heavy later cost to the party.

The union department was set up at the same time as the party to promote, train, guide, and co-ordinate the work of party members in the unions.[37] Real power lies in the elected Executive Council, a small group of thirteen unionists and the two union leaders elected by the party Junta to the National Council. The head of the union department is the national director, unpaid like his counterpart in the other parties. The department authorizes the creation of the Workers' Fronts set up by Christian Democrats in their respective occupations and controls the executive members of these fronts, whom it may dismiss if they are negligent. In theory the Executive Council advises the Political Commission on strategy and policy. But Christian Democratic unionists do not regard their department as particularly influential.[38] As an example, the departmental national director claimed that the government and the Minister of Labour hardly consulted them on the proposed reform of the labour code. The department resented this neglect for most of its members were opposed to the government's idea of

[37] For further details see *Reglamento del departamento nacional sindical del PDC* (1969, mimeo).

[38] An editorial in the Jesuit monthly *Mensaje* (Mar.–Apr. 1966) lamented that 'There exists a union department of the PDC, but this department is as abandoned as the union movement. It has very little economic assistance, and, even more important, minimal doctrinal and technical assistance. And the results are obvious. A year ago the Christian Democrats completely controlled the ETCE (state collective transportation company). Today the Marxists are in control. A year ago the Christian Democrats dominated the cement union. But the party decided to send the union president to Germany and now the marxists have the majority. Last year the elections in the railway unions were practically won, but the Communists annulled 150 votes. Nobody complained, nobody wanted to complain, and the marxists have taken control of the railway unions. And so we could continue' (p. 82).

allowing several unions to be created inside a plant, replacing the obligatory single union of the existing law.[39] In the 2nd congress of Christian Democratic trade unionists in 1966 the unions complained of their lack of representation in the government and in the party. Of the eighty-one deputies in 1967 only some eight had been union leaders, mostly in the state or white-collar sectors; no senators appear to have had this sort of background.[40] When the leadership of the union department passed into the hands of supporters of the rebel faction, the criticisms of the government grew sharper. Apparently the leaders of the department had no regular contacts with the Minister of Labour, nor were they consulted on matters of economic policy; the only time their help was sought was when there was an appeal to them to impede some strike called against the government's economic policy.[41]

There is no particular reason why the union department should be influential inside the party. The PDC makes no such claims as the Socialists or Communists to represent, above all, the working class. The unions do not finance the party (as they do the Labour party in Britain), and consequently they have no financial leverage. This situation parallels that in the Radical party. Unionists are more influential in the marxist parties because they constitute a great proportion of the membership and electorate, and because unions are more important in the overall strategy of the parties. Nevertheless, the leadership of the PDC does not seem to have been very skilful in wooing unionists either inside or outside the party.

For Christian Democratic unionists at large the union department performs the same sort of functions as its counterparts in the other parties though it seems to be able to do this more efficiently as it is better financed, and has more technical advisers. The

[39] Interview with the national director of the union department (Santiago) May 1967. The national director was also on the executive of the FIFch. These opinions were later confirmed in an interview with the national secretary (May 1967, Santiago). As early as 1959 the party had declared that union representation in it must be strengthened—though it added that this depended on unions developing 'politically and morally' (Resolución sobre política sindical, *Documentos de la 1º convención nacional, 1959*).

[40] As n. 28. Two were former *empleado* copper union leaders, 1 a former nitrate *obrero* union leader, 1 a former railway *obrero* union leader, 1 a former ANEF leader, 1 a former *empleado* union leader in Huachipato, and the notorious Ruben Hurtado of the Viña sugar refinery workers; 5 of them had been members of the Falange party.

[41] Interview, national director of the union dept, Santiago, Dec. 1968. Like the previous director he was also on the executive of the FIFch.

department is thus more active in helping to form new unions. Its representatives attend important meetings of the Christian Democratic Workers' Fronts (though members of its executive hold posts in Workers' Fronts as well). The department exercises some power over the choice of candidates for election to union executives, and is certainly active in this regard when contesting the elections in the CUT. The party also pays the expenses of at least some delegates to the CUT congresses, though it does not have as much money as it wishes. The national director of the union department in an interview in a party newspaper lamented that lack of funds prevented sixty delegates from Valdivia and sixty from Africa from travelling to the 1968 CUT congress.[42]

## The political evolution of Christian Democratic unionism

Christian Democratic trade unionists find it more difficult to establish their credentials as authentic members of the working class than most other political groups in Chile. One obstacle is the heavy weight of Christian Democratic theory about the role of trade unions. The theory stems from intellectuals in the party, and is based upon abstract concepts that rely little on the traditional notions of solidarity and class conflict that are in the stock-in-trade of most unionists in Chile. Prominent among the proponents of this theory was William Thayer, a lawyer and university lecturer who became an unpopular Minister of Labour, not least in the ranks of his own party. A second obstacle is the relatively recent development of Christian Democracy in the trade unions, added to the fact that its early policy was marked by attempts, not so much of the unionists as of the party leadership, to set up rival confederations to the marxist-dominated CUT. A third obstacle is the existence inside the Christian Democratic union group of a number of opportunistic and right-wing union leaders, very much disliked and mistrusted by the other political groups in the labour movement. The fourth, though by no means least important, obstacle was the fact that Christian Democratic unionists were of the same party as a government that had come to power by defeating the Socialist–Communist coalition. Though it promised revolution, the government was hardly able to sustain important reforms, and it lost union support by an economic policy that relied increasingly on the wage freeze as the basic instrument to contain inflation—

[42] Interview in *Flecha roja*, 27 Nov. 1968, p. 4.

though in practice wages were neither held down nor was inflation contained.

## 1. The theoretical framework

Christian Democratic theory on the correct role of unions has been expounded by Thayer in his *Trabajo, empresa, y revolución* (1968). Unions should be 'essentially economic and not ideological; free and not controlled; united and not divisionist; wide and open, not small and exclusive'; they should concentrate on improving living conditions and should not waste time on unfruitful discussions. They should respect democracy and the social, political, and religious beliefs of members and should not serve interests foreign to union objectives; they should be conscious of and press for a reform of enterprise structure and not confine themselves simply to immediate economic demands. He gave warning that a union movement that grows too powerful might have disastrous economic consequences for a country like Chile, for the unions would be able to make demands that the economic system could not bear. Union growth therefore can only be contemplated with equanimity if at the same time there is transformation to a situation where capital and labour instead of being in conflict work in harmony. Thayer is no advocate of workers' control and strongly criticized the application of this principle in large state enterprises as advocated by the rebel group of the PDC.

Thayer sponsored the project abolishing the closed-shop unions. His answer to the criticism that this would lead to the multiplication of politicized, and powerless small unions within factories, when the real problem is already that unions are too small, was unacceptable to his opponents and Christian Democratic unionists. He argued that he expected working men to refuse to support unions that would secure no benefit. A 'free' choice would mean support willingly given to strong unions and withdrawal of support from ineffective or politicized unions. He added, 'we cannot kill liberty in order to save unity. Unity must be free in order to maintain democracy.' The argument of those who effectively blocked this concept when it was embodied in the proposed labour code reform of 1965 was that they were afraid that the bill would kill the union movement.

Thayer was a leading member of ASICH, the Catholic union organization set up by Fr Hurtado in the early 1950s. He has always believed in the strong moral guidance of the workers by the teachers of their movement, which in practice meant an important role for the Catholic priests in ASICH who were in charge of its training programmes.[43] Because the marxists confuse the political world with union matters, i.e. regard party and union as a single organism, he held that workers of Christian belief must set up a Christian confederation in order to combat these false ideas. It is hardly surprising that Thayer has been closely associated with the various attempts by Christian Democracy to set up rival national confederations to the CUT.[44] Though he has expressed himself in favour of overall unity, he is not willing to make concessions to the marxists if this involves a violation of his concept of democratic and free unionism. As the Communists and Socialists strongly favour one-union plants, and oppose his ideas, practical co-operation is difficult.

Writing in 1957 on whether Catholic unionists should remain in the CUT or not, he argued that they should at least bargain from a position of strength; that is Catholic unionists should first of all form a strong and united organization to decide on tactics towards the CUT. In his opinion continuance in the CUT was impossible if the other members acted in an anti-democratic manner, adding that the mere fact of affiliation to Communism or Socialism did not necessarily mean that unionists would so act, though implying that if they were consistent with their party principles they could not but do so.

The programme of the Frei government was first outlined in detail in a report drawn up in December 1962.[45] This very long report deals with proposals for reform of enterprises and unions. Models of the enterprise or firm derived from capitalist and Communist societies are decisively rejected. The Christian Democratic conception is that the enterprise belongs exclusively neither to capital nor labour—though it should belong largely to labour. Both workers and the providers of capital should share power, ownership, and profits, but overall investment will be regulated by the state in the national interests. The capitalists will tend to dis-

[43] Thayer, 'Bases para una política sindical', *Política y espíritu*, 15 Aug., 1957, p. 14.

[44] e.g. the Federación Gremialista de Chile immediately following the establishment of the party in 1957, the MUTCH following the victory of Frei in 1964, and the UTRACH in the late 1960s.

[45] The report is called the *Informe preliminar para un programa de gobierno de la Democracia Cristiana*. This was the 'blue book' on which was largely based the 'white book' which constituted the actual programme of the government.

appear in favour of the new owners—both manual and intellectual workers in the enterprise. Thus the role of the union will be transformed, for it will now be part of the enterprise and not opposed to it. Nevertheless the union as such will survive, for it represents the work or labour part of the productive process, and should still continue to combine with similar organizations in other enterprises to represent this function nationally.

Nevertheless, until the communitarian society is fully realized there are numerous immediate and pressing tasks in the labour field. The difference between *empleado* and *obrero* must be gradually eliminated. The provisions of the labour code inhibiting the formation of federations and confederations must be repealed, and the public sector (apart from the police and armed forces) should be granted equal rights to form unions. The report does not envisage a completely uniform structure—remnants of the old and the new will mingle, different technological systems entail variations in the distribution of authority, etc. For unions to perform this future role properly they must be strong and free and they must participate in state bodies. Unions must spread to the unorganized; the system of a single obligatory union must disappear in favour of freely chosen unions (though it was recognized by the government when this principle was embodied in a proposed reform that to avoid the dangers of creating a large number of unions, legal recognition would be given only to those unions representing at least 30% of the workers, and that the largest union would be regarded as the agent for collective bargaining). Unions must be brought into active participation in the apparatus of state administration at all levels.

In the first years of the Frei government, the party returned continually to these themes outlined in the 1962 report. The 1966 congress denounced the antiquated nature of the existing labour code and called for its revision. It denounced (rather ambiguously, considering its own record) party interference in union affairs.[46] Yet in a relatively short time these demands became increasingly irrelevant. In very few of these objectives did the Frei government achieve any real success; in some it made no effort at all. Christian Democratic unionism swung away from these ideas to adopt a critique of society largely influenced by the rebel faction, and closer

---

[46] 'Congreso del PDC; política sindical', in *Politica y espiritu*, Oct. 1966, pp. 91–3. The official government newspaper, *La Nación*, in its issue of 1 May 1967 outlines the government's views on the role of unions in much the same terms.

to socialism than communitarianism. The original Christian Democratic position was contradictory. Unions should be independent of all parties—but to achieve this end the Christian Democrats must win power, and to win power they needed to build up the party position in unions. Then, had they ever achieved such authority, their control over unions would have been *weakened* by the implementation of their proposals on union freedom—a gesture somewhat difficult to imagine from any political party in a competitive situation. These original ideas on the role of unions always had a rather artificial relationship to reality, for the record of Christian Democracy in the unions reads rather less like a disinterested attempt to direct workers along the path of Christian inspiration and rather more like that of the other political parties, struggling to extend influence, to weaken the enemy, to co-ordinate the action of the unionists and the party, usually in the interests of the party. This can be illustrated by looking at the relationships between the Christian Democrats and the other parties in the CUT.

## 2. Christian Democracy and the CUT

The Christian Democrats have had a changing and on the whole rather unsatisfactory relationship with the CUT. On the one hand they do not wish to be excluded from the largest Chilean confederation; on the other they want to dictate their terms of entry and of continuing co-operation in the movement, terms that are not always acceptable to the other parties. They want to challenge marxist influence in the unions but also to co-operate with marxist unionists in the general interest of trade union unity. An additional complication arose when the Christian Democrats were in government, for the party unionists resented attacks on the government but felt increasingly unable to defend its incomes policy. Whether the emphasis is given to working with the marxists or to opposing them in a separate organization depends on the political circumstances of the time, though it is never a clear-cut choice. There are always those hostile to the CUT, and those who emphasize the need to work in it for the unity of the labour movement, a division that does not correspond to that between politicians and unionists, for members in both sectors have very different ideas on the correct Christian Democratic union policy.

When the move to set up the CUT was initiated there was an unusual degree of accord in the labour movement. The Communists at that time were outlawed, and the Socialists and Christian Democrats were opposed to the ban. As the condition of illegality hampered, though far from prevented, Communist activity in the unions, there was less concern about threats of Communist hegemony. The Radicals, gravely weakened by their loss of power in 1952 and internally confused and divided by the experience of government, especially after the President González Videla had moved to the right, were at that time working in alliance with the then Falange in the union movement. These four groups were able to agree to present a joint list of candidates for the first CUT executive, and the Falange elected two members.

This unusual unity did not last long. As Communist power grew in the labour movement with the slackening of the repression, the Falange asserted that the CUT was becoming little more than an instrument of the marxist parties.[47] The first real split occurred at the 1st congress in 1957 over the CUT's Declaration of Principles. The original Declaration was clearly marxist, with some anarcho-syndicalist influence. The newly formed Christian Democrats wanted a Declaration independent of party ideology. They alleged that the original Declaration was marxist, materialist, and, by its commitment to the class war, divided rather than united the working-class movement. The debate was not simply about the wording of a Declaration; it also reflected the conflict between two different approaches to unionism and the resentment of the Christian Democrats at the marxists.[48] The Socialists and Communists agreed to modify the text and the Christian Democrats attended the 1957 congress under that condition. At first the Communists proposed a Declaration even more moderate than that proposed by the Christian Democrats but as this was opposed by the Socialists, the combined marxist group produced another document, with some modifications which were not, however, drastic enough for the Christian Democrats, though they were too drastic for the anarcho-syndicalists who promptly withdrew. When, in addition, the marxists refused to make concessions to the Christian Democrats over the composition of the executive, the

[47] See, e.g., 'La CUT y los problemas politico-sindicales', *Política y espíritu*, 15 May 1955, pp. 3–4 for an attack on the 'growing and excessive influence' of the CP in the CUT.

[48] 'La CUT y sus problemas', *Política y espíritu*, 1 Sept. 1957, p. 22. This issue also contains the text of the Christian Democratic proposal for the new Declaration of Principles and the revised marxist one.

Christian Democrats withdrew from the congress, though not from the CUT itself. Although ASICH used the opportunity to try to draw the Christian Democrats into a separate Catholic union confederation, this overture was rejected as divisionist. The Christian Democrats emphasized the importance of respecting democracy in the union movement as a condition of their continuing participation in the CUT; their version of the Declaration of Principles even included a passage that stated that 'in general Chilean democracy guarantees human rights and permits working-class action'— which must have seemed a little strange to the outlawed Communists.

However, strong efforts on the part of the Communists did succeed in bringing back the Christian Democrats into the CUT, and they accepted the offer of four places on its executive. This unity did not last, for the Christian Democrats returned to the controversy with the 1959 congress. They argued that union democracy had been infringed by the imposition of various policies that 'threatened freedom of religious and philosophical thought' of the members.[49] The Radicals also used this pretext to withdraw from the proceedings though the real reason was that they were then beginning to collaborate with the President at a time when governmental policies were strongly opposed in the union movement. Another long debate on the Declaration, though leading to further changes, still resulted in a solution unacceptable to the Christian Democrats, as it was also, though for different reasons, to the anarcho-syndicalists and the Trotskyists.

A meeting of the PDC declared that if the CUT acted in accord with the ideas laid down in the Declaration, the party would find it impossible to continue collaboration. Although it had withdrawn from the 1959 congress it would remain in the CUT as long as Christian Democratic principles were respected. It recognized that most unions were members of the CUT not because of the Declaration but because of their desire for unity, a sentiment which the party shared. All parties must work to resolve the question of the Declaration at the next conference.[50]

The question was finally resolved to the satisfaction of the

---

[49] Barría, *Trayectoria*, p. 376. This was in reference to a decision of the congress in favour of secular education and of stopping state grants to religious schools.

[50] 'Resolución sobre política sindical', *Documentos de la 1º Convención nacional, 1959.*

Christian Democrats and the Radicals, and in the 1962 congress they presented a joint list of candidates for the executive, the Christian Democrats taking three places and the Radicals one. However, the exclusion of a large number of delegates from Catholic rural unions on the grounds that their credentials were not in order annoyed the Christian Democrats and it was obvious that their co-operation would be unwilling.

The changing political situation made co-operation difficult at the best of times, and now almost impossible. The presidential campaign of 1964 saw a sharp polarization of political forces between the marxists and the Christian Democrats. Frei's victory did not alleviate the tensions, partly because the congressional elections for 1965 were close, and the Communists and Socialists were anxious for revenge. The Christian Democrats felt that the opposition was trying to impede the progress of the government by using the CUT to foment strikes, make unreasonable wage demands, and so on.[51] The arrangements for the 1965 CUT congress brought the tensions into the open, and resulted in yet another division in the CUT.

When the Christian Democratic union department suggested modifying the representation and voting arrangements of the congress, the CUT secretariat accused it of trying to impose a Christian Democratic plan. The Christian Democrats replied that it was pure hypocrisy not to recognize that the unionists of every party co-ordinated and planned congress activities.[52] They accused the Socialists and Communists of using every opportunity in the CUT to impose their ideological preconceptions, from compulsory secular state education to support for the Cuban revolution. They particularly resented the attacks on the government. They argued that it was hardly appropriate for Communists and Socialists to accuse them of being divisionist and sectarians in view of the bitter history of Socialist–Communist relations, adding that because of party rivalries the CUT was almost completely ineffective in its efforts to improve the structure of Chilean unionism.

With such an atmosphere of bitterness, it was hardly possible that the congress should produce any semblance of unity. Indeed,

[51] 'Leo', 'Los planes de la oposición de Izquierda', *Política y espíritu*, May–June 1965, p. 18.
[52] The text of the reply of the union dept of the Christian Democrats to the CUT is contained in 'Carta a los Trabajadores Chilenos', ibid., pp. 55–62. The Christian Democrats also wanted national elections for the CUT executive.

for the third time in five congresses the Christian Democrats (half of whose delegation had even refused to attend) abstained from voting and effectively withdrew from participation in the CUT.

Though it was the advent to power of the Christian Democrats that in effect provoked that particular division in the ranks of the labour movement, it was, paradoxically, the policy pursued by that government that also brought back a semblance of unity to the union movement—enough at least for Christian Democrat unionists to agree to participate once more in the activities of the CUT, to attend the 1968 congress, and actually to remain to vote. The Frei administration was to see important developments inside the labour movement.

### 3. The Frei administration and the unions

The question of how far the Frei administration was successful is difficult to judge so soon after the event; it may be necessary to wait until the end of the Allende administration when the two can be compared.[53] But it is clear that the government was a disappointment to the Christian Democratic unionists. The reasons are clear enough—an unpopular attempt to impose the reformed labour code, a general feeling that the unions were neither consulted nor given greater representation in the new scheme of things, inability to contain inflation, and very unpopular policies of wage restraint.

The disappointment of the party members was probably more severe, for Frei had been a long-standing advocate of trade union reform. While in opposition he had presented a bill to the Senate (which was never considered) which would have permitted public employees to form unions.[54] He had also recommended that unions should be incorporated in Economic Councils (to plan and regulate economic development), in the administration of social security funds and of enterprises, in the educational system, and so on. He argued that 'unions must have a decisive role in the organization of the economic mechanism'.[55] But in power he did little to give unions that 'decisive role'—presumably because the marxists were too strong in the unions.

---

[53] The author has attempted an interim balance in 'Chile: from Christian Democracy to Marxism', *The World Today*, Nov. 1970 and 'Chile: the difficulties of democratic reform', *Internat. J.*, Summer, 1969, pp. 515–29.

[54] Frei, p. 87.                     [55] Ibid., pp. 88 & 92.

In office, most of Frei's policies, rather than stressing the 'communitarian' element of Christian Democratic thought, relied on a system of centralized control and planning that owed more to the ideas of the Economic Commission for Latin America than it did to those of Maritain or even Vekemans. Other Christian Democratic movements experienced similar problems. Fogarty writing of the French MRP, says:

Its history is . . . the clearest and most extreme tendency . . . for Christian Democrat politicians to treat politics as an exercise in pure principle on the one hand and day-to-day tactics on the other. The tendency is to forget, or not to think through sufficiently, the intermediate level of strategy—the hypotheses or middle principles.[56]

The actions of the government showed that they had not 'thought through sufficiently' their labour policies. The reform of the labour code ran up against strong union hostility because unionists in Chile, including Christian Democratic ones, did not want to see one of their strengths—the obligatory single plant union—eroded by allowing up to three unions to exist. They also united in opposition to the proposals that would have allowed the President to order back to work any group of strikers who were trying to get a bigger pay rise than that officially permitted, especially as these orders would be enforced by civil or military authorities and would be accompanied by compulsory arbitration.

Nor did the unionists take kindly to the government's attempt to support the initiative of some party members to create a rival confederation to the CUT. The Catholic unionists in ASICH were always anxious to attract to their small numbers the Christian Democratic unionists. ASICH strongly backed the creation of the MUTCH by a section of the party. Frei himself spoke at a May Day rally organized by the MUTCH to rival the traditional CUT rally, but the movement never really attracted support and quickly faded away. Yet it was not the only attempt to create such a rival. Santiago Pereira, a PDC deputy and a former member of the CUT executive and also of the ANEF executive, tried his hand with the Comando Nacional de Trabajo, which grew out of the 'unionists for Frei' movement in the campaign of 1964.[57] This organization was less opposed to the CUT than the MUTCH, and less enthusiastic

[56] Fogarty, pp. 338–9. Another, and equally sympathetic student of Christian Democracy, though this time of Latin American, shares this verdict (Williams, ch. 10, *passim*).
[57] Interview with Pereira, 17 May 1967 (Santiago).

about collaboration with the ASICh. But like its predecessor and successor, it never achieved much importance and in some ways was more of a nuisance than a help to the Christian Democratic unionists. This was even more the case for the UTRACh, the last attempt during the Frei administration to create a rival to the CUT. The UTRACh had some support from right-wing PDC leaders and the ASICh, but was opposed by the majority of the party unionists; and eventually the union department with the backing of the party (once it was clear that the movement was a non-starter) resolved that membership in the UTRACh was incompatible with militancy in the PDC.

In the increasingly bad relations between the unions and the government, the events of 1966 in the El Salvador copper mines played a prominent part. In that year the El Teniente copper miners struck in support of a wage claim, arguing that the increases proposed by the company (now jointly owned by the Chilean government and the original company) were only just sufficient to cover the increase in the cost of living and did not take account of increasing productivity and profits.[58] Copper miners in the North then struck in sympathy. This was declared illegal, and the government sent in the military, six miners being killed in the resulting clash. Frei defended the troops and accused the marxist parties of inciting the trouble. Whatever the rights and wrongs of the matter, Frei's defence of the troops increased the union's hostility to the government and provided a frequently brandished symbol of its alleged brutality and indifference to the labour movement.

The Jesuit monthly *Mensaje* severely criticized the government, and its strictures were undoubtedly shared by many on the left of the PDC, although *Mensaje* did not exonerate the marxists from responsibility. Frei regarded his copper policy as the keystone of his programme, so that it was to be expected that the marxists would use all their influence in the copper unions to hinder it. In the incident at El Salvador the miners did fire on the troops. But the central point of *Mensaje*'s criticism was that the government should never have come to this point in its relations with the labour movement.[59] It attacked the party for approaching the labour

[58] Petras, *Politics & Social Forces*, pp. 238–9. The incidents led to Castro's charge that Frei had promised revolution without bloodshed but had given Chile bloodshed without revolution.

[59] See the editorial, 'Huelgas y disparos' and the article by Gastón Cruzat,

movement in the same way as the other parties, as simply another area of inter-party struggle for domination. The general attitude of the government to labour was described as 'lack of understanding, and indifference'. *Mensaje* demanded that the government should do something to redeem its pledges to extend unionization and to reform the labour code.

The government and the party were not slow to defend their record. They pointed out that as early as 1966, a party congress blamed the intransigent opposition of the right and the marxists for the failure to reform the labour code.[60] However, the government's report to the congress maintained that the reform in the urban sector, though not that in the rural sector, had also been held up because the party was undecided.[61] The report pointed to a great deal of progress in the labour field—the rural unionization bill, the higher minimum wage, defence of workers against arbitrary dismissal—but indicated that many reforms were of such a profound nature that they needed a great deal of preparation. It was stated, for example, that the elimination of the difference between *obrero* and *empleado* partly depended on better educational facilities eliminating disparities in educational levels, and also on a thorough revision of the social security system, which had grown into an incredibly complex structure of differential privileges. Enterprise reform had been postponed because it had not been possible to proceed with the needed union reform and because the right attitude towards participation in enterprise management could not be expected from the present labour movement.[62] The assignment to all Chilean workers of a minimum wage at the level of the white-collar worker would, in the existing economic circumstances, mean a massive increase in inflation. Union reform could

---

'Huelgas y elecciones', in the same issue, Mar.–Apr. 1966, pp. 71–4 & 78–83. The sympathy strike was far from unanimously supported in the various mines —Chuquicamata mine, the largest, continued working normally. Frei's charge that the strike was politically motivated cannot of course be dismissed lightly; Cruzat in his article alleges (without reference to any source) that the majority of miners at El Salvador and El Teniente wanted to return to work but were held back by the leaders (quite how it is difficult to imagine).

[60] *Acuerdos del 2º Congreso*, 1966, pp. 31–2.

[61] PDC, *Informe: Programa de la revolución en libertad y su cumplimiento* (*Anexos del Tema no. 3*) (1966), p. 82.

[62] Ibid., p. 85. This sounds like the situation in Italy described by Margaret Lyon, 'Christian Democratic parties and politics', *J. Contemp. Hist.*, 2/4 (1967), p. 83.

not be considered in abstract; a great deal of other reform was necessary and until this was completed, the party ought not to make unrealistic demands on the government.

The Christian Democrats also took the offensive against the CUT, accusing the marxist parties of using the confederation to block the government's reform programme.[63] A magazine published by the office of the presidency accused the CUT of encouraging the presentation of excessive industry-wide wage demands. According to it, such demands had been made in the construction, metallurgical, and electricity-supply industries, by the shoe and leather workers, and so on—all calculated to break the government's wage-stabilization policy, for all far exceeded the rise in the cost of living.[64] The CUT replied—not without justice—that the official index was not an accurate measure of the real increase in the cost of living.

It was the question of the cost-of-living increase and the government's attempt to deal with inflation by wage-stabilization policies that brought about the sharpest confrontation in November 1967. The government proposed that for most of the public sector there should be a wage readjustment of 20% to take account of the inflation in 1967, but that 5% of it would not be paid in cash but into a special national savings account. The same was proposed for the private sector, except that employers would also pay an additional 5% into the savings account. The accumulated savings would then be used for national investments and would mean that the workers would be part-owners of the capital of the new enterprises. An interest of 5% per annum would be added to the accounts, but no withdrawals could be made except for unemployment or death.[65]

This proposal met a stormy reception in public and private sectors of the labour movement, and the support that labour received in Congress from the opposition parties, added to the uncertainty in the ranks of the government party, was enough to stop the proposals and lead to cabinet resignations. Not only did the

[63] See, e.g. the article by L. Ortega, 'Aspectos políticos de la crisis sindical chilena', *Política y espíritu*, Jan.–Mar. 1967, pp. 69–75.

[64] 'Pliegos únicos de peticiones', *Siempre el pueblo*, Feb. 1967, pp. 24–38.

[65] Though they could be used as security against mortgages, etc. For a general and critical account see Olavarría Bravo. For Frei's defence of his proposal see his speech on Television on 28 Nov. 1967, published as pamphlet by the government, *La unión hace la fuerza*.

unionists with good reason feel that such savings would soon dwindle to nothing with the normal Chilean inflation, but they also strongly opposed the proposals to link this scheme with restrictions on the right to strike. When this provision was voted on in the Congress, sixteen Christian Democrats opposed it and five more abstained.[66] The government was forced to drop the savings scheme and the limitations on the right to strike (partly, it was suggested, because the CP agreed to vote for the wage readjustment of 20% if the government would drop those two controversial items). Although, as usual, the extent of support for the November strikes was contested by the government, which claimed only a minority turnout, and by the CUT, which claimed overwhelming support, it was clear enough to the government that their proposals were so unpopular that they would be very difficult to enforce, and could never have obtained enough backing to be used as the basis of a new approach to the problems of investment and inflation. Frei was highly indignant at the way his proposals had been rejected. He pointed out that the workers themselves were to administer the fund. He accused the union leaders of irresponsibility, of working to provoke inflationary wage demands to serve their own political ends. The Radicals were indirectly attacked on the grounds of constantly restraining wages when in power but now presenting themselves as the champions of the unions. Frei strongly denied any government intention to suppress the right to strike; their intention was to limit its use in cases of excessive wage demands—and the ultimate beneficiaries of this scheme would be the workers.

No doubt many of Frei's points were justified. But such strong attacks on the unions hardly increased the government's popularity or made it easy for Christian Democratic unionists to defend it. There had been some redistribution of income to the working class in the first year or two of the Frei administration, but as there were no further benefits, the government's policy came under increasing attack. Neither had the government succeeded in winning union support. Thayer's policies as Minister of Labour had been almost as unpopular amongst his own party members as among unionists at large. He was accused by the rebel party faction of too regularly siding with the employers, of threatening reprisals against union leaders, of using the law in order to break

[66] Olavarría Bravo, p. 79. The rebel faction of the party campaigned strongly against the bill.

strikes.[67] Eventually his unpopularity led to his replacement by Eduardo León, who was more acceptable.

Unionists, both inside and outside the PDC felt that Frei had not lived up to his promises to consult the movement. This criticism was echoed in the presidential campaign of 1970 by the party candidate Tomic, complaining of lack of contact between the unions and the government. There were in fact a few overtures to the unions, but too few and too late. León instituted an open-door policy and claimed to have seen thirty-six different labour group representatives of over 300,000 workers, and he also tried to establish tripartite commissions of government, workers, and management to consider the problems of the gas and electricity industries.[68] But this was not until 1968, when the atmosphere had worsened too much to make these gestures effective. It was not until July 1969 that Frei addressed a meeting of copper workers to explain his policy in person.[69] He did promise to set up a grand Economic and Social Council with representatives from the unions to consider the problems of the nation, but this was not until his presidential message of May 1969.

*Mensaje*'s charges of lack of understanding and indifference may overstate the case. Basically it seems that government, after 1965, decided on a policy of conciliating investors, both private and foreign. It could not do that and continue to grant large wage increases and redistribute income—at least not in the short term, whatever its long-term intentions may have been. But a policy relying increasingly on private investment and private enterprise was forced to take tough measures against unions. There were also PDC trade unionists, however, and their mounting grievances against the government help to explain the leftward swing inside the party's union movement.

### 4. The process of radicalization

The PDC unionists have been subjected to conflicting pressures. On the one hand are the theorists like Thayer, the Catholic groups like ASICH, and right-wing union leaders like Moreno of COMACH, who believe that co-operation with marxist groups inside the

---

[67] L. Hernández Parker, article in *Desfile*, 21 Mar. 1967.

[68] 'Chile: a more flexible cabinet', *Latin America*, 8 Mar. 1968.

[69] This was at Chuquicamata, though the union leaders refused to meet him (*Ercilla*, 23–29 July 1969, p. 23).

unions is difficult, if not impossible, and that it is preferable for Christian Democrats to maintain their integrity even at the cost of complete separation from other groups. On the whole this group is associated with a less radical attitude to enterprise reform and union tactics generally. The cost to the unionist in joining this camp is that of ending up a member of a small sectarian group, trying to extend influence in ways that would be condemned if they were used by the marxists. The other wing in the party places far greater emphasis on the need for unity in the labour movement as a laudable and traditional aim of the working class, in the interests of which some doctrinal purity may have to be sacrificed. This group adopts a more militant attitude towards reform. The costs of following this policy are that it can put a great strain on party–union relations; one that is greatly increased when the party is in power.

This division does not correspond neatly to that between politicians and unionists. In the first camp fall some right-wing unionists and members of the more Catholic groups.[70] In the second camp are found not only those politicians who supported the rebel faction but a small number of one or two more prominent leaders, nearer to the corridors of power, who have always made a point of keeping in contact with the unions. Bernardo Leighton, when Minister of Interior in the Frei government, played an active role in labour disputes partly because he was respected and liked by unionists when they disliked Thayer.

The outlines of a new policy towards the unions was sketched by the rebel faction of the party in 1967.[71] They advocated a more

[70] Another prominent right wing unionist is the health workers' leader Waldo Grez, who caused a mild stir when he left the Socialist party in 1964 to support Frei's presidential campaign. The Christian Democratic union department subsequently resolved to send him before the party disciplinary tribunal for authoritarian methods he was using inside his union, including his habit of picking a fight whenever he was challenged (*Ultima hora*, 28 Aug. 1968).

[71] For full text see *Política y espiritu*, Oct. 1967, pp. 118–19. In the same issue of the journal Senator Patricio Aylwin criticized the report, arguing that it reversed the policy decision on union matters taken at the 2nd congress in 1966, and that a decision to recognize the CUT as the representative organ of Chilean labour would not have the support of the majority of the party. Senator Gumucio of the rebel faction replied to Aylwin in the same issue. For the views of the rebel faction on the use of the strike for political ends see, 'Las Huelgas Políticas', PEC., June 1967, pp. 7–8, reproduced from the rebel publication, *Documentación*.

'realistic' policy, involving recognizing and trying to work with the CUT. They argued that good relations with the unions were absolutely necessary for the government to carry out its promised reforms. The government was warned about the dangers of using provocative and bellicose language.

Their warnings were probably brought home to the government when in 1968 the PDC unionists in their congress gave a majority to a list of left-wing unionists, some closely identified with the rebel faction, to run the department. The congress decided to re-enter the CUT and began to issue radical declarations about the need for reform.[72] Shortly after the meeting the CUT postponed its 1968 congress, ostensibly to allow certain federations more time to organize their delegations, but actually in response to the Christian Democratic move to re-enter. The vote inside the unionists' meeting was decisive, though not unanimous—forty-four in favour, five against. The divisionist movement UTRACH was condemned and its leaders, among them Frei's adviser on labour matters, Emilio Caballero, were to be sent to the party's disciplinary tribunal. The meeting also resolved to ask the National Council of the party to order all Christian Democratic industrialists to hand over their enterprises, within six months, to be run by workers' representatives. Frei was reportedly very displeased with these decisions —his then Minister of the Interior, Pérez Zujovic, was a large industrialist who showed no signs of wishing to hand over his enterprises to his workers. Nor, apparently, was Frei particularly pleased with the decision to re-enter the CUT. Reflecting the move to the left, the new head of the union department, Alejandro Sepulveda, declared in an interview that the 'CUT should be made the instrument of the vanguard in the fight against the national oligarchy and American imperialism in order to realize a non-capitalist road of development'.[73]

The new leaders of the union department were clearly unhappy with the government. To emphasize that Christian Democratic unionists were expected to give their first loyalty to the union movement, the department issued a circular insisting that if the view of the Christian Democratic group in a union was not

[72] See the reports in *Ultima hora*, 16, 17, & 20 Sept. 1968, *La Nación* & *El Siglo* 18 Sept., and *Ercilla* 25 Sept. 1968. The left-wing list elected 3 national directors to the 2 of the minority list (including Waldo Grez) and 6 national councillors to the 4 of the minority list.

[73] Interview in *El Siglo*, 7 Nov. 1968.

accepted, it was to conform to the majority view. Local union leaders were not to take the initiative in deciding whether or not to support a strike; they should discuss with their followers if they considered the strike call to be justified or not and then report immediately to the executive of the union department, which would then decide the line of action.[74] Obviously the department was anxious to avoid the charge that, faced with industrial conflict, it acted on government instructions. In an interview the head of the department admitted that in the past Christian Democratic unionists had tried to prevent some strikes in the interests of the government's overall economic policy, but that in future they would not do so.[75] Asserting its new attitude of independence, the department defended a strike in the public sector in January 1969.

The most detailed exposition of the new ideas of the union department was contained in a long report, issued jointly with the youth and *campesino* departments, entitled 'Plan for a non-capitalist development: revolutionary strategy for the socialist transformation of the country'.[76] That it was issued jointly with two other departments shows that dissatisfaction with the government and party hierarchy was not confined to the union department; indeed the youth department had always been in the forefront of the radical movements in the party, the union department being the relative latecomer. The report began by stating that the first years of government revealed the inadequacies of the party principles and of the remedies generally accepted as instruments in the transformation of the country. The party had always rejected capitalism and had always offered as an alternative the communitarian society; what it lacked was a strategy to implement this. The inability to devise a strategy capable of attracting popular support was a criticism that could be levelled against the marxist parties as well; a totally new approach was necessary. The report denied that any of its inspiration came from communism, as the right alleged. On the contrary, if it derived inspiration from anywhere it was from the efforts of third-world countries to liberate themselves from imperialism and dependence. The report was concerned with the difficulties of the transition period between capitalism and socialism; it stressed that the final objective is socialism, and that

[74] Sec. Gen., Departamiento Nacional Sindical, *Normas para la acción sindical* (26 Sept. 1968, mimeo).

[75] Interview with the president of the union dept, Dec. 1968 (Santiago).

[76] The report is contained in *El Mercurio*, 26 Dec. 1968 & 3 Jan. 1969.

this can only be achieved by the masses taking power and transforming the state. When power has been achieved, there will follow a rapid extension of nationalization, of agrarian reform, and of economic planning involving control of the commercial and banking network. The transitional period will still see the survival of property forms appropriate to the bourgeoisie and petty bourgeoisie (capitalism and individual ownership), but the continuing process of class war and struggle will culminate in the victory of proletarian forms of production (state ownership, co-operatives).

The report seeks to minimize differences inside the party and between the party and government by arguing that all hold to a vision of the communitarian society; but little has been done to realize this vision in practice. The party needs a total strategy to transform capitalist society. This can be done only by transforming the basis of power, by making it popular, by involving the people and their representative organs such as unions, in the process of social transformation.

In many ways an odd mixture of socialism and Christian Democratic theory, the report emphasizes the class nature of society and the class struggle, but combines this with a peaceful, gradual, and co-operative plan of social transformation. It attacks capitalism and private property, but expects both to work in harmony with the state and socialist sector for their own destruction. In the transition period the centralized, planning bureaucratic state is the paramount instrument of transformation; but when this has performed its function it will be replaced by communitarian or socialist society—the words are used almost interchangeably.

The report is perhaps less important for what it says than for what it represents. The Frei government had had an important impact on the Christian Democratic trade union movement. It had grown larger and stronger and had become more mature and independent. It was less content to receive instructions and theoretical guidance from the party hierarchy. It emphasized its attachment to the party less and its links with the working-class movement more. It became more radical; under the pressure of attacks from the marxists and Radicals in the labour movement, it justified its allegiance to the movement by joining in the criticisms of the government's economic policy and by trying to devise alternative theoretical formulations which would bring the party back in line with its original promise of revolution.

This new trend is far from definitive. There are still strong groups that would prefer a unified Catholic labour movement to participation in the CUT. Nor is the move to the left necessarily irreversible. Chilean politics has seen far more dramatic and sudden changes. Nevertheless, the increasing radicalism of the Christian Democratic union movement is important, not merely because it demonstrates a greater degree of independence and maturity but also because it brings into question the doctrine and strategy of the party itself.

# 9. The Unions and the Parties

UNION activity in Chile could hardly fail to be political. Because the government plays such an important role in virtually all areas of industrial relations, and because at least the larger unions must be as active in Congress and in the ministerial departments as on the shop floor, industrial relations necessarily take on a political dimension. The question at issue is not so much whether unions are engaged in politics—for they obviously are—but the extent of their politicization. How far are the actions of unions, or their methods, or their general ideas derived from a political ideology or influenced by party rather than union considerations?

This question must be placed in the national political context. Unionists are also citizens and voters, and in a democratic, highly politicized and partisan society it is to be expected that this will be reflected in the union movement. Issues arising in unions need not necessarily take on a political character or become party matters, but can well be made political issues by parties and their spokesmen.[1] Where also the political divisions in a society are not simply between classes but also within them, as in the Chilean working class, naturally the larger partisan divisions are also reflected inside the labour movement.[2] One may compare Argentina, where the balance of power between the two groups is quite distinct, and

[1] Lipset & others, *Union Democracy*, pp. 208–9. They write that in the ITU chapels 'the open introduction of union politics is informally prohibited. Many union leaders explain this prohibition by noting that the issues of chapel politics—personalities and the administration of chapel affairs—are not related to the differences and issues between the two union parties. But as can be seen at the local and international levels of the ITU, almost any issue can be converted into a partisan issue.'

[2] Thus Di Tella & others (p. 58) explain the fact of politicization of Chilean unions largely in terms of the lack of a union bureaucracy, and the form of that politicization in terms of weak unions and strong parties, so that union groups have little independent influence over their parent parties.

where the labour movement is so overwhelmingly dominant that there is in effect an amalgamation of union and party, with the party's identity submerged in that of the unions.[3]

It is far more complicated than it seems to try to divide union activities into 'economic' and 'political', a point made by Eldridge when he summarizes the main explanations of active unrest leading to strikes. These are: (1) economic advantage—unions are in business to maximize wages; (2) job security; (3) class warfare—the unions are the embodiment of the working class reacting to capitalist exploitation; (4) political, emphasizing the primacy of political conflict (often stressing the influence of communism) whether between unions and management over the recognition of unions and over collective bargaining, or between unions over jurisdictional disputes, or inside unions over internal leadership rivalries; (5) human relations, i.e. explanations in terms of the breakdown of primary groups among workers or the lack of understanding between management and workers.[4] The difficulty is, as he points out, that *all* these elements may be present as causes, and that while some union leaders may have reformist–economic ends, others, engaged in the same strike, may well have revolutionary–political ends.

One cannot classify union leaders as politically motivated simply because they employ party rhetoric, unless it is possible to establish a clear line of authority between party and unionist. V. L. Allen writes that in practice real union militancy refers more to methods than to aims: 'it is not what unions are pressing for which matters so much as how they are pressing'.[5] This distinction is less applicable in the Chilean case, given the deep ideological divisions. Nevertheless, what matters is not so much what union spokesmen say in the open congresses of the CUT as to how they lead their unions, and this cannot be determined simply by examining their avowed political philosophies.

It is difficult to generalize about the whole labour movement and the extent of its politicization, for some sectors are undoubtedly more politicized than others. If the extent of politicization in the activities of the CUT is unmistakable, the significance of this for the

---

[3] E. Gallo, 'Divisions in the Argentine labour movement', *BOLSA R.*, Nov. 1968, p. 613.
[4] J. T. Eldridge (following Neil Smelser), *Industrial Disputes* (London, 1968), p. 57.
[5] *Militant Trade Unionism* (London, 1966), pp. 18–19.

labour movement as a whole depends on the importance of the CUT and the power or influence it has over its constituent members. Similarly, that there are individual union leaders who are highly politicized is beyond question, but what does remain a question is firstly how relevant their political beliefs are for their industrial action, and secondly how influential they are, in their capacity as unionist–politician, over the bulk of the rank and file. [6]

Politicization of unions is usually considered in relation to a labour movement where either one party or ideological movement enjoys overwhelming support in the union world, or where ideological divisions correspond to separate unions. Normally it is assumed that unions are one-party governments. Clark Kerr argues that 'there are no continuing conflicts except over ideology, and ideological conflicts tend to split unions rather than to create two-party systems within them'. Other issues, pay claims for example, may lead to factions and leadership rivalry but not to two-party systems. [7] Yet Chilean unions are not split into separate ideological entities; one of their most striking features is the continuing co-operation between supporters of different parties on the same executive. Politicization does not therefore automatically fragment the labour movement—though it is true enough that the major causes of disagreement in the Chilean movement are party disputes. If party interests push unionists apart, may there not also be a union interest or ideology that keeps them together, a sense of the tradition of working-class unity which acts against party attempts at division? This is not the only reason for the existence of multi-party executives; legal requirements keep plant unions united, and at present at any rate political pressures also generally work for a united labour movement. Nevertheless, simply because a union leader is a member of a political party it is wrong to assume that he acts as a party agent in his union—indeed, as we have seen, parties often complain that their unionist affiliates are far too bound up with their unions.

---

[6] That there are active partisans at all is of course of some importance. As Lipset & others write (pp. 214–15): 'By bringing union politics into the chapel in ways that force them upon the attention of less active and partisan men, the active partisans are important to their union's political processes far out of proportion to their numbers. These active partisans convert *potential* political arenas into *actual* ones by channeling union concerns into union politics and by injecting political issues into the networks of social relationships that flourish in the larger shops.' Their italics.

[7] Kerr, *Labor Management*, p. 31.

## The CUT

Several national confederations exist in Chile, but unquestionably the largest and most powerful is the CUT, founded in 1953.[8] Not long before the electoral victory of Allende, of the existing 79 federations 49 were affiliated to the CUT, bringing with them well over 60% of all unionists.[9] Exact figures of membership are vague, if only because the normally chaotic financial state of the CUT makes it virtually impossible to see which federations and unions have paid their dues; membership inflates rapidly as a congress approaches and declines thereafter—as the basic reason for paying dues for many unions (the right to attend a congress) ceases to be relevant for another three years. The CUT itself claims that the great majority of organized workers are members, and that of its members 60% are *obreros* and 40% *empleados*. Anxious to emphasize its proletarian base it also claims that 40% of its members are miners and industrial workers.[10] Rather more important than estimates of membership is the extent of support the CUT obtains for its activities and objectives, and this has varied as much as nominal affiliation.

The CUT's objectives, as set out in the Declaration of Principles, have continually been modified ever since 1953, largely in an effort by the CP to keep Christian Democrats and Radicals inside the organization.[11] The existing Declaration condemns the 'chronic incapacity of the capitalist regime that, based on the private ownership of land and the instruments and means of production, divides society into opposing classes'.[12] The enemy is defined—the landowning oligarchy, the capitalist bourgeoisie, imperialism—but the solution has been modified from 'complete socialism' to a less specific 'transformation of society'. These objectives are rather less pressing than the aims outlined by each congress when it discusses policy. In 1968, as always, an important

---

[8] The best single work on the CUT, a mine of information, is Barría's *Trayectoria*.

[9] US Dept of Labor, *Labor Law*, p. 39; Zapata, *Federaciones y centrales en el sindicalismo* (1968), p. 6. Since then CEPCH and COMACH have entered CUT, considerably increasing the official membership. Barría (*Trayectoria*, pp. 387–9) gives a list of the major federations and national unions in the CUT. Of the 49 federations, 36 were 'free' or not legally recognized, and 13 were legal.

[10] *Memoria del consejo directivo al 5° congreso*, p. 18.

[11] See ch. 8.

[12] CUT, *Declaración de principios y estatutos* (Santiago, 1965), p. 1.

P

preoccupation was union organization, and the executive proposed that great efforts should be made to bring into the CUT workers outside it and to reorganize existing structures into large industry-wide federations.[13] The executive stated it would work for a more rapid and drastic agrarian reform, would prevent penetration by imperialist interests, would advocate widespread nationalization and state control, would work for the direct representation of workers in the management and direction of state enterprises and social-security agencies; and it advocated financing new investment by stiffer taxes for foreign concerns and the rich. The government's wage policies were roundly condemned and the CUT called for tripartite commissions of its own representatives, employers, and the government to establish wage increases. The platform also contained a number of urgent suggestions for combating inflation and monopolies and issued a call for united action to almost all social sectors apart from the bourgeoisie.

The supreme authority is the national congress which is supposed to meet every three years. It consists of delegates elected by local trade unions and the members of the CUT executive (the Consejo Directivo Nacional), five members from each federation or national union and five delegates from the CUT provincial councils. The congress divides into a number of commissions to discuss various aspects of union affairs, but its most important function is that of electing the executive.

The number of unions attending the national congress varies considerably. In the founding congress 35 federations and national unions and 913 local unions were represented; in 1957 there were representatives from 41 national unions, but only 438 from local unions; but by 1962 the figures were 40 and 1,042 respectively.[14] Membership in CUT is not stable; COMACH, though a founder member, left the CUT in 1957 and did not return till ten years later; for a short period even the copper workers left the CUT; and the bank workers' federation also left it in 1957. The occupational background of the delegates to the congresses is shown opposite.

CUT congresses are notable not so much for the varying attendance of unions as for the different distribution of political forces. The CUT is an overwhelmingly political organization not only because most of its attention must be focused on, and its activities

[13] *Memoria del consejo directivo*, p. 4.

[14] Barría, *Trayectoria*, pp. 178–80. The information in this paragraph is based on this work.

directed at, the government rather than the employers, but more significantly because the major divisions inside it run along party lines. The main CUT groups are organized on a party political basis. Unionists meet with their party advisers before and during the congresses to discuss tactics, and the choice of candidates to be included in the list to be presented for election. Lists presented for election to the executive are not alliances of one union with another, but of members of the same party affiliation from different unions, and the ties that bind groups of union leaders together on the executive are political ones.

*Occupational distribution of delegates to* CUT *Congresses*

|  | *1957* | *1959* | *1962* |
|---|---|---|---|
| Industrial workers (*obreros*) | 526 | 540 | 836 |
| Miners | 138 | 163 | 214 |
| Total *obreros* | 664 | 703 | 1,050 |
| Private-sector employees | 26 | 38 | 121 |
| State employees | 401 | 364 | 641 |
| Municipal employees | 66 | 66 | 102 |
| Total public sector | 467 | 420 | 743 |
| Agricultural workers | 9 | 32 | 166 |
| Self-employed (*comerciantes*) in commerce | 14 | 35 | 80 |
| Pensioners | 7 | 19 | 41 |
|  | 1,187 | 1,257 | 2,201 |

*Source:* Barría, *Trayectoria*, p. 188.

It is obvious why the election of the executive should be the main function of the congress. Union affairs cannot be discussed properly in a meeting of 2,000 delegates. On political issues, each congress repeats the debate going on in the country at large between the parties. The importance of the congresses lies in the rise and fall of parties on the executive and in the political alliances that are made. The relative standing of the parties is shown in the tables on pp. 216 & 217.

The very formation of the CUT was evidence of the primacy of political over union factors. The impetus to repair the damage to the union movement caused by the bitter split in the CTCh came from the same political groups that had brought about those divisions. All political groups favoured unity. The Radicals, who

*Voting for, and composition of, the* CUT *executive*

| | 1953 | | | 1957 | | | 1959 | |
|---|---|---|---|---|---|---|---|---|
| *List 1* | *Votes* | *Councillors* | *List 1* | *Votes* | *Councillors* | *List 1* | *Votes* | *Councillors* |
| Anarchist | 188 | 3 | Socialist and Communists | 825 | 20 | Trotskyist | 17 | 0 |
| *List 2* | | | *List 2* | | | *List 2* | | |
| Communist Socialistas de Chile Radical Falangist | 903 | 13 | Radical Socialists-dissident | 163 | 4 | Communist | 645 | 12 |
| *List 3* | | | *List 3* | | | *List 3* | | |
| PSP Socialist-dissident Supporters of Ibáñez—the ('Independents') | 657 | 9 | Trotskyist | 18 | 0 | Socialist | 405 | 8 |
| *List 4* | | | | | | | | |
| Trotskyist | 18 | 0 | | | | | | |
| TOTAL | 1,766 | 25 | | 1,006 | 24 | | 1,067 | 20 |

Abstention 589
(many delegations could not get to the conference, or could not stay—largely because of financial reasons. Later on political impediments also played a part.)

Abstention 354
(mostly Christian Democrats and anarchists. PDC given 4 councillors to re-integrate them into CUT. Most anarchist groups had by 1957 withdrawn from CUT.)

Abstention 373
(mostly Christian Democrats and Radicals and anarchists.)

Sources: 1953–62 figures from Barría, *Trayectoria*. This is in turn based upon newspaper accounts, conference reports, and some inspired arithmetic. 1965 & 1968 figures compiled from newspaper reports and conference records. The number of councillors *directly* elected changed from conference to conference. The total vote is usually greater than the sum of the votes for the lists as it includes a small number of null or blank votes.

had lost power in 1952, were prepared to combine with other union groups to protect their interests. The temporarily revived anarcho-syndicalist movement hoped that sectarianism would be buried in a new move for unity and lent their enthusiastic support to the formation of the CUT. The Communists, then illegal, and once more following a change in the international line, were anxious to emerge from isolation. Even the followers of General Ibáñez formed a Front to participate in the new surge of united action and combined with the PSP. The one important block that was independent of these party positions consisted of a number of important federations—amongst them the copper, railway, and maritime unions—which had joined or at least sympathized with the ICFTU and its inter-American affiliate the ORIT. The leaders of these independent federations were in fact mostly former Socialists, disillusioned with both Socialist parties. However, their independence from party affiliations was not to last long, and with the exception of the maritime workers they soon left the ORIT

| 1962 | | | 1965 | | | 1968 | | |
|---|---|---|---|---|---|---|---|---|
| List 1 | Votes | Councillors | List 1 | Votes | Councillors | List 1 | Votes | Councillors |
| Revolutionary groups | Retired | | Communist | 890 | 11 | Communist | 134,250 | 14 |
| List 2 | | | List 2 | | | List 2 | | |
| Independent | 12 | 0 | Trotskyist | 20 | 0 | Socialist | 63,818 | 7 |
| List 3 | | | List 3 | | | List 3 | | |
| Communist | 751 | 6 | Socialist | 696 | 9 | Christian Democrats | 30,165 | 3 |
| List 4 | | | | | | List 4 | | |
| Socialists | 686 | 5 | | | | Radicals | 23,825 | 2 |
| List 5 | | | | | | List 5 | | |
| Christian Democrats and Radicals | 583 | 4 | | | | Popular Socialists (Ampuero's group) | 11,519 | 1 |
| | | | | | | List 6 | | |
| | | | | | | MIR | 4,067 | 1 |
| | 2,065 | 15 | | 1,670 | 20 | | 267,644 | 28 |
| Abstention | 349 | | Abstention | 434 | | Abstention | 277 | |

(1965) Abstention 434 (mostly Christian Democrats and Radicals.)

(1968) The voting system was changed for the 1968 congress; hence the larger number of votes cast, though the number of delegates (2,951 in all) had increased.

for the CUT, associated with one or other of the normal political participants.[15]

The tensions inside the CUT reflect the tensions between the political parties. Generally in the CUT the Socialists echo the party's insistence on revolutionary action (though likewise in a rather vague way); the Radicals and the Christian Democrats struggle to make their more moderate, if conflicting, views of unionism prevail; and the Communists, with a fair degree of success, attempt to act as brokers between the others.[16] Perhaps

[15] Barría, *Trayectoria*, p. 38–44. See also Oscar Núñez, *Diez años de lucha de los trabajadores* (1963), pp. 6–7. He also refers to the role of the students federation (the Federación de Estudiantes or FECH) which helped to create contacts between all these groups by bringing them into a 'Command against Price Rises and Speculations'.

[16] Thus Figueroa reported to the CP that the 'Organizing Commission of the 4th congress is composed of 11 members, of whom 3 are Communists, 3 Socialists, 3 Christian Democrats, and 2 Radicals which guarantees a widely representative Congress' (PCC, *Pleno de abril de 1965*, p. 41).

this CP role deserves special emphasis, for it has made great efforts to unite the labour movement, placating dissidents to the right and left, emphasizing the importance of respecting democratic principles and the right of dissent. It has been far more prepared to compromise than the Socialist party, partly because Communists, much more than Socialists, look back favourably on the Popular Front victory—a victory achieved because the Communists were prepared to be compromising and self-effacing.

*Political affiliation of delegates to CUT congresses (per cent)*

| Political allegiance | 1953 | 1957 | 1959 | 1962 | 1965 | 1968 |
|---|---|---|---|---|---|---|
| Communist | 21·3 | 39·9 | 44·7 | 31·1 | 42·3 | 45·5 |
| Socialist | | | | | | |
| Popular | 12·7 | 22·9 | 28·1 | 28·4 | 33·1 | 21·6[1] |
| de Chile | 4·2 | — | — | — | | 3·0[2] |
| Diss. | 8·4 | 3·0 | — | — | | |
| Radical | 6·3 | 9·0 | 4·1 | 6·2 | 4·8 | 8·1 |
| PDC | 6·3 | 14·7 | 14·6 | 17·9 | 11·9 | 10·2 |
| Anarchist | 7·9 | 2·2 | 2·0 | 2·0 | | 1·4[3] |
| Trotskyist | 0·7 | 1·3 | 1·1 | 0·8 | 1·0 | |
| Independent | 6·6 | — | — | 0·5 | | |
| Non-classifiable & absent | 25·6 | 8·8 | 5·0 | 12·9 | 7·2 | 9·4 |

[1] The main Socialist party     [2] Ampuero's USP     [3] MIR

*Source:* Ibid. Barría uses voting figures as an indication of political allegiance of delegates. By no means as accurate as the above table would seem to indicate, it is nonetheless, a broad guide. Percentages do not always add up to 100 because of rounding.

Divisions within parties also have repercussions in the CUT. When the Socialist party split in 1967, six CUT leaders who followed Ampuero, including the secretary-general, Oscar Núñez, were suspended from their duties, despite protests against this allegedly unconstitutional action.

Not only is the CUT executive divided up between party groups; even the election of delegates from the base unions appears to reflect the same sort of division. The CP repeatedly criticizes the widespread practice of composing delegations according to the distribution of political forces inside the local union instead of allowing for free and open elections of the delegates.[17]

[17] Astudillo, 'Perspectivas del 2° congreso de la CUT', *Principios*, Feb. 1960, pp. 14–15.

The parties do not only arrange for the election of delegates but are active during the whole congress proceedings, including its various commissions. Party technicians draft reports to be discussed and help edit the final versions and brief the often uninformed delegates on what to say and who to vote for. The discussions and speeches in the general meetings and in the commissions are more often of a political than a union nature; speakers are as likely to identify themselves by their political affiliation as their union membership—though the Communists disapprove of this. There are also ideological disagreements at the congresses; at the 1968 congress, for example, the Socialists held up the proceedings for several hours because they argued that the terms of reference of the various commissions were not sufficiently anti-imperialist and were too technocratic and class collaborationist.[18]

This party domination is criticized from inside the union movement as well as from outside. The first CUT president, Blest, a radical but non-aligned leader, constantly opposed the influence of the parties. In a May Day speech in 1957 he declared that the CUT 'must renovate itself or fade away . . . the union movement has been transformed into a purely economic body. . . . Party action has divided up the CUT into sectarian parcels and has prevented any real and positive action.'[19] Blest was useful to the marxist parties as a kind of non-political front to deflect right-wing accusations that the CUT was simply the extension of the parties. But when the CP was no longer banned and when Blest became rather more dangerous as his increasingly violent message gained in credibility after the Cuban revolution, as has been seen, he was quickly and brutally dropped. The specific cause was disagreement when he wished to extend and make general strike action

---

[18] The author was present at the 5th congress in Santiago in November 1968 and felt he had to agree with the rapporteur of the First Commission that this was the worst organized conference he had ever attended (the rapporteur's comment provoked furious booing from the audience). I would estimate that 25% of the time of the 4½-day congress was spent waiting for something to happen (halls due to be open at 9 a.m. for a commission to start proceedings opened at 11 a.m.); 25% on formalities like fraternal greetings from various national and foreign delegations—including an hour-long speech in Korean; 40% on procedural wrangling—who should compose commissions, who could vote, etc.; and 10% on debating and discussing issues, which were mostly occasions for Communist–Socialist confrontation.

[19] Vitale, p. 101.

that the marxist parties wished to call off, but there were, as he indicated in his resignation speech, more basic disagreements as well. 'I believe in direct massive action; others in legalism and co-operation with the pseudo-democratic bourgeoisie. The CUT ought to be the leader and vanguard of the working class and not the simple plaything of events and circumstances, and what is worse, an instrument of organizations alien to the Chilean labour movement.'[20]

If the CUT had been constantly strong and united as well as politicized, it could have been a very influential body in the Chilean political system. It became stronger and more influential during the last years of the Frei administration—not only through its own efforts but because the government's wages policy made it more important.[21] Even so, for most of its life its weaknesses were more evident than its strengths.

One of these weaknesses has been revealed by the need to change, at nearly every congress, the method of forming the executive in order to try to secure a more active body. Inevitably a number of executive members hardly bothered with the CUT activities. The reports of the executive to the national congresses usually criticized the failure of some CUT departments because those leaders nominally in charge were busy elsewhere. The problem is especially acute when executive members are also leaders of important federations or unions, for in these cases the federation or union takes first place and the CUT second place. To try to inculcate greater responsibility the statutes were changed at the 3rd congress to allow each federation with more than 3,000 paid-up members to nominate a representative to the executive, but at the 4th congress it was reported that 'the majority of the federations did not have permanent representatives. The comrades who were nominated only maintained sporadic contact'.[22]

[20] His speech is contained in the *Memoria del CDN al 3° CUT congreso nacional ordinario 1–5 Aug. 1962* (1962), pp. 23–4. The Socialist party for all its self-announced revolutionary aims joined with the Communists in getting rid of Blest.

[21] It will undoubtedly become even more influential during the Allende administration. But there are obvious constraints on its growth, such as continuing party rivalry, the ability and intention of the PDC to block pro-CUT legislation in Congress, and the Chilean tendency to view the executive and Congress as the focus of political activity and importance.

[22] *Memoria del consejo directivo nacional al 4° CUT congreso nacional ordinario, 25–8 Aug. 1965* (1965), p. 25.

A similar problem arises with the body which is intended to put the CUT executive in touch with representatives of the major unions. This body was supposed to advise the CUT executive of views in the federations and then to transmit to the federations the decisions of the joint meetings of the CUT executive and federation leaders. Unfortunately the federations largely ignored the meetings. The delegates who did attend had no authority to commit their unions and made no real attempts to report back the results of the meetings. The leaders of the federations were usually too much occupied with their own union business to attend the meetings. Rarely are the leading executive members of the CUT itself prominent leaders of large federations. The present president, Figueroa, though technically a printing worker, has in practice been a CP functionary for many years and is now also a deputy; the secretary-general, the Socialist Hernán del Canto, a former leader of the Socialist Youth, is a young employee of the municipality of San Miguel in Santiago; the previous Socialist secretary-general was a primary schoolteacher, more prominent in the activities of the party than the teachers' union. The CUT can afford to pay salaries to only a small and varying number of its executive (between four and seven), and it is not important enough for a major federation to pay a union leader only to represent it before the CUT. State employees—Blest is an obvious example—have always been prominent in the CUT leadership, partly because the political involvement of the CUT makes its activities very relevant for them and because, like the CUT itself, unions in that sector operate outside the framework of the labour code.[23]

The structural weakness of the CUT is also reflected in its regional organization. The 3rd congress resolved that there should be a special effort to revive the regional organization, but the executive's report to the 4th congress indicated little success. Most of the provincial CUTs—with the exception of a few mining and industrial areas—have a very irregular life and lack funds and organizers. Unions and federations that are affiliated to the CUT nationally are often not affiliated to their local branch. The reluctance of unions to bother with their local CUT is understandable. If the importance of CUT lies in its national political role, then only the national body

[23] The report of the Izquierda Sindical y Partido Obrero Revolucionaria (1959) (a Trotskyist group) to the 3rd congress, criticizes the over-representation of artisanal and *empleado* sectors on the CUT executive and the lack of representatives from industrial and mining unions (p. 17).

can be of much use to unions. Those that do exist are often very narrow sectarian bodies that have been captured for the exclusive use of a political faction.[24]

Perhaps the weakness of the CUT is shown most clearly in its poverty. Starting reasonably well it could afford to pay modest salaries to seven leaders, soon to be reduced to four.[25] Unions do not pay the dues set by the national congresses. At first the situation was not critical, and for three years 70% of expenditure could be met out of income; after that up to 70% had to be met out of extraordinary measures such as loans, special collections, and so on, including a loan from the WFTU. The CUT treasurer at the 1957 congress denounced those federations and provincial organizations which, when they (infrequently) collected dues for the CUT, usually appropriated them for their own use.

Attempts to produce a newspaper or periodical have always failed for lack of finance, and the only vehicle it has ever possessed was the car presented by the Soviet Embassy in Santiago on behalf of the Soviet trade unions. Even by 1968, when the CUT was becoming increasingly important, it was reported that only 85,000 workers on average were paying monthly dues. One reason why the CUT has sought legal recognition is that this would permit it to request employers to deduct union dues at source. Otherwise it is difficult to see any solution to its financial weakness; and party influence is strengthened by the fact that many of the financial obligations of the CUT and the payment of its leaders, even of union dues just before congresses, is undertaken by parties and not by unions.

This financial weakness, apart from any other factor, has hindered any attempt the CUT might wish to make to transform union organization in Chile or to organize the unorganized. Congress after congress hears the call for the creation of nation-wide unions, for the formation of larger federations, for industry-wide bargaining, but there have been no initiatives worthy of note. In the first place, the organization of the CUT itself, especially of the often lifeless departments, is hardly an advertisement for

[24] *Memoria del CDN al 4° congreso*, p. 25. See also O. Núñez, 'Balance del paro nacional', *Arauco*, Nov. 1962, p. 20.

[25] Barría, *Trayectoria*, p. 305. Even here political considerations were important; the original seven posts had to be divided carefully between 3 Communists, 1 Socialista de Chile, 1 Socialista Popular, 1 anarcho-syndicalist, and 1 Christian Democrat.

union organization.[26] The report of the CTC 1955 conference strongly criticized the CUT, pointing out the

annoyance and ill-feeling felt in the bases of the CTC for the lack of interest, lack of directness, lack of solidarity shown by some of the national leaders of the CUT on repeated occasions, in a way that has damaged the material and economic interests of the copper workers and even contributed in very large part to the adoption of repressive measures on the part of the government.[27]

Even if there did exist, as one executive report put it a 'certain bureaucratic tendency to direct the CUT by circular instead of direct contact with provincial leaders',[28] the CUT still lacks financial means and an administrative structure anywhere near adequate to set about transforming the trade unions.

Until relatively recently the stronger federations tended to ignore the CUT when they were engaged in the process of collective bargaining, even if this process broke down and resulted in a strike. There was little consultation about the overall nature of union demands to be put to employers and no co-ordinated plan of action to oppose the capitalist system.[29] The CUT executive continually issued warnings about the uselessness of fighting the economic battle on a large number of tiny fronts, and criticized the lack of solidarity of most unions with their comrades. The executive accused union leaders of egotism and mistrust, and referred to 'the incomprehensible attitude of respected leaders who stick to the belief that they have the obligation of ensuring

[26] Barría (ibid., p. 260) writes that 'in spite of the resolutions taken and the interest that has been aroused, little has been done in this field (i.e. the formation of single industry-wide unions) and the CDN as a body has taken no positive action, except for sending around circulars and propaganda.' Moreover, he writes that nothing has been done about trying to spread union organization to the unorganized, partly because the CUT has not succeeded in organizing itself properly.

[27] *Estatutos y informe del 2° CUT congreso ordinario* (La Serena, 1955), p. 21. The copper union leaders felt that they had not received much support in a strike; though they also admitted that they had hardly been active in supporting the CUT.

[28] *Memoria del CDN al 3° congreso*, p. 19.

[29] Barría (*Trayectoria*, p. 264) quotes the report of the president of the CDN to the 2nd CUT national congress to the effect that few unions bother to consult the CUT about their strike proposal, and that even worse, when they do so, and the CDN opposes them, they still carry out the strike. 'In spite of the fact that there are very precise instructions in this matter, member unions ignore them. This has been the cause of the gravest internal difficulties inside the CUT.'

that the workers do not rise above their local cares to contemplate the need to overthrow the exploiting regime'.[30]

The CUT was, until the last year or so of the Frei administration, largely ignored by the PDC government. Unlike the earlier CTCH (and before the Allende government), it had no permanent representatives on any of the planning organs of the state or on any of the social security boards; only by a legal technicality was it able for a short time to elect a representative to the board of the Central Bank. Relations between the unions and the Frei government were generally bad; relations between it and the CUT were even worse. In 1968 the CUT president referred bitterly to a circular issued by the Ministry of Labour expressly forbidding legal unions to organize payment of dues to the CUT. This was in spite of repeated offers by the CUT to collaborate with the government over such matters as wage policies, social-security legislation, and so on.[31] No doubt many Christian Democrats read this offer as a hope by the unions to embarrass the government still more by making unreasonable demands in any commissions set up. That this was not necessarily the case was shown by the agreement reached by the government and the CUT to fix the level of salary readjustments for the public sector for 1969. The strongest group in the CUT are undoubtedly the Communists. While they naturally hoped for the electoral defeat of the Christian Democrats, they were very firmly committed to the maintenance of the electoral process; hence the strong solidarity expressed by the CUT and the CP, though not by the Socialist party, with the government when there was an unsuccessful military threat not long before the end of the Frei government.

Perhaps the Christian Democrats took the public utterances of the CUT leaders too seriously. During most of its history the CUT has been more noted for making declarations of faith than for putting its strength to the test. It has often seemed to be torn between the anti-capitalist character of its Declaration of Principles and the day-to-day needs of a fragmented union movement fighting not one battle but a large number of skirmishes which are often more of a holding operation than an advance. Yet in some ways this approximates to Lenin's recommendations for building a united union movement—a combination of concrete struggles for immediate objectives plus a long-term unifying ideological vision

[30] *Memoria del CDN al 3° congreso*, p. 12.
[31] *Informe del consejo directivo al 5° congreso nacional*, p. 4.

which gives a greater sense of purpose to the daily struggles. The persistent problem for the CUT has been to relate the long-term political vision to the daily struggles—but no revolutionary expects victory to come easily and smoothly.

The CUT has had most success in mobilizing workers for political action when the call to arms has coincided with the desire of some powerful single federation or group of unions to strike for economic ends, as increasingly occurred in the last two years of the PDC government. But in earlier times the CUT call to action was often unsuccessful, and the failures resulted in real setbacks for the union movement. For example, in 1956 it called for a general strike to protest against the anti-inflationary measures of President Ibáñez, taken on the advice of the controversial Klein–Saks mission to Chile. Not only was the strike poorly supported, but Ibáñez, using his powers under the Law for Defence of Democracy, arrested many national and local labour leaders and succeeded in disrupting the CUT national and local organizations. The strike was badly planned (it had already been preceded by a number of limited strikes) and the call for a general, unlimited strike which Blest advocated had less than an enthusiastic reception in the CP.[32] Moreover, the results of the anti-inflationary measures were not completely predictable and many unionists preferred to adopt a wait-and-see attitude. An even more dismal failure—which this time merely brought about a loss of prestige, not reprisals—was the call for a strike in May 1961 in support of the Cuban revolution.

The help of the CUT was not always very effective in supporting strikes by its members. If a union is strong enough it will not need CUT help; if it is weak, then the help of Congressmen is likely to be more useful than that of the CUT. In a prolonged strike of the health workers' union in 1963 the CUT talked of calling sympathy strikes. But without the support of its constituent federations the only result was that it gave the opportunity to the government to com-

---

[32] Thus incidentally demonstrating that CUT action, to be successful, needs the prior approval and backing of the major parties. On the strike see Burnett, pp. 157–9 & Barría, *Trayectoria*, pp. 103 & 283. Blest accused the marxist parties of destroying the strike by issuing a return to work only a few hours after the strike was due to start—not that many had supported the call anyhow. Blest himself had called off a strike in July 1955 when the federations favoured prolonging it, as he thought he had received assurances from an intermediary of President Ibáñez of the President's willingness to seek agreement (Zapata, *Federaciones y centrales*, p. 12).

plain of political interference.[33] Though the strike lasted for twenty-five days and involved bitter street clashes, it was obvious that the crucial support for the health workers came from the political parties (decisive when the Radicals in Congress opposed their colleagues in the cabinet who were supporting Alessandri's stand against the union) rather than from other unions.

Yet like its predecessor the CTCh, the CUT has enjoyed good years as well as bad, and a combination of increasing inflation and official attempts to contain it of necessity brought the CUT more into the centre of affairs. National opposition was needed to national plans, and for all its faults the CUT was the only instrument available to bring together public and private-sector unions in, for example, the successful opposition to the forced savings-scheme tax of November 1967. Indeed, the success of that venture did much good to the CUT; it became more optimistic and confident, as was reflected in the more hopeful executive report to the 1968 congress.[34] This optimism had firm political foundations. The Communists were well organized and growing; the Socialists had lost their chief theoretician, Ampuero, and were consequently less vigorous in their opposition to some of the moderate aims of the Communists; the Radicals were firmly lined up against the government; and even the Christian Democratic trade unionists were moving to a position of almost consistent opposition to the government's economic policies.

The CUT therefore felt increasingly confident about being able to perform its functions. These were not particularly new functions—what was new was the degree of success. The CUT had performed a useful role in the past. Though its efforts at mediation with governments were not always fruitful, sometimes it did produce results; at the very least it brought publicity to a strike, sometimes it attracted more attention from congressmen than might otherwise have been the case, and it was occasionally able to provide legal or technical advice to unions lacking funds to retain their own advisers.[35] The CUT also helped unions to resolve their own internal

[33] Burnett (pp. 234–45) has an interesting and detailed description of the strike.

[34] *Memoria del CDN al 5° congreso*, p. 29.

[35] A question was put to workers of modern, traditional, and small enterprises about whether, if they were engaged in collective bargaining, it would be useful to seek the aid of the CUT. Compared with 31% of workers in the modern enterprises who thought it would be useful, and 49% in small enterprises, the figure rose to 54% in traditional enterprises—obviously showing that workers

problems, or, more important, conflicts with other unions.[36] If it can combine its opposition with support from the parties, and if the government is not prepared to use measures of repression as drastic as those of Ibáñez in 1956, then the CUT can become very important in co-ordinating, leading, and informing opposition to government policies, for it is the body that transforms unions' economic demands into political pressure, as in 1967.

Politically the CUT reflects the traditions, characteristics, and structure of the Chilean labour movement. If it is a mistake, as some analysts argue, to regard it simply as an external structure imposed on the unions by the parties, it is an even more obvious mistake to examine it purely as a union movement. For the CUT is the meeting place of parties and the unions (though whether they meet amicably or not depends more on the state of relations between the parties than anything else). In this sense it provides a sort of forum within which the chief ideological groups may debate policies and tactics. It also provides a forum for the various parties active in the labour movement where they can focus their attention on objectives of obvious interest to ordinary workers, and where the importance of unity is constantly emphasized. Thus the CUT helps to unite the left-wing parties and to win progressive elements from the Christian Democrats and Radicals over to the common cause.

The question for the future is how far the CUT will change under Allende's administration. This cannot be answered in the abstract; changes in its position will reflect changes in the union movement and the structure of the economy, and they may take a long time to come about. Nevertheless, some preliminary points can be made. In the first place, the Chilean union movement is not a complete stranger to political power; the CTCh had representation in the government and in Congress. Two factors that brought about the collapse of the CTCh—party competition in the unions, and the failure to contain inflation for long—are, if not to the same degree, potential threats to the present system. Moreover, there are limits to the expansion of Chilean unionism; the 30% of the labour force

---

in big modern plants feel they can rely on their own strength, while those in small plants feel they need support (Gurrieri, *Aportes*, 9 July 1968, p. 111).

[36] Burnett (p. 135) quotes the president of the FIFch: 'The major value of the CUT is that when there are conflicts among labor groups, they can go to CUT where they have facilities and techniques to act as a sounding board and help to resolve inter-union disagreements.'

now in unions cannot, apart from the rural sector, easily be expanded, though what might happen is the consolidation of the union movement into a small number of powerful federations. That, however, will take time and involve legal changes, and though the government has signed an agreement with the CUT to co-operate for common purposes, the majority in Congress has already turned down proposals to legalize the CUT so that it could collect dues more easily.[37] In addition, any process of reorganization of unions will involve dismantling some unions' structures, and of all social institutions few exhibit so much desire to carry on in existence than trade unions. Reform of enterprise structure to allow workers' representatives more power is, similarly, a long process dependent on other changes in the economic and political system.

The CUT has been and will be incorporated much more into the apparatus of state planning, though how far it will have to advocate the point of view of the workers to a government that is committed to their point of view in any case is not easy to see. But the Allende government will be under pressure from many underprivileged sectors of Chilean society—and far from all of them are trade unionists. And Allende has made it clear that his vision of socialism rests basically on centralized planning, naturally with representatives of the unions, but not on some sort of workers' control on the Yugoslav model.[38] If unions will have new privileges and rights in the new regime, they will also have heavy responsibilities, especially in the overall task of national development, even if this threatens their short-term advantages. While it is to be expected that the CUT and the union movement generally will become more powerful and more established under the present government there are also good reasons for thinking that the

[37] However, on 12 May 1971 Allende signed another project granting legal status and providing for adequate methods of financing, to be sent to Congress for approval (*El Mercurio*, 13 May 1971).

[38] Régis Debray, *Conversations with Allende* (London, 1971), p. 111. In Allende's own (translated) words: 'We are and always shall be in favour of a centralized economy, and companies will have to conform to the Government's production planning. To achieve this, we shall maintain a continuous dialogue with the workers. But we are not going to hand over a company to the workers just so that they can produce what they want or to let them turn the fact that they control a company which is of vital importance to their country to their own personal advantage in order to demand higher earnings than other people. We are against any policy of that nature.'

process will be long and difficult, and there is no reason to foresee an end to the political divisions in the labour movement.

## Unions and leaders

It is very difficult to offer general propositions about the nature and characteristics of a national labour movement. Thus although this study has largely dealt with independent unions, because many unions are small in Chile there are numerous situations where the union is dominated by the employer. A large powerful federation like that of the copper workers is the exception. But the fact that the small plant union is the most common industrial unit in Chile makes generalization a little easier. Many Chilean unions would fall into the category described by H. A. Turner as 'exclusive democracy'. The

> unions are generally marked by a high membership participation in their affairs and management. They usually have relatively few full time officials. And . . . the official is very much one of themselves . . . So that there is also little distinction of status or interest between the members themselves.[39]

It is generally accepted that there is an association between the size of firm, the degree of unionization, and a left-wing vote. Very small establishments often have a pattern of relationships which binds employers and employees together rather than separates them into potentially antagonistic social sectors. A minimum size is necessary to create a viable trade union with some degree of autonomy from the managerial sector. Among factors predisposing workers in large plants to join trade unions are:

> the more routinized and disciplined nature of work, the physical and symbolic segregation of manual from non-manual employees, the collective pressure of workmate opinion, and the probability that un-

[39] *Trade Union Growth*, p. 289. His third type of union structure, the opposite of the 'exclusive democracy', is the open one, and 'such unions are marked by a generally low level of membership participation, and by the greatest difference between the members and the professional officials on which they depend. In their case, the full-time officers' expertise is quite beyond the ordinary member's experience. And there is often a distinct hierarchy among the officials themselves'. Few such unions exist in Chile—even the copper workers union only numbers some 18,000 members broken up into important constituent unions, a far cry from the mass unions of Argentina.

satisfying jobs make the extrinsic rewards of pay and conditions very prominent in the worker's mind.[40]

On the other hand participation and politicization do not always increase with size. Large national federations may be more obviously political in the aims they espouse and the area of their activities; but this may be because a politicized leadership is directing a largely apathetic mass membership. Lipset found that in the ITU the most politicized shops, where this also meant active membership participation, were in fact the medium-sized shops of between 100 and 200 members—a common union size in Chile. Such plants, especially where there is compulsory union membership, favour close relationships between leader and led, and discussion of issues by a large number of the members. The fact that the unions are generally autonomous—for even those that are members of federations are often only slightly restricted by that—makes for genuine participation.[41] In Chile, the small size of the unions, their financial weakness, and the legal restrictions on payment of leaders inhibits the development of an institutionalized bureaucratic leadership which elsewhere often replaces democracy by oligarchy in the labour movement. Leaders in Chilean unions rarely feel a status differentiation between themselves and their members, and move back to the rank of ordinary worker without any apparent strain, financial or otherwise. This is important for maintaining participation and democracy in union movements.

If these are the conditions that permit a high degree of membership activity in union affairs, it is political competition that mobilizes the membership and provides a real choice between those competing for leadership. For leaders are competing for office not just on a platform based on narrow union activities but also in the name of diffuse and general political ideologies. In making his choice the unionist is not only acting in his capacity as member of an occupational group; he is also in effect acting in his general political capacity. This is not without its reciprocal effects on the political scene. High participation in union elections, fought along party lines, strengthens worker identification with left-wing parties and so aids the parties in their task of building up a loyal following.

[40] Goldthorpe & others, *Affluent Worker*, ii. 51.
[41] Kerr writes that 'the one plant local with real authority is the most democratic entity in the trade union movement' (*Labor & Management*, p. 35).

If union elections contested by lists of candidates known to be members or supporters of a particular political party are an index of the politicization of unions, then Chilean unions are very politicized indeed. The larger the union the more evident will this be, but even at the plant level, many if not most union elections have some political element, though there are many independents, or candidates whose popularity is such that they are sought out by the parties rather than seek office because they are political partisans.[42]

Parties take an active interest in union elections encouraging participation, and often they give advice on tactics, provide financial or legal assistance, and help to select the list of candidates to represent the party. Certainly such party intervention helps to increase electoral participation, and turnouts of the order of 60% and above are very common in union elections, a much higher figure than is usual in many other countries.[43] Elections in Chilean unions are a genuine choice, and more than that, can be perceived by the rank and file as a genuine choice because candidates are identified by party labels. The fact that it is the local plant union that engages in collective bargaining, adds further incentive to participate. Union leaders make no secret about their party affiliations, and even though the CP leadership likes to create the impression that it plays a far less active role than it does, Communist union leaders rarely make any effort to conceal their allegiances —and even if they did their fellow unionists would be quick to point them out.

Union leadership does not constitute a bureaucracy in the way that it does in Argentina; there is nothing comparable in Chile to the power, financial benefits, and improvement in status that

[42] It is not possible to be very precise about the number of candidates in all elections to union office in any one year who are 'political' rather than 'independent'. But the delegates to CUT congresses are nearly all 'political' and they do represent most of organized labour. Moreover, union leaders and observers of the labour scene corroborate these assertions; and of course evidence like the Landsberger survey showed that only 19% of the sample did not support any political tendency.

[43] For similar high participation in union elections in another country where political divisions are strong in the labour movement see, G. Adam, 'La representativité des organisations syndicales', *R. française de sci. pol.*, Apr. 1968, pp. 278–31 . For evidence of low participation in unions where politicization is not a factor encouraging competition see M. van de Vall, *Labor Organizations* (London, 1970), chs. 3 & 5.

accrue to the leader of a large Argentinian union. There are some union offices which may lead to better things (perhaps a seat in Congress), but these are so few and far between that they can hardly enter into the calculation of many candidates. Many unionists stand for office because they are party militants; but this does not mean that union leaders see their offices mainly in political terms. Most leaders when asked why they sought union office gave economic reasons. This is not surprising: a hard-working union president is unlikely to think that his union of perhaps a hundred workers is going to make a frontal assault on the class and power system of the country. Union leaders often hold views that seem politically incompatible, but so do many politicians presumably more educated and sophisticated (and certainly not least of all Chilean politicians). Though political commitment may be an important impetus in seeking union office, it is rarely a complete explanation of behaviour once office has been secured (except in organizations like the CUT, for which collective bargaining is not normally the central activity), because a whole range of other forces and pressures come into play—which is not to say that political commitment becomes irrelevant.

This bears on the question, often answered affirmatively in Chile, whether parties *control* unions. However, there is a strong tendency, even for the most politicized union leaders—those in the union departments of the party—to act primarily as unionists and secondarily as party members; if this is marked at the top level, then it can be expected to be even more marked at the lower levels. Again, Chilean parties are not strong enough, nor do they have enough manpower, to control unions systematically and widely, even if they wished to do so. Here the CP is to some extent different, but one often hears the party leadership complain of lack of control over their unionist members. Nor do parties always have a clear notion of what they want their unionists to do, apart from holding office. Even if union leaders obeyed party orders, it does not follow that they could translate them automatically into union action; the rank and file of Chilean unions can rarely be mobilized for action outside their perception of a threat to their economic interests. Union leaders may be able to amalgamate a union issue with a party one, but there are fairly strict limits to the number of occasions on which this can be done. Moreover, overt party manipulation is impeded by the fact that very few executives are made up entirely of one political party; most of them are not.

Though parties do co-operate, even at their friendliest they are hardly likely to lose the opportunity to make gains in union as well as national elections. This helps to keep the unions democratic, for there frequently exists an opposition keen to expose the mistakes of the leadership and take up the reins of office.

These generalizations hide the differences inside the Chilean labour movement. Widespread politicization far from implies complete uniformity, though given the differences between white- and blue-collar sectors, between state and private-sector workers, between large and small factories, between traditional and modern industries, the uniformity of politicization is striking.

There are naturally variations on this pattern of party influence in the unions. For many years COMACH was dominated by Wenceslao Moreno, who placed membership of the ORIT above affiliation to any Chilean political party, though he joined the PDC after its electoral triumph. The maritime workers are notoriously susceptible to union dictatorship (as in Britain for many years), but even here Moreno's rule has been threatened by Socialists and Communists combining to defeat him in important constituent unions of the federation. Another case where a union bureaucracy enjoys an unusually firm degree of control is in the Sindicato Ganadero de Magallanes, the union of sheep workers on the huge ranches in the far south of Chile. The conditions of work here too are favourable to union oligarchy. In the same way that in the merchant marine it is difficult to contest the leadership because so many of the members are at sea at any given time, workers on the huge estates are widely scattered and separated; and as the union bureaucracy manages to hold elections for the union in mid-winter, before the activities in the meat-packing stations bring large numbers of workers together, they manage to keep control relatively easily. It has even been alleged that the union leaders opposed the expropriation of one of the largest estates (and perhaps the largest ranch in the world) for fear that this would undermine their power in the union.[44]

A great deal of attention has naturally been paid to the political role of the copper workers' unions. Although their leadership is largely marxist, it is often argued that the workers constitute a 'labour aristocracy' indifferent to the fate of their class and essentially petty bourgeois. It is true that in the large mines they are much better paid than most workers in Chile and their unions

[44] Ampuero, *Izquierda*, pp. 139–40.

are stronger. But it cannot be argued that simply because the unions are more successful in their basic function of getting higher salaries, they are a petty-bourgeois labour aristocracy, separated from the rest of the labour movement. What may be surprising, considering their privileged economic position, is their attachment to the radical tradition, whether measured by the political affiliations of their leaders, by the voting habits of their members,[45] by their support for the cut, by their militant strike record, or by their hostility to the agreements made by the pdc government with the American-owned companies.

One interesting hypothesis explaining miners' solidarity has been advanced by Dillon Soares,[46] who argues that the occupational structure in mining and quarrying, including copper mining, is less favourable to individual economic betterment than in other sectors of the economy. In mining and quarrying, 83% of the labour force is classified as *obrero*, compared with 56% in manufacturing industry, 48% in services, and 17% in commerce. Though copper workers earn more than many *empleados*, this was achieved through union solidarity rather than by an upgrading of occupational status. Nor do living conditions of the copper workers resemble those of a labour aristocracy; the men are grouped in insanitary barracks or inadequate houses, compared with the managerial grades, who occupy far superior houses, have separate schools for their children, and so on.[47] This helps to explain the militancy of the copper unionists. In fact they behave in a rather similar way to most Chilean unionists. No doubt they could give more to the cut, they could use their power to support more solidarity strikes, they could be more active in union affairs generally (as could many other unions). That they do not do any of these things to the limits of their capacities does not make them by definition a labour aristocracy. In a way they can be seen as the heirs of the radical tradition of the early nitrate workers. There is a complex relationship between militancy and radicalism. The

[45] Chuquicamata is something of an exception here. In 1964 in Chuquicamata Frei had a slight majority over Allende (though in the department of El Loa as a whole, where miners also reside and vote, Allende had a majority). See the discussion of Chuquicamata below.

[46] 'Desenvolvimiento económico e radicalismo político', *América Latina*, July–Sept. 1962.

[47] T. G. Sanders, *Chile and its copper*, American Universities Field Staff, West Coast S. Amer. Ser., 16/1, p. 4; also Petras, *Politics & Social Forces*, p. 243 and *Ercilla*, 15–21 July, 1970.

copper unions are certainly militant in their pursuit of their union objectives. Strikes are well supported, usually successful, sometimes violent. In this way the copper unions are an example to the rest of the labour force; it is important for the Chilean union movement that the best paid and best organized sector of the working class should be seen to have achieved success largely because of its militancy. But are the copper workers politically radical? The fact that their unions elect to their leadership a majority of Socialists and Communists is not conclusive.[48] The copper mining areas normally turn in a large vote in elections for the two marxist parties, even if they are not so solid as the coal-mining areas (there is still a strong Radical tradition in certain Northern mining areas) and even if the PDC made inroads on the marxist support in 1964 and 1965. There are, too, deviant cases like that of Chuquicamata in 1970 where the male vote for Alessandri was almost as high as that for Allende, partly it seems because of the local success of right-wing propaganda maintaining that a victory for Allende would be less favourable for the copper workers; but even here the male vote for Allende still exceeded, if only by a slight margin, that for Alessandri, and not all the voters were copper workers. Allende was hurt by the results at Chuquicamata—the largest open copper mine in the world and the source of half of Chile's production, and when he attacks the 'workers oligarchy' in Chile, he is evidently referring to Chuquicamata. In this case he is arguing that because Chuquicamata is completely dominated by the American company, and isolated from the rest of Chile, the 'imperialists' have been able to prevent the workers from developing a revolutionary class consciousness.[49] Yet a glance at Chuquicamata's voting record makes this criticism seem too severe. In 1953, for example,

[48] As further proof of copper union radicalism Petras & Zeitlin argue that the evidence that rural municipalities that have a common boundary with mining municipalities produce a higher pro-FRAP vote than rural municipalities that have no common boundary, indicates proselytizing activities on the part of copper unionists ('Miners and agrarian radicalism', *Am. J. Sociol.*, Aug. 1967). However the higher vote could be due to other factors—miners residing in rural municipalities, seasonal employment of rural labourers in mines, 'demonstration effect'. I asked a number of copper union leaders if they engaged in such activities—helping to form rural unions, trying to convert peasants—and their response was invariably that they did not.

[49] Partly, in Allende's view, because the owners have bought off a large part of the workforce by paying them high wages, and in dollars—which are then sold on the black market (Debray, *Conversations*, pp. 110-11).

the combined Socialist vote in the congressional elections was 1,726 out of a total of 2,854 (though of the two Socialist parties, Allende's Socialistas de Chile did very badly with only 130 votes—part of the reason for his animosity?). In the 1958 presidential elections Allende polled close on 50% of the vote—over 50% if confined to male voters alone—well ahead of any of his rivals. Although Frei's vote narrowly exceeded that of Allende in the presidential election of 1964, by the 1965 congressional elections the combined Socialist–Communist vote was again close on 50% of the total poll, with the Socialists as the most popular party well ahead of the PDC, even on the female vote.[50]

However, even if this seems to show that the copper unionists are not deserting the working class and the union movement by becoming an aristocracy of labour, it may still be true that their attachment is changing, becoming more instrumental and less a question of emotional allegiance, that is 'one devoid of all sense of participation in a class *movement* seeking structural changes in society or even pursuing more limited ends through concerted class action'.[51]

The condition of the copper workers is unusual and not typical of the majority of Chilean industrial workers, who can never hope to approach their pay scales. The Allende government recognized —and rejected—their privileged position by refusing to include, as part of the constitutional amendments necessary to nationalize the copper industry, a special statute safeguarding the position of the workers; in Allende's opinion, this would create a legally privileged sector of the working class, and that was unacceptable to a government pursuing social equality.

### Unions and members

The precise role that unions should play in the seizure of power by a marxist movement has been a subject of long debate. But, at least in the orthodox marxist camp, the assumption has been that the unions must be subordinate to a directing, elitist party. If this guidance were lacking, then, as Marx argued, even at their best unions would 'fail generally from limiting themselves to a guerrilla war against the effects of the existing system instead of simul-

---

[50] Perhaps Allende's strictures are not intended to be a historical comment, but more a warning to the copper workers that they cannot expect to maintain such high wage differentials from the rest of the workers under his government.

[51] Goldthorpe & others, *Affluent Worker*, iii. 178–9. Their italics.

taneously trying to change it'.[52] In a revolutionary movement the unions' role, while fundamental, would nevertheless be subsidiary. As one marxist, following Lenin, writes,

> trade unions everywhere produce working class consciousness—that is awareness of the separate identity of the proletariat as a social force with its own corporate interests in society. This is not the same thing as socialist consciousness—the hegemonic vision and will to create a new social order which only a revolutionary party can create.[53]

In Chile, however, a marxist President came to power by democratic elections. The ability to conspire, to use force, to overthrow the system—tasks of the revolutionary party—were far less important than the ability to build up a large, loyal electoral following—a task in which the unions, producing the 'working-class consciousness', played no small part. For the rank-and-file member of a small union, the union and its leaders are often more concrete entities, more capable of arousing personal loyalty, than the political party. In this sense, the role of the unions in mobilizing support for the marxist parties is of fundamental importance in building up the electoral clientele of those parties. The table on p. 238 shows the relative support for the three presidential candidates in 1970 in the chief mining areas—the heart of marxist strength in Chile, where trade unions are strong and closely allied with the Socialist and Communist parties.

If it is not difficult to demonstrate statistically that the left does better in areas of high unionization, the interpretation is not quite so straightforward. The question of the impact of unionization on political attitudes is far from simple, if only because it is very difficult to separate out the factor of unionization from all the other influences that combine to produce political attitudes and behaviour. It may be the case that political attitudes precede union involvement, and certainly for the leadership this is often likely to be so. But if the importance of the union in shaping the general values of its members varies a great deal from country to country, in Chile it would seem to be a significant influence.[54]

[52] Quoted from Marx's 'Value, Price and Profit', in Kerr, *Marshall, Marx and Modern Times* (London, 1969), p. 44.

[53] P. Anderson, 'The Limits and Possibilities of Trade Union Action', in R. Blackburn & A. Cockburn, eds., *Incompatibles: trade union militancy and the consensus* (London, 1967), p. 274.

[54] In Brazil the dominant social framework would appear to be that of urban community rather than trade union (A. de Simão, 'Industrialización y sindi-

*Male Voting in Mining Centres in 1970*

| Mining zones | Votes for Allende for each 100 votes for Alessandri | Votes for Allende for each 100 votes for Tomic |
|---|---|---|
| **Mining zones** **(*copper*)** | | |
| Chuquicamata | 106 ⎫ | 301 ⎫ |
| Potrerillos | 232 ⎪ | 225 ⎪ |
| | ⎬ 265* | ⎬ 303 |
| Sewell | 406 ⎪ | 307 ⎪ |
| El Salvador | 319 ⎭ | 381 ⎭ |
| **Mining zones** **(*nitrates*)** | | |
| Iquique | 194 ⎫ | 258 ⎫ |
| Pozo Almonte | 300 ⎪ | 289 ⎪ |
| Lagunas | 130 ⎬ 325 | 163 ⎬ 337 |
| Toco | 412 ⎪ | 541 ⎪ |
| Pedro de Valdivia | 591 ⎭ | 426 ⎭ |
| **Mining zones** **(*coal*)** | | |
| Coronel | 640 ⎫ | 448 ⎫ |
| Lota | 916 ⎬ 794 | 658 ⎬ 571 |
| Curanilhue | 827 ⎭ | 608 ⎭ |

\* Average.

*Source:* Petras, in *Punto final*, 5 Jan. 1971, p. 4.

There is evidence that Chilean workers place a high value on their union. Certainly they claim high participation—over two-thirds said that they attended union meetings regularly, and that they viewed the benefits produced by union membership favourably. Over three-quarters of union presidents questioned replied that in their union at least half of the members took an active interest in union affairs—by, for example, attending meetings regularly. A similar proportion—close on 70%—of the rank and file questioned replied that they nearly always attended union meetings—perhaps because these meetings are important in deciding the union's bargaining position with the employers.

---

calismo en Brasil', in *Sindicalismo en América Latina* (Barcelona, 1965), pp. 39–59, reprinted from *Sociol. du Travail* (Paris), 4 (1961). See also, J. R. Brandão Lopes, 'Aspects of the Adjustment of Rural Migrants to Urban-Industrial Conditions in São Paulo, Brazil', in P. M. Hauser ed., *Urbanization in Latin America* (UNESCO, 1961), pp. 234–48.

Unionists also agreed strongly with the proposition that their leaders work for the interests of the unions and not for personal gain, and they felt that relations between rank and file and the leaders were close and good.[55] The responses showed that most workers saw their problems as similar to those of rural labour rather than to those of white-collar workers or the middle class.

The impression that emerges from this and other surveys is of a fairly high degree of class-consciousness, in the creation of which the union plays a fundamental role. In this sense the union is an important agent of politicization and political mobilization of the rank and file. Even in a more specific sense, unions would be politically important as electoral agents in many practical ways—for example, they would remind members about elections, about the need to support the working class, and if the union as a whole did not come out officially for one candidate, leaders would certainly create electoral campaign groups to activate the membership, to persuade it to vote for a particular party.

These general propositions tend to hang in the air until they have been empirically proved or disproved, especially since, despite the number of surveys of leaders and members, there are few case studies of particular unions. One such study, however, was of the coal-mining town of Lota and the steel mill at Huachipato,[56] an excellent choice for comparison, for the two are geographically very close, but industrially distant, since the Lota coal mines are old, poor, and depressed whereas the Huachipato steel industry is the epitome (for Chile) of modern, capital-intensive technology. The survey was not conducted at the most suitable time to examine political attitudes, for the date of fieldwork, 1955, coincided with the period when the cp was still illegal, although by then it was functioning fairly regularly.

Lota is almost a classic traditional mining town. Over 90% of the workforce is classified as *obrero*, and there are only slight status and occupational distinctions to vary its essential homogeneity, though there is an enormous social gulf between it and the

[55] Nazar, n.p. Nazar uses the survey directed by A. Gurrieri of ECLA for A. Touraine's comparative study of working-class attitudes. Over 900 workers were interviewed from a variety of industrial (but not artisanal) settings. Recent migrants, long-term urban dwellers, and various occupational strata were included—making the survey less representative of the working class as a whole for the sake of providing information about different strata inside it. Fieldwork was conducted in 1966–7. See also Barrera, *Participación*, pp. 45–8.

[56] Di Tella & others.

management.[57] The links between the union and the municipality are very close; workforce and community are largely the same. Union leaders direct the affairs of the municipality and most are Communists, with a minority of Socialists. It is not surprising that in Lota the CUT should have one of its strongest local organizations. The solidarity of the community with the marxist parties is shown by its electoral behaviour, for it regularly returns a very large majority for these parties. The repression of the post-1947 period and the Law for the Defence of Democracy temporarily weakened the power of the union and the left-wing leadership, but only temporarily. The Lota worker has a polarized view of his social situation—either he is with the union or with the enterprise. Union membership is associated with a high degree of emotional attachment. Individuals (a small minority) who desire social advancement see the route not through the union, but by becoming independent and self-employed, abandoning the union and the political attitudes associated with it. In Lota it is the worker who shows himself most dissatisfied with his position who is most active in the union; hence there is a predominance in it of workers from the lowest social and occupational strata. Participation in union affairs is high; approximately 17% are very active, and a further 52% participate regularly.[58] The rank and file feels generally satisfied with the leadership and with the closeness of contacts between leaders and members. The relationship between attitudes towards the union and the parties is more complicated. For the worker in Lota the union is his central interest; political parties are somewhat distant and abstract entities. Workers who hold strong political beliefs are not necessarily active in the unions, though union leaders are certainly active in the parties.

Although Huachipato differs so much from Lota in its technology, occupational structure, and working conditions, the role of the union is not dissimilar. There are differences of course, but one striking similarity is that marxists have dominated the leadership, though not so completely. Unlike Lota, however, in Huachipato union leaders come from the higher occupational groups in the enterprise, and union activity is associated with a greater

---

[57] Ibid., pp. 70 & 74. The author visited Lota and Huachipato in 1967 and conducted interviews with union leaders. The picture that emerged was not very different from the Di Tella study.

[58] Ibid., p. 184 & appendix for a discussion of the exact meaning of the terms.

acceptance of middle-class norms and values. Thus union leaders there come from the ranks of those keen to rise in the enterprise rather than those who oppose it, as in Lota. While in general among the workers in Huachipato there has existed a tendency to see society at large and the enterprise in particular in polarized terms, this was less marked among the leaders than among the followers—the reverse of the Lota situation. Participation in the union in Huachipato is more instrumental and less emotional than in Lota; solidarity with the union is weaker partly because of the complex occupational hierarchy, which, as long ago as 1955, was tending to fragment the union situation and which by the mid-1960s had produced a number of specialized union groups (though by 1969 the process of upgrading from *obrero* to *empleado* had gone so far that a new unity movement was spreading, but based this time on the *empleado* rather than the *obrero* grades). Although the same proportion of workers as in Lota was very active in the Huachipato unions, the number who merely participated was less —37% compared with 52%. Huachipato workers were a little less favourably inclined towards parties than Lota workers, though the fact that the CP was illegal at the time makes answers to this question less reliable.

Like the copper workers, the Huachipato steel workers are exceptionally privileged compared with the rest of the Chilean working class. The Lota coal miners also differ in their conditions of isolation, of union dominance over the community and munici-pality, of dangerous and poorly paid work. But as both extremes exhibit certain common features, it is probable that other unions will do likewise. For these features are partly a product of a long tradition of working-class history, partly of close union relations with marxist political parties, partly of the legal system, partly of a certain cultural homogeneity, and partly derive from the economic structure itself. Whatever the causes of the present structure and behaviour of Chilean trade unions, one effect of that structure and behaviour is clear—the creation of a strong electoral base for the Chilean Communist and Socialist parties.

## Conclusion

The revolutionary left in Chile has often criticized the role of the trade unions, arguing that they have retarded revolutionary development and, by creating a 'privileged' sector of the working class, have divided that class and reduced its political unity and power. This point of view has been shared by some theorists far removed from the revolutionary left, who point out that the existence of strong unions can reduce the possibilities of social tension developing into mass violence.

The view that the existence of trade unions contributes to regulate conflict between labour on one hand and employers and government on the other is not a novel one. Whatever the contributions of unions to economic development or to the industrialization process, their existence does make it easier for governments to deal with the demands of the working population. As Almond notes, groups like trade unions provide 'orderly procedures for the formulation of interests and demands . . . and the transmission of these demands to other political structures'.[59] Urrutia argues a similar case for the role of the Colombian labour movement.[60] The repeated demands by Chilean unions for consultation and participation in the decision-making process indicates that they too are anxious to share in the regulation of conflict. That governments in the past have so often excluded them contributed to the radicalism of the labour movement. Its fragmentation into small plant unions undoubtedly helped the government to resolve conflict on its own terms, and incidentally helped to politicize the unions as they found it necessary to undertake political activities in self-defence.

Analysts who see the role of unions as conflict regulators often assume also that it is somehow in 'the nature' of unionism to be reformist, democratic, and economic rather than revolutionary and political; the parallel assumption, of course, is that revolution is by definition a violent and chaotic process. Yet J. A. Banks rejects this use of the concept of revolution and argues that the history of trade union participation in British politics before 1926 (the year of the General Strike) and afterwards is one of 'acceptance of the constitutional machinery with the express purpose of using it legally to improve the situation of the working class'. If, deliberately or willy nilly, 'this has actually resulted in the piecemeal erosion of the capitalist system of exploitation', such partici-

[59] Cited by R. H. Bates in his interesting *Critique of the Major Approaches to the Study of Labour and Development* (Cambridge, Mass., 1969), pp. 25–6, who writes (p. 25): 'Perhaps the most energetic proponents of this view are those who ponder the failure of the Marxian prophecy.'

[60] *Development of the Colombian Labor Movement*, pp. 256–7.

pation is revolutionary.[61] If this may be thought to stretch the definition of revolution rather far, these criteria seem to apply more convincingly to the Chilean case. Here is a union movement a majority of which supports political parties whose aim is to overthrow the capitalist system, led by members of parties who demand profound transformations in society, and which mobilizes its members to vote for such a programme. Many observers have denied that the Chilean union movement is radical, since most union activities are concerned with pay and conditions of labour, but a union that did not fight for the improvement of living standards would be anomalous. Even if the leaders spent most of their time in these activities, nevertheless their message to the union rank and file to support the left in elections took strong root in the organized working class.

The election of Allende in 1970 was widely noted as the first democratic election of a marxist President anywhere in the world. To that election the contribution of unions has been substantial. If it can be argued that the existence of unions helped to prevent the social situation degenerating into violence, and that by their very existence unions helped to resolve conflict, it is just as true that those unions formed the base of two powerful radical parties and helped to build up mass support for a successful marxist presidential candidate. In this sense the claim to have brought about revolution with liberty can be made with more justice by the trade unions than by the Christian Democrats, who coined the phrase.

[61] *Marxist Sociology in Action* (London, 1970), p. 111.

# Appendix I[1]
# Rural Unionism

WITH the rural labour law of 1967, with increasing unrest in the countryside, with competition for control over the peasantry between the parties, agrarian reform institutes, Catholic organizations (and landowners), with the impact of agrarian reform itself, and finally with Allende's election, change has been rapid, widespread, and confusing. This alone would be sufficient reason for not trying to deal with both urban and rural labour in a single book, and another good reason is that there is very little contact between the two sectors. Urban and rural unionists have not co-operated; indeed they have rarely had any contact apart from occasional CUT meetings.

Nevertheless, one common feature of rural and urban unions is a similar relationship with the parties, for politicization is now as much in evidence in the countryside as in the towns. Socialists, Communists, and Christian Democrats all have a *campesino* department, as actively concerned with the relations between the party and rural unions as is the union department between the party and the urban unions, although in some ways the task of the organizers of the peasant departments is more difficult as peasants are more mobile between parties, lacking the traditional party loyalties of many urban and mining unionists. One other difference in the rural areas is that the parties face additional competitors for influence and control, notably the ASICH-dominated unions and also, at least during the Frei administration, the government agency INDAP (Institute for Agricultural Development).

Rural unionism in Latin America is generally a weaker and more recent development than industrial or mining unionism. One reason is that peasant organizations are much more vulnerable to opposition from state and employer.[2] The first Chilean law in 1947 regulating the

[1] I am indebted to David Lehmann for comments on this appendix, many of which have been incorporated in the text.

[2] For the disastrous consequences on rural unions of the change from a favourable regime to an unfavourable one—from that of Goulart to the post-1964 Brazilian military governments—see de Kadt, *Catholic Radicals*.

R

formation of rural unions was in practice intended to prevent, not encourage, such unions.[3] Landowners had earlier blocked all attempts to loosen their control over their rural labourers, and it was not until the presidential election of 1952, and later with a reformed electoral system providing for a genuinely secret ballot, that rural voters shook off their traditional allegiances to the Conservative and Liberal parties. The spokesman of the large landowners, the SNA (National Agricultural Society), consistently opposed attempts at peasant organization, except those that landowners could control themselves.[4]

The concentration of power in the Chilean countryside was such that efforts by peasants alone, without the strong support of such forces as the government and parties, could hardly have started to change the structure of power. According to the 1955 census—and the ex-vice-president of INDAP, Jacques Chonchol, argues that the position has changed little since then[5]—the rural population was about 2 m., or 350,000 families. Of these families 3% could be classed as large landowners, and another 7% as medium-sized proprietors, and these two groups employed some 7,000 families as administrators of their estates. Outside this rural upper class there were 60,000 families of small proprietors; 60,000 families in communities—including those of the Araucanian Indians—but who were largely minifundistas, the 'community' being a legal definition rather than a social reality; 22,000 families of *minifundistas*; 30,000 families of *medieros*—independent landless workers who work the large estates on sharecropping tenancies; 30,000 families of specialized workers on the large estates; 82,000 families of *inquilinos*—the resident rural labourers on the large estates paid partly in kind, partly in cash, and partly in usufruct; and 25,000 families of landless labourers.[6]

[3] See ch. 4.

[4] Comité Interamericana de Desarrollo Agrícola, *Chile: tenencia de la tierra y desarrollo socio-económico del sector agrícola* (1966), pp. 33–6. In the 1920s when the SNA was worried that unionism might spread as a result of the developments in the urban sector following the formation of the CP, it wrote to Alessandri: 'The needs of the rural proletariat are not the same as the city proletariat, because their way of life is different, their needs are distinct and they have a different level of culture. There is no reason at all why the worker in the countryside should join and make common cause with the urban worker.' Alessandri agreed, though urging landowners to pay more attention to their peasants' grievances by setting up landowner dominated federations (cited in A. Affonso & others, *Movimiento campesino chileno* (1970).

[5] 'Poder y reforma agraria', in *Chile Hoy*, p. 277.

[6] Ibid., pp. 277–8. The figures are by no means exact and there is considerable debate amongst agrarian reform specialists on the true proportion of, especially, inquilinos to day-labourers. For a detailed analysis of the figures see the CIDA report (n. 4 above), pp. 291–4, where they estimate that in 1965, 12·4% of the active rural population were *inquilinos*, and 27·2% were *afuerinos*

The lower class constitutes the overwhelming majority of the labour force in the countryside, but there are important divisions within it. Between those who have land and the landless, between those with fixed employment on estates and those seasonally employed there are distinctions that are difficult to overcome in any one rural organization. For the purposes of unionization, one crucial distinction is that between resident permanent workers and temporary non-resident workers—i.e. between on the one hand *inquilinos*, specialized workers, and *voluntarios* (who do not enjoy the usufruct of a small piece of land, and are therefore not obliged to work in theory, though in practice economic necessity is a strong enough inducement, especially as they often receive higher wages than *inquilinos* in compensation for not having land), and, on the other hand, the *afuerinos*, literally 'foreigners' or 'outsiders'. The other crucial distinction is between estate workers in general, and peasant smallholders, tenant farmers, or sharecroppers, for though *inquilinos* do enjoy access to land, the amount is generally so small that *inquilinos* are better classified with other estate labourers than with other small farmers or minifundistas. In fact so far unionization as such has been largely confined to the resident workers on the estates; the non-resident labourers are mainly unorganized; and the small proprietors have their separate Comités de Pequeños Proprietarios (committees of small landowners).

Yet historically the outstanding division in rural society was between the large landowners and the rest of the labour force. The large landowners received the officially-provided credit,[7] they alone enjoyed political power, they were the spokesmen on the state planning agencies, and the rural ruling class established a system of social relationships hardly conducive to independent peasant organizations. In the 1930s George MacBride wrote of the sharp division into two classes, master

---

(non-resident labourers) or *voluntarios* (labourers often resident in the houses of *inquilinos*, but theoretically not obliged to work for the estate owners). Other sources point to the general substitution of *inquilino* labour by wage labour, estimating the *inquilino* proportion of the active rural labour force at only 6% (see Cristobal Kay, *Theory of Agrarian Change: manorial or hacienda system*, Ph.D. Thesis, Univ. Sussex, 1971, p. 127).

[7] Approximately 30% of the total rural population are clients of state financial institutions, reform agencies, commercial banks—the remaining 70% have no access to the formal credit market, and the informal credit market extorts usurous real interest rates, because 'the typical rural commercial lender is either an oligopolist, a duopolist, or an outright monopolist, and his market for loans is confined to the small geographical region in which he lives and operates. The demand curve facing the money-lender is interest-inelastic' (C. Nisbet, *Interest Rates and Imperfect Competition in the Informal Credit Market of Rural Chile* (Wisconsin Univ., Land Tenure Center, reprint ser., 1967, p. 84).

and man, pointing out that the hacienda system had tended to perpetuate the division: 'it has kept the lower class down and has made it servile at the same time that it has fostered aristocratic tendencies among the land-holding group'.[8] The landowner controlled the life of his tenant by a system of economic sanction and patronage, he mediated between his tenant and the outside world and excluded influences that would weaken his authority. Chonchol describes the Chilean peasantry as lacking in self-confidence, dominated by a psychology of dependence, mistrustful of change, concerned much more to have a good *patrón* than anything else—if the peasants rebelled it was against a bad *patrón*, not against the system.[9] If the peasantry was exploited economically, this was no less true politically and socially.

Before the recent changes in the countryside there had been some attempts to organize the peasantry. Ramírez estimates that 5,000 peasants were in unions in 1925; and four years earlier the FOCH had held a peasant congress in Santiago in which eleven unions, representing 2,600 peasants, participated.[10] That these were not entirely idle claims is shown by the anxious messages in which the SNA urged Alessandri to take strong action against the 'Communist agitators' stirring up the countryside. Before the Popular Front a Liga Nacional de Campesinos Pobres was set up, and during the Popular Front administration Communists and Socialists were active in the countryside.[11] These movements were no match for opposition from government and landowners. The landowners demonstrated their power even over the Popular Front government when, in 1939, the government ordered all activities connected with the formation of rural unions to be suspended—a concession to the right that the Socialists and Communists agreed to make, in the interest of the fragile unity of the Front, and in order to concentrate attention on the growing urban labour force, whose demands for cheap food might suffer a setback if rural unionization led to higher wages and consequently higher prices.[12]

Above all peasant leaders were the target for victimization, and of all unions, leadership in peasant organizations is very vulnerable to such sanctions; a persecuted urban union leader stands to lose employment, a rural peasant leader his house, land, and property as well.[13]

[8] *Chile: land and society* (New York, 1936), pp. 12–13.

[9] Chonchol, pp. 285–7.

[10] Ramírez, *Origen*, p. 105. Poblete writes that there were 10 unions with 5,000 members in the Valle de Choapa in 1925 (cited in Affonso).

[11] In late 1939 the CP claimed to have encouraged the formation of nearly 400 unions with 60,000 members (Affonso).

[12] A. Mattelart & others, *Ideología de la dominación en una sociedad dependiente* (1971), pp. 117 & 137.

[13] For the general problem of leadership in rural unions see Landsberger & C. A. Hewitt, 'Ten Sources of Weakness and Cleavage in Latin American

Such movements that were formed were more often than not creations of the political parties, and even if some gained genuine support among the peasantry, the loss of national political support—a frequent occurrence in the unstable Chilean political world of the 1920s and 1930s—usually meant the decline of the rural movement.

Since the Socialists and Communists largely abandoned their attempts to organize the rural workers, first in the interests of Popular Front unity and then because they were too busy attacking each other, real changes in the countryside had to wait for a weakening of the power of the landowners in the state as the rural sector became less important, for the spread of effective suffrage with electoral reform and the popular radical parties' heightened interest in the rural vote, for changes in peasant mentality, for general acceptance of the need for agrarian reform, and for the PDC government's wish to build up a large rural following. These processes gathered momentum after World War II.

Renewed attempts to organize the peasantry began in the 1950s, when Catholic groups like ASICH and the IER (Instituto de Educación Rural) hoped to win them over to the cause of moderation, of change through education, and, in the case of the IER, of co-operation with landowners. Political parties again began to set up organizations, but it was the PDC government's commitment to agrarian reform and peasant unionization which was crucial in effecting change.

Agrarian reform and peasant unionization are not necessarily complementary aims—indeed in the Frei administration they tended to conflict. The confusion and complexities of the debate over the nature of the changes needed in the countryside were reflected in the policy of the Frei administration. The agrarian reform tried to be both capitalist and popular. It expressed a desire to disturb efficient landowners as little as possible, indeed to help them with technical advice, better marketing arrangements, etc. Yet it also promised to distribute land to 100,000 peasant families (in fact the achievement was nearer 20,000). These two aims were contradictory enough, given the shortage of funds, irrigated land, and trained administrators, but the policy also aimed at social justice through encouraging peasants to form unions, by establishing higher minimum wages, better conditions, etc. In its second objective the government's performance was better—figures for rural unionization and redistribution of income are more impressive than those for agricultural productivity or land redistribution.[14]

---

Peasant Movements', in R. Stavenhagen ed., *Agrarian Problems and Peasant Movements in Latin America* (New York, 1970), pp. 559–83.

[14] This is not the place to go into the problems of Chilean agrarian reform; the Chonchol article in *Chile Hoy* is a good and recent discussion.

On wages, R. P. Echeverría writes: 'The policy regarding remuneration was based on the granting of wage adjustments equivalent to 100% of the increase

The development of rural unionism must be seen against this background of general expectation of agrarian reform, of new interest in the problems of land tenure and rural labour, of growing pressure from expanding peasant organizations.

## The Catholic organizations

Though there had been previous church-sponsored attempts at union organization, the first of any note was the ASICH set up in 1947, which formed the UCC (Unión de Campesinos Cristianos), in 1960. Inspired by Hurtado, it was at first dedicated to training potential union leaders, but in 1956 converted itself into a union organization as such.[15] Though at the start it maintained friendly relations with the CUT, doctrinal incompatibility between its Catholic reformism and the CUT's views on class conflict soon led to a break, after which ASICH made a point of denouncing communism. It also began by having friendly relations with the Christian Democrats, but they too fell out when ASICH opposed what it saw as attempts to control unions for party ends, while the Christian Democrats came to denounce ASICH as a clerical and conservative body.[16]

ASICH played a prominent role in settling the strike of vineyard workers in Molina in 1953, an event which was something of a watershed in the life of the organization.[17] The strike was revealing. Molina was not a typical rural area, for its vineyard workers were organized more like an industrial than a rural proletariat. The wine industry was growing and prosperous, labour costs were relatively low, the area was fairly urbanized, and the vineyards employed a high proportion of the local labour force. There was also some tradition of early unionism and

in the cost of living during the previous period for everyone. . . . The exception was to be farm workers, for whom substantial increases were contemplated to the point where they would be level with urban workers in terms of minimum wage and family allowances, together with legislation for all of their minimum wages to be paid in cash. And in the period 1964–67, the income of agricultural workers relative to other groups went up by 31·3% (and 25·5% for non-agricultural workers; whereas the large agricultural producers' relative income fell by −3·8%) (*Effect of Agricultural Price Policies on Intersectoral Income Transfers*, Cornell Univ. L. A. Stud. Program, dissertation Ser. no. 13. June 1969, p. 187).

[15] ASICH, *Lo que es—lo que pretende* (1962).

[16] See the general account of ASICH contained in the ASICH-CCT, *Estudios y resoluciónes, 9° congreso nacional ordinario, 9–12 nov. 1966* (1966).

[17] The strike is described in great detail in Landsberger & F. Canitrot, *Iglesia, intellectuales y campesinos* (1967); a shorter English version appears in the volume edited by Landsberger, *Latin American Peasant Movements* (New York, 1969). Page references are to this version, unless otherwise indicated.

agitation by the CP, and a number of workers had experienced working in the copper mines.[18] Yet under the most favourable conditions there was practically no union organization, the 1953 movement would have been ineffective without outside help, and agreement was possible only by flouting the legal code on many points.[19] And even after the success of 1953, unions were not permanently established until under the PDC government.

The strike showed ASICH as basically an urban movement of middle-class intellectuals. One of the two leaders it sent to Molina was an official of the Bank Employees' Union, the other was a young but retired army colonel (instructed to prevent Communist infiltration). On its leadership Landsberger has stated that at no time, even at the local level, was an important position held by anyone who was earning his living as a *campesino*; with two exceptions, none of the leaders came from peasant stock, but most were professionals with an intellectual bent. 'The composition of this leadership is not accidental . . . the total absence of peasants probably bespeaks a lack of leadership potential within that large stratum.' There was no indication that the marxist groups had succeeded better than the Catholics in attracting peasant leaders.

Though one of the strike organizers, Emilio Lorenzini, was a Falangist (and later a PDC congressman), membership in ASICH and the Falange did not overlap much. This was especially true after a major conflict inside ASICH over whether it should convert itself into a federation of trade unions (and part of the Catholic international trade union movement—IFCTU) or whether it should continue as an organization of individuals basically concerned with education, training, and indoctrination. Apparently 'those with most trade union experience and most sympathy with the Falange as well as the clergy most involved, leaned towards the latter policy but lost, and withdrew at tremendous cost in leadership resources'.[20]

The UCC was created at the 5th ASICH congress in 1960. Of its first executive of ten members, seven were urban based and of urban origin, in part because the aims of the UCC included also political, economic, and social assistance. ASICH had found that coercion by state and employer made it impossible to organize unions in the countryside, so using the UCC, it decided to establish small cells on estates to propagate its ideas and to prepare the way for union organization. By 1961 the UCC claimed to have an effective strength of 20,000 rural militants,[21] by

[18] Ibid., p. 86 (in the Spanish version).

[19] e.g., the code forbade negotiations or strike threats at harvest time, the signing of agreements covering several estates, and so on (ibid., p. 34).

[20] Ibid., p. 247.

[21] C. Menges, *Peasant Organisations and Politics in Chile* (1968), p. 27.

1966 it claimed—probably with some exaggeration—to have organized 209 rural unions, 15 co-operatives, 453 pre-union committees, and 7 overall regional federations; over 15,000 peasants had passed through its training schools.[22]

To establish rural unions successfully it is necessary to have a number of full-time organizers, and because the peasantry can rarely supply them or the funds needed, the way is open for groups like the UCC to exert influence. Added to its sophistication and financial resources was the prestige of the church and the energy of the local clergy, for UCC branches were almost always created with the active support of the local priest. Dues from peasant affiliates were clearly inadequate to meet the costs of the organization, and funds were raised from a number of sources, such as the Chilean National Bishops' Conference, the US Point IV programme, Catholic international labour organizations, and German sources.[23] (After 1966 substantial sums came from the International Development Foundation, later discovered to be a front organization for the CIA.)[24]

The activities of the UCC were wide ranging. It attempted to enlist the help of employers to establish co-operatives and various youth and social clubs. At first it tried to restrain strikes and discourage 'excessive' demands, but the mounting tide of peasant pressures later pushed it in a more militant direction. Its strong anti-communism was reinforced when its delegation to the 1963 CUT Congress was denied credentials on the grounds that many of the delegates were not unionists. The UCC alleged that the real reason was that the Communists were afraid of losing control of the CUT to the Christian organizations.

UCC policy on agrarian matters was until recently only mildly reformist, supporting the PDC wing which favoured an agrarian reform based on small, individual peasant proprietors, and opposing the wing which favoured a more co-operative, even collectivist, solution. It opposed the creation of unions by INDAP on the grounds that unions should be set up by the peasantry themselves. INDAP, dominated by the more radical Christian Democrats, largely ignored the UCC, sponsoring a separate federation El Triunfo Campesino, which it encouraged peasant unions to join.[25] The UCC was strongly opposed to the collectivization of agriculture and argued for private family property as the basis of agrarian reform. It opposed any obligation to make peasants join a co-operative. It disapproved of seizures of estates by peasants as a

[22] ASICH, 5° congreso, p. 5.

[23] Affonso. The rest of this discussion of the UCC relies heavily on this report.

[24] M. Wolpin, 'Some problems of the left in Chile', in R. Miliband & J. Saville, eds., The Socialist Register 1969 (1969), p. 227.

[25] D. Lehmann, 'Political Incorporation versus Political Stability: the case of the Chilean agrarian reform' (mimeo, 1971), p. 100. This article has been published in the J. Development Stud., July 1971.

means of exerting pressure for reform, though it was to witness some of its affiliates engaging in these practices. Its expensive operating costs could hardly bear a continuous increase in its relatively well-paid and numerous advisers. When INDAP entered the union field, many UCC local branches simply moved over to it, the UCC retaining local strength only in the province of Talca.

The UCC was to form in 1965 the CNC (Confederación Nacional Campesina), with the other major Catholic groups the ANOC (Asociación Nacional de Campesinos Cristianos), and the MCI (Movimiento Campesino Independiente). These movements were offshoots of the IER, which itself was the product of a combined effort of the church hierarchy and the landowners organized in the SNA to develop a form of 'responsible' peasant organization and head off the marxists.

In 1952 the Chilean Bishops had set up the ACR (Acción Católica Rural) to attend to the spiritual needs of the peasantry.[26] Influenced by the Molina strike to take more positive action, ACR decided to set up the IER with the explicit co-operation of a faction of the SNA. The IER's three main purposes were to expand the programme of agricultural, technical, and general education offered to selected peasants, to provide a forum for co-operation with the large landowners so as to forestall their active opposition to the peasant movement, and to provide an independent body that could contract with the national and international organizations for financial assistance and technical help.[27] The IER executive included a number of prominent Conservative landowners, though after the PDC electoral victory in 1964 and 1965 the majority were Christian Democrats. Financial support came partly from the SNA itself, partly from the governments of Alessandri and Frei, the AID, the International Development Foundation, and other external sources.[28]

The main activities of the IER consist in providing technical and ideological training for potential peasant leaders. By 1965 it had 23 centres scattered throughout the country which had taught over 4,000 peasants, and some 400 full-time officials attending over 1,000 local communities; it had set up over 200 co-operatives with 5,000 members; and it had issued a number of widely distributed periodicals and had given regular broadcasts.[29] The content of its courses was heavily

[26] The ideas of the movement are outlined in O. Domínguez, *Campesino chileno y la Acción Católica rural* (1961).

[27] Menges, p. 10.

[28] E. Labarca, *Chile invadido: reportaje a la intromisión extranjera* (1967), p. 174. This book is a denunciation of American imperialism written by a Communist journalist in Chile. Though some of the accusations are wild, by no means all of the book—especially in its section on the unions—is wide of the mark. For the executive of the IER and its sources of finance, see also Menges, p. 15.

[29] Affonso.

anti-Communist, and invariably its local groups sought the help of landowners. Courses on union organization were included only after 1964. Its policy on agrarian reform involved modest redistributions to peasant families but it stressed much more the need for technical changes and modernization.

However, in 1962 a group on the IER felt the need for more positive action and set up the ANOC. This was supposed to organize the various regional and co-operative groups created by the IER, to help solve peasant problems and secure effective representation of the peasantry on official bodies. But ANOC quickly took on an independent life, and the landowners on the IER succeeded in reducing its funds, so that the IER local organizers no longer worked for ANOC as well. While the ANOC leadership was prepared to face conflicts with landowners, and even to use strikes against them, the IER was not and eventually the two groups split. As ANOC grouped local units that were essentially offsprings of the IER, its prospects for growth were not good. By 1966 it claimed to have as affiliates 76 unions, 149 pre-union committees, 19 co-operatives, 8 committees of small producers, and various other groups—a total of 10,000 members.[30] At this point, however, it had entered the CNC, along with the UCC.

The ANOC was not the only group set up by the IER, for it also created a more explicitly political group, the MCI, designed to oppose the activities of the marxist groups among the peasantry and to support the Christian Democrats in 1964 and 1965, not as a permanent measure but as the best way to defeat the left. The MCI was given the use of all IER facilities, and most of its activists were IER trained.[31] But the manoeuvre was too subtle. Temporary identification with the Christian Democrats led to a closer working relationship with them than with the IER, which now lost control over the second of its union groups.

The MCI entered the CNC with the other two groups but soon disagreed over union tactics, as it wished to pursue a more radical policy. Another reason for the dispute was MCI suspicion of the source of CNC funds and of their misuse,[32] and less than a year after joining the CNC, the MCI left it. Though the MCI leaders were more in sympathy with the PDC than with any other political party, they remained independent of the party, somewhat to the right of it on rural matters, and not particularly strong.[33]

[30] Ibid.

[31] Menges, pp. 22–3.

[32] Labarca (p. 184) claims that Chonchol and members of the PDC *campesino* dept discovered that some equipment, especially jeeps, given by the AID carried the obligation to report fully on the activities of the organizers. He also alleges that the MCI was more aggrieved because it didn't get any of the jeeps.

[33] Interview, president of PDC *campesino* dept (Santiago, May 1967).

## The marxist organizations

The history of Communist and Socialist attempts to organize the peasantry is scattered with large sounding names of rather flimsy organizations. The two parties did not confine themselves only to organizing resident farm workers but also worked among the small proprietors and the Mapuche Indians in Southern Chile, whose strong desire for the restitution of their communal lands made them more militant than most of the peasants.[34] Though their organizations suffered heavily from attacks by landowners and the government, their efforts cannot be dismissed as completely unsuccessful. They helped to train leaders who were later to become prominent, and they made the peasantry more aware of its situation of exploitation and of possible remedies for it. However, the main focus of attention of both parties was the urban worker, not the peasant, and leaders of the marxist rural organizations often complained of the indifference of the main party. Nor did the rural unions receive any assistance from the CUT.

The various marxist groups in the countryside came together in 1961 to form the FCI (Federación Nacional Campesina e Indígena). The revived interest of the parties in the peasant movement came as a result of the high FRAP vote in rural areas in 1958.[35] It is difficult to estimate the extent of the activities of the FCI and its rural support in the early 1960s because many of its operations were conducted in secrecy. Concealment was necessary because the type of union organization it set up was illegal, because any such attempts would have immediately brought repression from landowners and police, and because of fear of infiltration by Christian Democratic organizers.[36] As with the other organizations, financial support had to come from outside the peasantry, and the FRAP parties more or less openly admitted to supporting the FCI.

The ideas of the FCI are naturally heavily influenced by its close relationship with the marxist parties. It opposes the right-wing Catholic

[34] For the background on Mapuches see W. C. Thiesehusen, 'Grassroots economic pressures in Chile', *Econ. Dev. & Cult. Change*, 16/3 (1968).

[35] Affonso, citing the president of the FCI, Communist José Campusano, from *El Siglo*, 15 Apr. 1962.

[36] Menges (pp. 39–40) writes: 'The Christian Democrats estimated that between 700 and 1,500 Communist and Socialist volunteers worked in the countryside during 1963 and 1964. A source very close to FRAP, however, mentioned a two or three years effort (1961–64) involving about 100 to 400 organizers annually. As to numbers of peasants formed into cells, the best guess could be that more than the 20,000 claimed by ASICH/UCC cells must have joined FRAP's groups because of the greater manpower resources of the Socialist–Communist movement'. Menges's best guess is almost certainly too high. When the FCI became legal it claimed considerably fewer than 20,000 members, and Affonso reports only a 'handful of full-time organizers'.

organizations, denouncing them as the agents of American imperialism, though local circumstances have sometimes forced the groups to co-operate. It emphasizes the importance of the union as the best weapon of the peasantry, especially the single union of all members of estates in a locality. Possibly realizing the advantages of unity and solidarity stemming from the single union in the industrial enterprise, the FCI opposed that part of the 1967 law allowing for more than one union in the rural communes, on the grounds that this would lead to fragmentation of the rural unions along party lines. Its view of agrarian reform is more radical than that of the Catholic groups, but not as drastic, for example, as the Cuban model. It would expropriate well-managed farms if this was in the public interest, but not necessarily all of them; nor does it insist on, though it prefers, communal working of expropriated estates. It does not advocate estate seizures as a regular tactic, though certainly Socialists in the FCI approve of this.[37]

There have been famous occasions when prominent Socialist parliamentarians have led estate seizures. Oscar Naranjo, the Socialist deputy for Curicó, played a leading role in the seizure of the 'Los Cristales' estate, and generally 'helped peasants form unions, write petitions, plan strikes, and ultimately used his privilege of parliamentary immunity from arrest to plan and direct illegal seizures of property'.[38] Such seizures can be successful—in the case of 'Los Cristales', McCoy writes that

since the peasants took over, the fundo has been transformed from a community eyesore into a profitable agricultural enterprise, [and] as an instrument of political penetration, 'Los Cristales' is ideal. Not only does its mere existence serve to remind the peasantry in Curicó of the Socialist party, but peasants on the fundo are proud and eager to spread the story of how the party helped them become real owners of the land they work. Each member of the peasant union is a card-carrying Socialist militant, and the president ran as candidate for office on the Socialist ticket.

Such seizures obviously put the Christian Democrats in an awkward position—recognition of the peasants' claims would have conceded victory to the Socialists, forcible ejection of the peasants would have damaged the Christian Democrats' claim to have been a popular party of reform.

[37] T. L. McCoy writes that the FCI 'had the potential for overloading the reform agencies with an excess of demands but Marxist leaders urged moderation and discouraged illegal challenges to the reform process; while maintaining constant pressure on CORA and INDAP, the Marxists stayed within the bounds of legitimate behaviour' (*Politics of Structural Change in Latin America* (1969), p. 33).

[38] 'The Seizure of Los Cristales', *Inter-American Econ. Aff.*, 21/1 (1967), provides the details.

But seizures such as 'Los Cristales' are exceptional. They demand a great deal of preparation and very favourable circumstances if they are not to misfire and discredit the party or union initiating them. 'Los Cristales' had been rented for several years to a prominent Socialist who had freely allowed political activity on the fundo—not a typical case. There are few deputies like Naranjo in the Socialist party, and the Communists in the FCI did not favour seizures—and have criticized him for *caudillismo* (nor indeed has he escaped criticism from inside his own party).

Members of the FCI played no small part in developing the notion adopted by the PDC government of *Asentamientos*, or co-operatively-run properties (which were to be a transitional method of operation before handing over estates to individual proprietors, a PDC addition to the formula not liked by the FCI). This happened when a number of expropriated estates in the Valle de Choapa came into the hands of the CORA (the state agrarian reform agency) and where there was strong local pressure for co-operatively run farms.[39]

Below the national leadership level, competition between the two parties for control does not seem to be very marked, though the National Council itself, divided between four Communists and three Socialists, often repeats and reflects the arguments between the two national parties. At the provincial and regional level, writes David Lehmann, 'each party seemed to leave the other to foster its own clientele without interfering. Party affiliation did not affect bargaining policies, or the policy of attempting united action with *Triunfo*'.[40] And both parties, at least at the provincial and local level, realize that at the present time unity of action, or at least tolerance towards the actions of the other party in the FCI, is crucial for the development of rural unionism if the challenge of the Christian Democrats is to be effectively met.

The FCI, like the other organizations, tends to have particularly strong regions or localities, and one factor in creating them is the energy and enthusiasm of an influential local congressman. In the province of Colchagua, where the FCI is especially strong, the activities of former Senator Salomón Corbalán, and then Deputy Joel Marambio, both

[39] *Asentamientos*, moreover, unlike unions, are highly dependent on the state, not least of all financially. As D. Lehmann writes: 'The *asentamiento* itself was constituted as an association between CORA and the workers concerned, who were selected on certain criteria by CORA. The land was owned by CORA, though eventually it was to pass to the workers, and CORA had control over credit, as well as veto-power over all decisions' ('Political incorporation versus political 'stability''', *J. Dev. Stud.*, July 1971, p. 12). Thus *asentamientos* became a method of integration of the peasantry into the state apparatus rather than a method of increasing the power and independence of the peasantry as a separate group.

[40] Ibid., p. 11.

Socialists, were important in creating an active union movement.[41] The fact that the UCC was also active locally created a competitive spirit amongst the unions.

## Rural unionism under the Christian Democrats

The strongest force in the countryside for unionization was, in fact, the INDAP, which played a very important role in creating unions, training leaders, giving advice, providing finance, and so on. In the early days of the Frei government, union leaders and INDAP officials were often the same people. Many of the unions so created remained loyal to the party that had passed the law of 1967 and that had provided the means to form unions. The MCI became associated with the work of the INDAP, though the relationship between the two and the *campesino* department of the PDC was one between complementary and parallel bodies rather than between three branches of the same organization. As an official agency INDAP was in theory politically neutral, but naturally the conception and aims and methods of unionization that it put across were more akin to those of the Christian Democrats than those of any other group. Though union leaders at the farm level are normally resident workers, at the provincial level they are often full-time employees of the union. The expenses are best met by the agency most able and most willing to provide the finance—the PDC government through its agency, INDAP, and its national union confederation, El Triunfo Campesino. The leaders of El Triunfo were INDAP-trained and often irreplaceable because they had developed a whole series of contacts with the government, politicians, and agrarian reform agencies essential to the welfare of the peasantry. With the 1967 law rural unionization spread widely, as is shown below (though many of the unions registered in 1967 had in some cases been formed previously, when they were illegal).

*Growth of rural unions*

|  | Unions | Members |
|---|---|---|
| 1964 | 24 | 1,658 |
| 1967 | 211 | 47,473 |
| 1968 | 369 | 83,472 |
| 1969 | 421 | 104,666 |

Source: *Sexto mensaje del Presidente Frei*, ii. 266. There were also 59 committees of small producers, with 37,741 members. INDAP was advising 186 unions with 55,748 members and 173 co-operatives with 26,525 members.

With the 1967 law the existing federations also transformed themselves into legal organizations. The CNC was the basis of the new Confederación Nacional Sindical Campesina 'Libertad', the FCI became

[41] 'Colchagua: provincia con dueños', *Punto final*, June 1967, p. 31.

the Confederación Nacional Campesina e Indígena 'Ranquil', and the INDAP unions and the MCI the Confederación Nacional de Trabajadores Agrícolas 'El Triunfo Campesino de Chile'. Their size in late 1968 was:

*Rural confederations, 1968*

|  | Federations | Unions | Members 1968 | 1969 |
|---|---|---|---|---|
| 'Triunfo Campesino' | 20 | 166 | 39,770 | 47,610 |
| 'Libertad' | 11 | 66 | 16,539 | 23,024 |
| 'Ranquil' | 12 | 77 | 17,197 | 30,912 |

Sources: *Quinto mensaje del Presidente Frei*, p. 369, and, for 1969, Lehmann, *Political Incorporation*, p. 10.

Though the growth of rural unionism is impressive, it cannot necessarily be assumed that it will continue at the same rate or that the simple fact of calling an organization of rural workers a union immediately converts it into something like its urban counterpart. Those urban counterparts have had very few contacts with the rural unions. Chonchol states that he has had dealings with industrial unions that were supposed to be highly politicized and progressive but which had no idea of what was happening in the countryside.[42]

Union organization has not spread equally to all strata of rural society. The easiest to organize have been the more prosperous *inquilinos* and permanent workers on the large estates; the non-resident wage-labourers have been hardly organized at all. There is a danger that unionization may widen the social divisions in peasant society. Those who work the more backward estates, or estates where landowner control is at its most repressive, those who neither reside on the estate nor participate in sharecropping agreements (let alone the minifundistas who lack an immediate *patrón* to organize against) are in danger of being left behind in the process of social change, while the minority of unionized workers secure greater benefits.[43] Any policy of changing the social system in the countryside that relies too heavily on the existing pattern of unionization is in danger of erecting a new system of privilege.

It cannot be assumed either that unions are necessarily opposed to their *patrones*. The cleverer landowners have worked to try to create a rural parallel to the 'business union', and while it is impossible to estimate the number of unions that fall into this category, it is not insignifi-

[42] Chonchol, p. 314.
[43] Juan Marin argues from survey work in Central Chile that unionisation, while it continues largely to pursue better salary settlements, may well lead to a strengthening of the existing social and productive structure in the Chilean countryside ('Asalariados rurales en Chile', *R. Latinoamericana de sociol.* (Buenos Aires), 1969, p. 340.

cant. Moreover, the process of agrarian reform itself has led to the dissolution of some rural unions. When an expropriated estate has been transferred to the peasantry, albeit in the co-operative *asentamiento* form, there is a danger that the peasants will regard the function of the union as completed and disregard the more general problems of the peasantry and its representation in society and government.

There is always the possibility that when unionization spreads for the first time to unorganized and relatively backward groups like the peasantry, it will continue to be a form of external control, of something representing what others think is good for the members, not what the members want themselves; or there may be a difference between the national headquarters of a federation which says one thing and the local branches which, nearer the source of peasant demands, do another. The national leadership, though most politicized, is less powerful than some provincial and local leaderships. Thus in Colchagua in 1969 the FCI and the provincial Triunfo, against the desire of the national Triunfo leadership, organized a strike for common wage demands. But the national Triunfo leadership prevented a common national wage demand with the FCI, after strong INDAP opposition to the idea.

The provision of the rural labour code allowing for several local unions obviously increases party competition for control over unions without, as in the urban sector, forcing partisan groups to co-operate on a single executive. This is especially marked in a country where ideological groups have actively competed in rural areas to build up unions reflecting their own particular ideas.[44] David Lehmann found that rural union leaders tended to form a union bureaucracy, partly because they were full-time paid employees of the union and were so enmeshed in the centres of political power that they became indispensable mediators between the peasantry and those who could solve their problems, whether government representatives or opposition congressmen.[45] This may not be the old-style paternalism, but it does in some ways resemble

[44] See for an example of the PDC programme of party activities in the countryside, the *Plan de trabajo de Verano* of the *campesino* dept (mimeo. 1967). Interestingly enough, most of the regional meetings of the campaign were to be held in the local headquarters of the IER. The CORA used the IER facilities and lecturers to give courses to members of the *asentamientos*.

[45] *Hacia un análisis de la conciencia de los campesinos* (1970), p. 19. Thus the president of one of the provincial federations was also a member of the PDC Communal and Provincial Council; the president of the other federation was a Socialist party activist and worked closely with the local Socialist deputy. Lehmann writes: 'In the mind of the peasants the union was "with" the Deputy, and linked with support for the union went support for the politician. In the same way the members of the other union were identified above all with the government because the union had had support from INDAP and at times they replied "we are of INDAP" when they were asked to what union they belonged.'

it; not so much the patron–dependent relationship of the traditional estate as the patron–client relationship of the more developed clientelistic system, where the 'client' has much more freedom to influence his *patrón*, or even to choose another one, than the 'dependent' in the traditional system. Ideology counts for very little here; what matters is that the *patrón* can solve the problems, and it is unimportant whether the source of his patronage is control over land, political power, or union authority.[46] This relationship is not inconsistent with strong and militant unions, which some provincial federations undoubtedly are.

Because of the recent development of rural unionism there are few empirical studies of organization. The chief study, that of Affonso carried out in 1967, produced some interesting results. The survey found, not surprisingly, that of the sample of 301 local union leaders, the great majority were better educated than their fellow peasants, and 35% of them had worked in towns. Only 15% of the total sample of 348 (i.e. including national and provincial leaders) had been *afuerinos*, or day-labourers. The major preoccupations of unions when presenting their *pliegos* was with wage increases rather than with demands for land or *regalías* (roughly benefits such as housing, a small plot of land, share of the crops, social security, etc.). This Affonso interprets as the influence of the advice of the national federations transferring their urban values (in this case the importance of the salary) to the peasantry. Writing at a later date Lehmann, on the other hand, found that unions placed strong emphasis on *regalías*—because, he argues this kind of payment is less vulnerable to inflation than cash, and also because the small plot of land is the core of the worker's family livelihood.[47]

The replies of the union leaders sampled by Affonso read very much like those of their urban counterparts. They are moderate, concerned with salaries, and seemingly concerned to improve conditions rather than to revolutionize them. Thus over 80% mentioned wage-claims and working conditions as the major function of their union; only 1% mentioned activities concerned with land redistribution. Their image of the employer was not as critical as one might suppose; asked about the reasons for obstacles to the development of unions, 38% of leaders blamed the peasants themselves, 32% the public authorities, and 28%

[46] Thus Chonchol (p. 309) writes that for most of the peasantry 'their vision of the politician is restricted to the traditional politician who renders personal services'.

[47] Perhaps this dilemma—land or wages—is not so clearly defined as it seems. J. Martínez-Alier writes: 'therefore when the question is asked, as it is many times asked, are agricultural workers interested in higher wages and assured work, or are they interested in land? The answer must be that they are interested in both, or in either. They can go quite easily, it would seem, in one or other direction' ('The Peasantry and the Cuban Revolution', in R. Carr ed., *Latin American Affairs*, St Antony's Papers, no. 22 (London, 1970), p. 151).

S

the *patrones*. Practically none saw the organization of the peasantry as an important factor in accelerating the agrarian reform, and only some 12% thought that a union objective ought to be to get land for the peasantry. Although there were no national leaders of the FCI in the sample, local FCI leaders differed little in their opinions from leaders of the other unions. In practice Triunfo unions sometimes went farther in their actions against employers—perhaps because they expected a more tolerant attitude from the PDC government.

The report also analysed close on 1,000 *pliegos* recently presented. None made any demand for land redistribution, though as *pliegos* are basically intended, by law, to be wage claims presented to employers, this is less surprising than it seems. It was impossible to see anything distinctive about the *pliegos* presented by the local FCI unions.[48] Analysing strikes in the period 1960–6, 621 were classified as having economic causes, 58 were caused by complaints about the conditions of life and labour, 105 were due to causes such as solidarity with dismissed workers and only 9 to pressure for land distribution (and 8 of those were strikes in 1964 in the Valle de Choapa). Most lasted only a day or even less, and almost all admitted to some advice or help from a national organization. Though land seizures are widely publicized in Chile, their occurrence is not frequent, nor are their objectives necessarily revolutionary. Only three of the seventeen seizures examined in the report could be described as aimed at land redistribution. Outside these cases, by far the most frequent land seizures occur amongst the Mapuche Indians in the South—and many of them after Allende's election—who regard them as the rightful restitution of usurped lands. According to Affonso's findings, few petitions for expropriations of estates were presented to the CORA but Lehmann states that these demands increased considerably in the last two years of the PDC government. Affonso and his colleagues conclude that 'the action at the grass roots is determined much more by the desires of the peasantry than by the formal ideology of the national organization of which their unions form a part'; while true up to a point, this seems to play down the importance of national organization in mobilizing and organizing the peasantry.

There are obvious points of similarity between the way rural unions are developing and the way the urban-sector unions have developed. In both sectors external political influences are very marked, especially at the national level. The union on the estate in many ways resembles the plant union. The unorganized in the towns and in the countryside are alike in constituting a majority, in both composed of similar social

---

[48] Thus the *Plataforma de lucha* for 1969 of the former FCI deals very largely with wage problems; agrarian reform is added almost, it seems, as an afterthought.

sectors—artisans and minifundistas, marginals and day-labourers, workers in small enterprises and on small farms, isolated workers. In town and countryside unions and parties form interdependent parts of the labour movement.

Nevertheless, there are marked differences. There are more varied ideological influences in the countryside. Since 1964 the attitude of the government to rural unionization has been much more favourable and rural confederations have advanced quickly along the road of presenting provincial and even national wage demands. Rural areas have no traditions of working-class unionism such as are strong in mining and manufacturing; neither are the political traditions of the urban working class shared by the peasantry except in very few areas. There is more danger of exploitation of the peasantry by unscrupulous employers, government officials, or union bosses. Lehmann believes that at least up to 1970, the Chilean peasants were in alliance with the urban middle class; hence many of the clientelistic characteristics of the relationship. He also believes that political competition reinforces patterns of dependence between peasants and political parties and divides the peasantry.[49] Yet this seems to discount the strength of grassroots pressures. Even if the alliances of the peasantry have been with the urban middle class rather than with the working class, even if old-style *patrón*-dependent relations have been replaced by a more modern clientelistic system rather than by independent, autonomous unions, this does not lessen the political impact of rural organization, or preclude the eventual development of independent, non-clientelistic unions. Once started, the process may flow into more radical channels than its originators intended; certainly the Allende government was caught off balance by the wave of land seizures following its election, after it had committed itself in the campaign to a much more rapid land distribution than the previous government. The biggest uncertainty may be the somewhat ambiguous future role of the peasant unions in the light of agrarian reform. In a largely collectivized rural economy, if this is Allende's aim, the role of the peasant union will be very different from one where the normal unit is the family estate. Thus the future development of rural unionism in Chile is intimately bound up with the future of agrarian reform, and it is possible that rural unionism may have to make further changes of a not less striking nature.

[49] *Peasant Consciousness*, p. 32.

# Appendix II
# External Influences in the Chilean Labour Movement

IT is not easy to label some influences as 'external' and others as 'domestic'. For example, right-wingers in Chile would regard both Christian Democracy and Communism as essentially alien (and undesirable) influences. However, this appendix concentrates on North American influences, and, to a lesser extent, on the Catholic international labour organization, the CLASC (Confederación Latinamericana Sindical Cristiana). The international Communist movement no longer has a Latin American affiliate,[1] and relations between the Chilean CP and the Comintern have already been discussed. German activity in the labour movement has increased but is not very important,[2] and Peronist attempts to gain a foothold in Chile were similarly unsuccessful.[3]

[1] The regional affiliate in Latin America was the CTAL, directed by V. Lombardo Toledano. It succumbed to the heavy onslaughts of ORIT and the Peronist movements and most of its chief affiliates deserted. In 1964, at a meeting in Brazil, it was formally dissolved. Attempts to establish a replacement have so far been prevented by disputes between Castroites and the orthodox Moscow supporters.

[2] The German Social Democrat party via the Friedrich Ebert Foundation has tried to steer the Chilean movement away from communism. Overtures to the Socialists were turned down; the Christian Democrats by and large ignored them, and only the Radicals looked interested for a while, until their move towards the marxists precluded further contacts. Apparently the German group in Chile has now switched its attention to university students (Labarca, *Chile invadado*, p. 159).

[3] President Ibáñez hoped to use Perón's ATLAS (his Latin American organization of pro-Perón unionists) to control Chilean unions. Rubén Hurtado, later a PDC deputy, was the most prominent ally with his Confederación Nacional de Sindicatos Obreros de Viña del Mar; but the creation of the CUT consolidated Chilean unionists in an anti-Perón organization (S. Baily, *Labor, Nationalism and Politics in Argentina* (New Brunswick, 1967), p. 151). Ibáñez established a labour office in the presidential palace under his naval aide-de-camp; and the

North American influence has worked largely through the ORIT and later through the AIFLD.[4] The ORIT was founded in 1951 in Mexico largely through the efforts of the American Federation of Labor (AFL). It is the Western Hemisphere affiliate of the ICFTU and is partly financed by that body but mostly by US affiliates and by the US government and American business corporations. It was founded largely as an anti-Communist force and has remained loyal to its original conception, in the process supporting several dictatorial regimes in Latin America.[5] It champions the free-enterprise system.

Influenced by the new climate of opinion with the Kennedy proposal for the Alliance for Progress, it began to discuss social reform, though its definition of reform is rather restricted and broadly conforms with the ideas of its closest political associates, the Mexican PRI, the Peruvian APRA, and the Venezuelan AD, all parties with strong anti-Communist sentiments. ORIT is even narrower in its ideas on who may be allowed to carry out reform, and, emphatically, Communists, Socialists, and even Catholic radicals are suspect. It is more concerned to oust opponents than to help labour.

In Latin America as a whole ORIT has an impressive number of affiliates in important countries like Mexico, Venezuela, Colombia, Peru, and Brazil. Though the figures are far from precise, at least formally in 1964 its members numbered something like half of all Latin American unionists.[6]

If it has had little lasting success in Chile, it has not been for want of trying. Even before it was formed, the AFL was active in Chile. Bernardo Ibáñez had very friendly relations with the AFL, and with their support stood against the Communist-sponsored Mexican labour leader Lombardo Toledano, for membership on the governing body of the ILO in 1944. The head of the AFL's Latin American department considers that Ibáñez's CTCH would have disappeared had it not been for AFL's help.[7] The kind of support given by ORIT and its lack of results is

---

Argentinian secretary-general of the CGT co-operated in trying to found a Peronist base, but to little avail (D. W. Bray, 'Peronism in Chile', *HAHR*, Feb. 1967, p. 44).

[4] A useful account of ORIT is Carroll Hawkin's, 'The ORIT and the CLASC', *Inter-American Econ. Aff.*, Winter 1966, pp. 39–53. See also, Landsberger, 'International Labor Organizations', in S. Shapiro, ed., *Integration of Man and Society in Latin America* (Indiana, 1967).

[5] It supported the action of its Brazilian affiliates who welcomed the overthrow of the pro-labour Goulart government in 1964 for the military regime that subsequently proved anything but pro-labour (Hawkins, p. 51).

[6] Ibid., p. 114.

[7] S. Romualdi, *Presidents and Peons* (New York, 1967), p. 303 & 326. Romualdi was the AFL's chief organizer for Latin America.

neatly captured in the following extract from Romualdi's auto-biography.

In 1956 an ORIT–ICFTU office was opened in Chile. With the co-operation of the AFL–CIO and the Cuban Confederation of Labor it launched a full-fledged campaign designed to rally the independents around a program of non-political, nonsectarian trade unionism, strongly opposed to the Communist-dominated left alliance. In view of our previous failures to recommend the investment of additional AFL–CIO funds, in a memorandum sent to President George Meany in March, 1956, I wrote:

'In order to understand my cautiousness in relation to Chile, I must remind you that the AFL, as early as 1946, contributed substantial amounts of money to the "anti-Communist" elements in Chile; that the CIT kept its head-quarters in that country for two years devoting a large share of its income and personnel to the support of the local "anti-Communists"; that later the ORIT and the Cuban CTC sent organizers and spent many thousands of dollars in similar work; that the United Mine Workers contributed like-wise thousands of dollars; and that finally the ICFTU, after keeping its Latin American representative in Chile for several months, installed an office and allotted to its maintenance a considerable amount of money. All these efforts have produced nothing more than a series of uninterrupted failures, dis-appointments, bickerings, and resentment, for various reasons that would be too long to enumerate. Nevertheless, if we find that this time there is really "a will to fight" I am in favor of giving all the support we can muster.'[8]

Campaigning against the CUT was a constant feature of ORIT's activities in Chile. Even though officially there was no love lost between ORIT and the CLASC, they were prepared to overcome their mutual dis-like in order to combat the far greater evil of communism in the unions. It is as well to let the official voice of the ORIT speak again:

Talks were again resumed, first informally and then officially, between rep-resentatives of ORIT and Christian Democratic trade union leaders, including officers of CLASC—the Latin American Confederation of Christian Trade Unionists—with the view of breaking the Christian Democratic unions away from CUT at its III Convention scheduled to meet in Santiago, August 1–5, 1962. However, at the very last moment, even after everything had been agreed upon, the Christian Democrats backed away. Here is how the events de-veloped.

Preliminary talks were held between Julio Etcheverry Espínola, then ORIT Representative in Chile, and José Goldsack, President of CLASC. An agreement was reached in principle, but CLASC asked to finalize the matter with a top officer of ORIT. On July 29, Morris Paladino, then ORIT Assistant General Secretary, arrived in Santiago. On August 1, a meeting between representa-tives of ORIT and CLASC was held at the Hotel Carrera. It adjourned after hav-ing reached the following agreements:

1. In the event the Communists, who controlled the Convention Credential Committee, refused to accept the credentials of about four hundred del-

8 Ibid., p. 332.

egates representing agricultural workers' unions that were bitterly opposed to the Communists, the democratic forces would leave the Convention en masse. All expected the Communists to refuse to validate these credentials because they represented the balance of power.

2. To strengthen the democratic forces inside the Convention, it was agreed that COMACH, the Federation of Taxi Drivers, and other democratic unions would take part in the Convention with voice and vote. *To make this possible, the ORIT representative agreed to pay the arrears in dues owed CUT by these organizations.* The CNT also agreed to send out immediate instructions to all its affiliated organizations to regularize their situation with CUT so as to be able to take part in the Convention and thus increase the democratic strength.

3. If they abandoned the site of the CUT Convention, which was to meet in the Caupolicán Theater, the democratic delegates would assemble in another hall, to be selected by CLASC, but whose rent would be paid by ORIT.

4. A New National Democratic Labor Confederation would be launched. The convention itself would decide whether it should join the ORIT or CLASC. It was agreed, however, among the participants in the Hotel Carrera meeting, that they would recommend, for the time being, independence from both— in other words, the solution advanced six years before, in 1956, which was then dropped because of opposition from the ICFTU. To defray the immediate urgent expenditures for the planned operation, Paladino authorized Etcheverry to give Goldsack an advance, for which he signed a receipt.

On that same afternoon, however, Goldsack received orders from the Christian Democratic Party leadership not to break with the CUT Convention. For several days Etcheverry and Paladino were unable to contact him, not even by phone. After the CUT Convention ended, with the Communists in solid control as before, Goldsack did tell Paladino the whole story of how he had been prevented by orders from the Party from going through with the agreement.[9]

The ORIT did secure a notable number of Chilean affiliates immediately after its foundation, when the marxists were in a state of great internal disarray. Important federations, such as the copper workers, railway workers, and maritime workers, were affiliated with or sympathetic to it. But with the formation of the CUT and the resurgence of marxism as a force, the temporary flirtation came to end, with the exception of the COMACH led by Moreno.[10] Thus at its 1955 congress the CTC recommended disaffiliation from the ORIT on the grounds that it had received no benefit from membership, that the Chilean offices of the ORIT had not only failed to support the strikes of the copper workers but had even opposed them.[11]

Since the heyday of the early 1950s the ORIT has enjoyed support only among unions and unionists that are regarded somewhat as outcasts in the labour movement. Three supposedly anarcho-syndicalists were expelled from the CUT executive in 1957, according to that body because

[9] Ibid., p. 335.          [10] Barría, *Trayectoria*, p. 375.

[11] CTC, *Estatutos . . . del 2° congreso ordinario*, p. 22. It did, however, recommend affiliation to the Miners' International based in London.

they were too 'spontaneous' and 'irresponsible'. The expelled leaders alleged that the CUT was collaborating with the bourgeoisie,[12] but only a year later they were organizing a Confederación Nacional de Trabajo (CNT) with support from Moreno and Carlos Ibáñez King, of the Federación de Choferes y Cobradores de la Locomoción Colectiva Particular. The CNT became the Chilean affiliate of the ORIT but never gained much support, and in 1965 ORIT resolved to disown it because of its unrepresentative nature.[13] Apart from this group, the main Chilean supporters of ORIT are Moreno, Ibáñez King, and Hurtado of the Viña del Mar sugar workers. All run, or ran rather unusual 'boss' type unions and are fiercely mistrusted by Chilean unionists, including those of the party to which all three belong, the PDC. Moreno came to power in COMACH in 1950 when many of the left-wing leaders were removed by González Videla under his Law for the Defence of Democracy. Moreno has been, to put it mildly, politically flexible; a Radical under González Videla, he became a supporter of General Ibáñez and Alessandri when they respectively became President, and then joined the PDC band-wagon. His union has received considerable sums of money from various US sources. He is on the governing body of the Chilean branch of AIFLD, is a vice-president of ORIT, is on the executive committee of the ICFTU, and is vice-president of the International Secretariat of Transport Workers. Union leaders in COMACH tend to enjoy great power, partly because those of their members at sea cannot participate in union business and because they have great power in deciding who works amongst the dock workers.[14] But Moreno's position in the party suffered a setback when the 1966 party congress passed a resolution prohibiting membership in, and any type of collaboration with, bodies like the ORIT and the AIFLD.[15] Moreno has been under increasing attack in his own union, and his power base has apparently been reduced to the port workers of Valparaíso.[16] Hurtado, too, suffered from the reaction against leaders of his sort, as well as the added complication of being involved in financial scandals. He lost control over his union in 1967 and was not again chosen as candidate for Congress by the PDC in March 1969. Ibáñez King, however, did become a party candidate in that election, though he received a very small vote.

It is not difficult to see why ORIT has been unsuccessful in Chile. Its

[12] Labarca, p. 167; Romualdi, p. 334. One of the three 'anarcho-syndicalists' later became a lecturer at the AIFLD.

[13] Burnett (p. 118) writes: 'Its leadership claims 126 unions with a total of 80,000 members, though other estimates suggest that 35 directly affiliated unions and 20,000 adherents may be nearer the truth'. That was in 1964—the numbers are certainly even smaller at present.

[14] Labarca, pp. 134–5.

[15] *Acuerdos del 2° congreso*, p. 56. See also Romualdi, p. 340.

[16] *Ultima hora*, 5 May 1967; *El Siglo*, 16 Jan. 1969.

non-political (or supposedly non-political) approach to unionism has little appeal and makes little sense in Chilean conditions. The participation of American business in its activities is an embarrassment for it in a country where attacks on American imperialism are common and where American corporations have been large employers of labour (including some of the most militant groups). Its anti-communism is not likely to take it far where communism is both strong and in working agreement with the other important political forces in the labour movement. Its association with some of the most unpopular of Chilean unionists and its free use of American funds add to the general suspicion that it is more concerned with political espionage than industrial relations.[17]

Much more directly under the control of the AFL–CIO, which experiences some problems with Latin American unionists in the ORIT, is the AIFLD, founded in 1961 by the AFL–CIO with which it works closely. George Meany was the president of both bodies. Formally outside ORIT, in practice it works closely with it and shares the same ideas and often the same officials, but it is also very closely connected with the US government and American business. Its chairman is the president of W. R. Grace and Co., and on its board are representatives of US corporations active along the west coast of South America for the last eighty years and, until recently, enemies of independent trade unionism. Most of its funds (92%) in 1967 came from AID and the rest from business and labour. It spends far more than ORIT. In Chile alone its expenditure went up from $18,785 in 1962 to $197,097 in 1967, which is fairly big money in the not rich world of Chilean labour.[18]

The AIFLD is basically a training and indoctrination institution, aiming to promote a strictly economic vision of unionism, emphasizing harmony in industrial relations and the follies of the class war and communism. Well over 3,000 unionists had gone through its courses by 1967, and it had sent some on special scholarships to Puerto Rico and the US.[19] It also finances social projects, such as housing schemes for selected unions. But it has achieved no notable successes, at least in the

---

[17] See also Landsberger, in Zañartu & Kennedy, p. 116. ORIT also works through the various trade secretariats of the ICFTU. The ICTT (the secretariat concerned with postal and telegraphic workers) has been active in Chile and had some success in the companies then owned by American interests (*El Siglo*, 5 Oct. 1968; Labarca, p. 130).

[18] These figures come from *Survey of the Alliance for Progress: Labor Policies and Programs*, a study by the staff of the Committee on Foreign Relations of the US Senate, 15 July, 1968 (1968), pp. 10 & 86. Total expenditure in Latin America for 1967 was $5,273,365, compared with $323,000 for ORIT. Central America received the largest amount, $568,197, and then Brazil with $499,961 —not countries noted for their free and independent unions.

[19] P. O'Brien, *AID and Trade Union Development*, MS., Santiago, 1967.

urban sphere. The US Senate Committee report on it concluded that 'our review showed that AIFLD social projects have in Chile resulted in few tangible results'.[20] It attracts support from the same unionists who support ORIT. It suffers from the same drawbacks too, and has spent a great deal of money to little effect. It was beginning to make some progress among the rural unions, where considerable sums had been given by AID to the IER and its unions, but Allende's election will probably put an effective end to its activities in Chile.

The CLASC was founded in Santiago in 1954. Most of its finances come from European sources, principally the solidarity fund of the ICFTU and even more so from the West German foundation known as International Solidarity, financed by the Federal government.[21] It is not a clerical or confessional organization and welcomes people of different faiths, although naturally the great majority of its members are Catholics. Though it attacks communism, it also attacks the values that ORIT propagates, and regards the model of 'neutral unionism' as inappropriate for Latin America. ORIT from time to time accuses it of serving the interests of communism.

Like many Catholic organizations it is divided. Its secretary-general, Emilio Máspero, an Argentinian, leads the radical wing, and its Chilean affiliate, ASICH, tends to support its more moderate rural majority. A dispute between the two led to removal of the CLASC offices, along with Máspero, from Santiago to Caracas, and ASICH has at present no representatives on the CLASC executive, though for many years it had been very prominent. William Thayer was the first president of the CLASC, and he was succeeded by José Goldsack, a bank employee who was also president of the ASICH. After CLASC went to Caracas, its educational offspring, the Instituto de Capacitación Sindical y Social (INCASIS) remained in Chile, directed by Father Vekemans, most incongruously occupying the neighbouring building to the CUT headquarters. CLASC and the ASICH have several times collaborated in trying to build up a separate confederation to rival the CUT, but unsuccessfully partly because no rival organization could succeed without the full support of the Christian Democrats, and this was forthcoming neither for the MUTCH nor for the UTRACH, though some Christian Democrats were involved in both.[22]

---

[20] *Survey of Alliance for Progress.* Thus houses promised for COMACH workers and started in 1963 were not completed by mid-1968. A massive $2 m. loan sought by AIFLD from the AFL–CIO could not be arranged as the American Confederation demanded a market rate of interest, which was too high. The failure was a setback to the AIFLD.

[21] See a useful article on the CLASC by M. J. Francis, 'Revolutionary Labor in Latin America', *J. Inter-American Stud.*, Oct. 1968, pp. 597–616.

[22] ASICH, *9° congreso nacional*, pp. 21–2. When the MUTCH was transformed, on a Christian Democratic initiative, into a confederation of unions rather than a

It may be objected that the ASICh is hardly an external influence on the Chilean labour movement, though it certainly receives external financial support.[23] Whether it is or not, the fact remains that both the marxists and the Christian Democrats regard it as such, pointing to its financial sources, its efforts to split the labour movement, and its scanty success apart from the rural areas, where, again, its success is mostly attributed to the greater financial resources that the ASICh affiliate, the UCC, received from abroad.

Relations between the ASICh and the Christian Democrats have never been particularly good. At one time militancy in both groups was held to be incompatible by Christian Democrats, though this decision seems to have been quietly put aside.[24] Towards the CLASC the Christian Democrats are a little less hostile. It was declared at the second congress that militancy in the CLASC was not incompatible with membership in the party, and the congress agreed to study means of possible further contacts, while pointing out that it objected strongly to the activities and tactics of the local Chilean affiliates of the CLASC.[25] However, many Christian Democratic unionists feel that membership in CLASC would impede them in the domestic labour field and would give other groups the opportunity to attack them as stooges of Catholic imperialism; too close contact with ASICh would open them to the charge of being stooges of American imperialism as well. As long as the Christian Democrats continue to value participation in the CUT more than association with other Catholic groups, they are unlikely to seek any agreement with them. And as long as the Catholic organizations are deprived of Christian Democratic support, they are unlikely to expand in the labour movement.

---

co-ordinating body, ASICh saw a rival to its own standing and withdrew. The UTRACh was launched at a time when Christian Democratic unionists had moved to the left, so the majority response it aroused in the party was hostility. Both the peasant department and the union department attacked it strongly and succeeded in getting the party to declare that Christian Democratic members could not participate in UTRACh (Labarca, p. 171).

[23] Burnett (p. 139) writes that 'ASICh's overseas sources are located primarily in Europe, especially among trade unionists who pay solidarity dues to African, Asian and Latin American labor. Inasmuch as Latin America offered the best hope in the 1960's for Christian Democratic expansion, more than 60% of that total amount reached the Western Hemisphere, and a large portion of that stopped in Chile.'

[24] Interview, president of ASICh (Santiago, 1968).

[25] PDC, *Acuerdos del 2° congreso*, pp. 56–7.

# Select Bibliography

*Note:* This bibliography contains only the most important books and articles on Chile used in this study. Footnotes contain the references to the party and union pamphlets and documents, and to unpublished theses. Unless otherwise indicated, books and periodicals are published in Santiago.

Abbott, R. The role of contemporary political parties in Chile. *American Polit. Science R.*, June 1951.

Affonso, Almino & others. *Movimiento campesino chileno.* ICIRA, 1970. 2 vols.

Aguilar, Luis. *Marxism in Latin America.* New York, 1968.

Alexander, Robert. *Communism in Latin America.* New Jersey, 1957.

—— *Labor relations in Argentina, Brazil and Chile.* New York, 1962.

Allende, Salvador. Homenaje a la memoria del ex-Senador Salomón Corbalán. *Arauco*, Apr. 1967.

Ampuero, Raúl. *Carácter de la revolución chilena.* n.d.

—— *La izquierda en punto muerto.* 1969.

—— 1964: Año de prueba para la revolución chilena. *Arauco*, Feb. 1964.

Arroyo, G. Sindicalismo y promoción campesina. *Mensaje*, June 1966.

Barrera Romero, Manuel. *El Sindicato industrial chileno* INSORA, 1965.

—— *La participación social y los sindicatos industriales en Chile.* Geneva, Internat. Inst. for Labour Studies, 1970, mimeo.

—— Participation by occupational organizations in economic and social planning in Chile. *Internat. Labour R.* (Geneva), Aug. 1967.

Barría Serón, Jorge. *Breve historia del sindicalismo chileno.* INSORA, 1967.

—— *El convenio colectivo en la industria de Cuero y Calzado.* INSORA, 1967.

—— *Las relaciones colectivas del trabajo en Chile.* INSORA, 1967.

—— *Trayectoria y estructura del movimiento sindical chileno.* INSORA, 1963.

Bermúdez Miral, Oscar. *El drama político de Chile.* 1947.

Boizard, Ricardo. *La democracia cristiana en Chile.* 1963.

Bowers, Claude. *Chile through embassy windows.* New York, 1958.

Briones, Guillermo. La estructura social y la participación política. *R. interamerica de ciencias sociales*, 2/3, 1963.

Burnett, Ben G. *Political groups in Chile*. Texas, 1970.

Chelén Rojas, Alejandro. *Trayectoria de socialismo*. Buenos Aires, 1968[?].

Chonchol, Jacques. Poder y reforma agraria, *Chile, Hoy*. Centro de Estudios Socio-Económicos, Univ. Chile, 1970.

Clissold, Stephen. *Soviet relations with Latin America*. London, 1970.

Comité Interamericana de Desarrollo Agricola, *Chile: Tenencia de la tierra y desarrollo socio-económico del sector agrícola*. 1966.

Contreras Labarca, Carlos. La gran experiencia del frente popular. *Principios*, July–Aug. 1967.

Corbalán, Salomón. Las bases técnicas de la revolución chilena en la política de frente de trabajadores, *Arauco*, Nov. 1961.

Corvalán, Luis. Strengthening the national liberation front. *World Marxist R.* Apr. 1959.

Cruz-Coke, Ricardo. *Geografía electoral de Chile*. 1952.

Debray, Régis. *Conversations with Allende*. London, 1971.

Escobar, Aristodemo. *Compendio de la legislación social y desarrollo del movimiento obrero en Chile*. 1940.

Faletto, Enzo & Eduardo Ruiz. Conflicto político y estructura social, in *Chile, Hoy* (Centro de Estudios Socio-Economicos, Univ. Chile) 1970.

Figueroa, Luis. La clase obrera y la elección presidencial. *Principios*, Jan.–Feb., 1964.

Frei, Eduardo. *Pensamiento y acción*. 1958.

Fuchs, Claudio & Luis Santibáñez. *Pensamiento, política, y acción del ejecutivo industrial chileno*. INSORA, 1967.

Garay, Mario. *La crisis política y el PSP*. 1969.

Gil, Federico. *The political system of Chile*. Boston, 1966.

González Díaz, Galo. *La Lucha por la formación del partido comunista de Chile*. 1958.

Grayson, George. *El partido demócrata cristiano chileno*. Buenos Aires, 1968.

Gregory, Peter. *Industrial wages in Chile*. New York, 1967.

Gurrieri, Adolfo. Consideraciones sobre los sindicatos chilenos. *Aportes* (Paris), July 1968.

—— & Zapata, Francisco. *Sectores obreros y desarrollo en Chile*, ILPES, 1967, mimeo.

Halperin, Ernst. *Nationalism and communism in Chile*. Cambridge, Mass., 1965.

Heredia M., Luis. *Como se construirá el socialismo*. Valparaíso, 1936.

Herrick, Bruce. *Urban migration and economic development in Chile*. Cambridge, Mass., 1965.

Hinojosa Robles, Francisco. *El libro de oro de los empleados particulares*. 1967.

Hirschman, Albert. *Journeys toward progress*. New York, 1963.

Hurtado Cruchaga, Alberto. *Sindicalismo: historia, teoría, práctica*. 1950.

Jobet, Julio César. *Ensayo crítico del desarrollo económico-social de Chile.* 1955.
—— El movimiento obrero mundial, la realidad chilena y la fundación del partido socialista. *Arauco*, Mar. 1967.
—— El partido socialista y el frente popular en Chile. *Arauco*, Feb. 1967.
—— El socialismo chileno a través de sus congresos. 1965.
—— Recabarren: los orígenes del movimiento obrero y del socialismo chileno. 1955.
Kaempffer Villagrán, Guillermo. *Así sucedió.* 1962.
Kaldor, Nicholas. Problemas económicos de Chile. *El Trimestre económico* (Mexico), Apr.–June 1969.
Labarca Godard, Eduardo. *Chile invadido: reportaje a la intromisión extranjera.* 1967.
Lafertte, Elías. *Vida de un comunista.* 1961.
Landsberger, Henry & Canitrot Fernando. *Iglesia, intellectuales y campesinos.* INSORA, 1967.
—— Do ideological differences have personal correlates? A study of Chilean labor union leaders at the local level. *Econ Dev & Cult Change* 16/2, 1968.
—— & others. *El pensamiento del dirigente sindical chileno.* INSORA, 1963.
—— & others. The Chilean labour union leader. *Industrial & Labor Relations R.*, Apr. 1964.
Lehmann, David. *Hacia un análisis de la conciencia de los campesinos.* ICIRA, 1970.
—— Peasant consciousness and agrarian reform in Chile. Sussex Univ., Inst. Development Stud., 1970, mimeo.
—— Political incorporation versus political 'stability': the case of the Chilean agrarian reform. *J. Development Stud.*, July 1971.
Mattelart, Armand, & others. *La ideología de la dominación en una sociedad dependiente.* Buenos Aires, 1970.
McCoy, Terry L. *The politics of structural change in Latin America: the case of agrarian reform in Chile.* Wisconsin Univ., Land Tenure Centre, Research Paper 37, 1969.
—— The seizure of 'Los Cristales'. *Inter American Econ. Aff.* 21/1, 1967.
Menges, Constantine. Public policy and organized business in Chile: a preliminary analysis. *J. Internat. Aff.* (Princeton), 20/2, 1966.
—— Peasant organizations and politics in Chile, *1958–64.* Rand Corporation, Dec. 1968.
Millas, Orlando. Medio siglo de partido obrero en Chile. *Principios.* July–Aug. 1962.
Morgado, Emilio. *Libertad sindical.* INSORA, 1967.
Morris, James. *Elites, intellectuals and consensus.* New York, 1966.
—— & Oyaneder, Roberto. *Afiliación y finanzas sindicales en Chile.* INSORA, 1961.

Nuñez Bravo, Oscar. Balance del paro nacional. *Arauco*, Nov. 1962.

—— *Diez años de lucha de los trabajadores.* 1963.

Olavarría Bravo, Arturo. *Chile bajo la democracia cristiana.* 1966.

Ortúzar, Gregorio & Isaac Puente. *Hacia un mundo nuevo: teoría y práctica del anarco-sindicalismo.* Valparaíso, 1938.

Petras, James. *Chilean Christian Democracy: politics and social forces.* Berkeley, 1967.

—— *Politics and social forces in Chilean development.* Berkeley, 1969.

—— *La clase obrera chilena. Punto final,* Jan. 1971.

—— & Zeitlin, Maurice. Miners and agrarian radicalism. *American J. Sociology,* Aug. 1967.

Petris Giesen, Hector de. *Historia del partido democrático.* 1942.

Pike, Frederick. *Chile and the United States.* Indiana, 1963.

Pinto, Aníbal. *Chile: una economía difícil.* Mexico, 1964.

Pizarro Novea, Eduardo. *Victoria al amanecer; intimidades y trayectoria de la huelga general de 1950.* 1950.

Poblete Troncoso, Moisés. El movimiento de asociación profesional obrera en Chile. *Jornadas* (Colegio de Mexico), 29 (1945).

—— *La organización sindical en Chile y otros estudios sociales.* 1926.

—— El movimiento sindical en Chile. *Combate* (Costa Rica), July–Aug. 1962.

Ramírez Necochea, Hernán. *Historia del movimiento obrero en Chile: siglo diez y nueve.* 1956.

—— *Origen y formación del partido comunista de Chile.* 1965.

—— El movimiento obrero chileno desde 1917 a 1922. *Principios,* Jan. 1960.

—— Tuvo influencia la primera internacional en Chile? *Principios,* Sept.–Oct. 1969.

Ravines, Eudocio. *La gran estafa.* 1954.

Recabarren, Luis Emilio. *Obras escogidas,* vol. i. 1965.

Romualdi, Serafino. *Presidents and peons.* New York, 1967.

Segall, Marcelo. *Desarrollo del capitalismo en Chile.* 1953.

Sepúlveda, Armando. *Historia social de los ferraviarios.* 1959.

Simon, Fanny. Anarchism and anarcho-syndicalism in South America. *HAHR,* Feb. 1946.

Soares, Glaucio Dillon. Desenvolvimiento económico e radicalismo político. *América Latina,* July–Sept. 1962.

Solar, Julio Silva & Jacques, Chonchol. *El desarrollo de la nueva sociedad en América Latina.* 1965.

Solberg, Carl. Immigration and social problems in Argentina and Chile. *HAHR,* May 1969.

Sunkel, Osvaldo. La inflación chilena: un enfoque heterodoxo. *El Trimestre económico,* Oct.–Dec. 1958.

Tella, Torcuato Di & others. *Huachipato et Lota: étude sur la conscience ouvrière dans deux entreprises chiliennes.* Paris, 1966. (Spanish ed., *Sindicato y comunidad.* Buenos Aires.)

Thayer, William. *Trabajo, empresa y revolución.* 1968.

—— Bases para una política sindical. *Política y espíritu,* 15 Aug. 1957.

Thomas, Jack Ray. The evolution of a Chilean socialist: Marmaduke Grove. *HAHR,* Feb. 1967.

Urzua Valenzuela, Germán. *Los partidos políticos chilenos.* 1968.

US Dept of Labor. *Labor in Chile.* Washington, 1962.

—— *Labor law and practice in Chile.* Washington, 1969.

Varas, José Miguel. *Chacón.* 1968.

Véliz, Claudio. The Chilean experiment. *Foreign Affairs,* Mar. 1971.

Vidal, Gustavo & Guillermo Barría. *Doce días que estremecieron al país.* 1950.

Vitale, Luis. *Los discursos de Clotario Blest y la revolución chilena.* 1961.

Waiss, Oscar. *El drama socialista.* 1948.

—— *Socialismo sin gerentes.* 1961[?].

Walker Linares, Francisco. Trade unionism among agricultural workers in Chile, *Internat. Labor R.* Dec., lxviii/6, 1953.

Wolpin, Miles. 'Some problems of the left in Chile', in R. Miliband & J. Saville, *The Socialist Register 1969.* London, 1969.

Zapata, Francisco. *Estructura y representatividad del sindicalismo chileno.* ILPES, 1968.

—— *Federaciones y centrales en el sindicalismo chileno.* Geneva, Internat. Inst. for Labour Stud. 1970, mimeo.

Zañartu, Mario & J. J. Kennedy, eds. *The overall development of Chile.* Indiana, 1969.

Zeitlin, Maurice & James Petras. The working class vote in Chile. *British J. Sociology,* Mar. 1970.

# Index

201; wage freeze, 144, 154 ff.,
190–1; white-collar workers, 148
f., 152, 154 f.; rural workers, 249
n., 260 f.
Waiss, O., 136, 145
WFTU, 145
white-collar workers (*empleados*), 38,
109; distinction between blue-
collar workers and, 66–8, 110,

149–50, 156, 159, 167, 193, 201;
share of national income, 72 f.;
growth in militancy, 148–54;
PDS supporters in, 185, 186–7,
189; *see also* ANEF; CEPch;
Radical party; *sindicatos profesionales*

Zeitlin, M., 184, 235 n.

CHILE:
Regions and Provinces

PERU

BOLIVIA

ARGENTINA

Pacific

Ocean

TARAPACÁ

ANTOFAGASTA

ATACAMA

COQUIMBO

ACONCAGUA
VALPARAÍSO
SANTIAGO
COLCHAGUA
MAULE
CONCEPCIÓN
ARAUCO
CAUTÍN
VALDIVIA
OSORNO
LLANQUIHUE

O'HIGGINS
CURICÓ
TALCA
LINARES
ÑUBLE
BÍO-BÍO
MALLECO

CHILOÉ

AISÉN

MAGALLANES

GREAT NORTH

LITTLE NORTH

CENTRAL URBAN

NORTH CENTRAL

SOUTH CENTRAL

THE FRONTIER

N

| 0 | 100 | 200 | 300 | 400 | 500 |
miles

| 0 | 200 | 400 | 600 | 800 |
km